The Solitary Druid

Walking the Path of Wisdom and Spirit

Revised and updated edition

By Rev. Robert (Skip) Ellison

ADF Publishing
Tucson, AZ

The Solitary Druid:
Walking the Path of Wisdom and Spirit
By Rev. Robert Lee (Skip) Ellison

Published by:
Ár nDraíocht Féin Publishing
Tuscon, AZ
ISBN: 0-9765681-7-9
ISBN-13: 978-0-9765681-7-9
Library of Congress Control Number: 2013940349
www.adf.org/publications/books/

Cover Design: Willow Nimfeach
Index: A.G. Vanidottir
Layout: Steph Gooch

This book was first published under the same name by Citadel Press under ISBN 0-8065267-5-0 ©2005. This edition has been revised, updated and expanded.

Some of the information on holidays in chapters six and seven first appeared in the book *The Wheel of the Year at Muin Mound Grove, ADF: A Cycle of Druid Rituals* by Rev. Robert Lee (Skip) Ellison, published by Dragons Keep Publishing, 1999. Some of the modified rituals in chapters 6 and 7 have been adapted from ones found in the same book. Used with permission.

Dedication:

This book is dedicated to the solitaries in ADF, whose questions and comments led to this book, and to the members of Muin Mound Grove, ADF.

Table of Contents

Chapter 1
What is a Druid?

I t was a dark, cloudless night, six nights after the new moon. A group of people dressed in white met in a glade of oaks in the middle of a dense forest. As they gathered around the base of an ancient tree, one of them, a priest, climbed up to a branch with large mistletoe plants hanging down from it. After prayers to the Gods and to the Spirits of the tree and the plant, the priest cut off the mistle-toe with a gold-clad sickle, and allowed it to drop into a white cloth being held by the others at the base of the tree.

The Path of Druidry

The above description is based on a section in Natural History, by one of the most frequently quoted Roman writers, Pliny the Elder, who lived from about 23-24 CE[1] to 79 CE. In section 16.24 Pliny goes on to say:

Not to be overlooked is the admiration of the Gauls for this plant [mistletoe]. The Druids—as their magicians are called—hold nothing more sacred than this plant and the tree on which it grows, as if it grew only on oaks. They choose only groves of oak and perform no rites unless a branch from that tree is present. Thus it seems that Druids are so called from the Greek name of the oak [drus]. Truly they believe that anything which grows on the tree is sent from heaven and is a sign that the tree was chosen by the god himself. However, mistletoe rarely grows on oaks, but is sought with reverence and cut only on the sixth day of the moon, as it is then that the moon is powerful but not yet halfway in its course (it is by the moon they measure days, years, and their cycle of thirty years). In their language the mistletoe is called "the healer of all." When preparations for a sacrifice and feast beneath the tree have been made, they lead forward two white bulls with horns bound for the first time. A

---

[1]Current Era. This usage is preferred by scholars over AD.

priest in white clothing climbs the tree and cuts the mistletoe with a golden sickle, and it is caught in a white cloak. They then sacrifice the bulls while praying that the god will grant the gift of prosperity to those whom he has given it [mistletoe]. They believe that mistletoe, when taken in a drink, will restore fertility to barren animals, and is a remedy for all poisons. Such is the dedication to trifling affairs displayed by many peoples.[2]

Pliny tells us much about the people we call the Druids. We learn that they reckon time by nights instead of days, that they revere the oak and the mistletoe, and that they give sacrifices to their Gods. Other writings from Classical, Irish, and Welsh authors, along with archaeological evidence, help round out the picture of who the Druids were, what they believed, and how they lived. In this book, we will explore what is known about the Druids and find ways for you to use their wisdom and skills in your own life.

People choose the solitary Path of Druidry for many different reasons. It may be because they live in an area where others do not feel the same. It may be because others where they live may follow a Druidic Path, but you do not like them or cannot work with them. Or, they simply feel the need to worship alone. These and many others are perfectly valid reasons for choosing to follow a solitary path.

The Path of Druidry is not always easy, however. It is a way that requires you to dedicate your life to learning and to the Mighty Kindred. The Mighty Kindred are the Spirits of Nature, the Ancestors and the Goddesses and Gods around us. The Spirits of Nature include those beings—including all living non-human beings—and the Spirits that inhabit the land, forests, and waters. The Ancestors include your own ancestors, those of the people you know and love, and the Ancestors of the land, the people who, in days gone by, have lived where you live and worship. The Gods and Goddesses are those you honor and worship.

The skills necessary to walk that Path of Druidry are not that hard to learn but they are many, and the path is long. There is no "instant gratification," no "one-stop-shop" to be a Druid. Indeed, given the amount of knowledge and the many different abilities that the ancient Druids possessed—their photographic memory, language skills, magical skills, etc.—it's doubtful that anyone today can actually be called a fully

---

[2]John Koch, *The Celtic Heroic Age: Literary Sources for Ancient Celtic Europe and Early Ireland and Wales* (Malden Mass.: Celtic Studies Publications, 1995), 26.

functioning Druid. In my opinion the most that can be said for present-day Druids is that we are following the "Path of Druidry" and learning the myriad skills necessary.

This is a path for those who value learning, the world around them, and the knowledge that what our ancestors have done can be relearned. Many are already on that path and their company makes the journey easier for those just starting. What I can do, is begin to lead you through this world in this book.

During my many years as a member of, and then for nine years as the head of, Ár nDraíocht Féin (ADF—pronounced "arn ree-ocht fane"), a NeoPagan religious organization that represents one tradition of modem Druidry, I have had the opportunity to observe many people starting out along this path. For the past fifteen years, I have been developing and teaching work-shops on various aspects of the journey. In this book, the instruction in those workshops have been brought together to assist people to more easily take their first steps along the path. The journey should be a pleasant one, not something that requires you to race through it or to see how fast you can finish. So read on and see where the path will lead before you make the decision to follow.

Definitions of a Druid

Who were the Druids? Most scholars believe that the first Druids were the priests and intelligentsia of the ancient Celts. The Celts are the peoples that spoke, or speak, one of the languages derived from the proto-Celtic branch of the western grouping of the Indo-European language tree. The list of those languages is long, especially those that have died out, but the modern languages include Manx, Scots Gaelic, and Irish from the Goidelic branch; and Breton, Cornish, and Welsh from the Brythonic branch. This definition, accepted by many scholars today, simply means that the Celts were identified mainly by language rather than culture, because the Celts saw themselves as individual tribes only, not as an empire or even as a race of people, and many Celtic tribes' cultures differed from each other.

As the priests of the Celts, the Druids were the men and women who led the main rituals for their village, performed sacrifices for the tribe or village, and read the omens and signs from the Gods. It is unlikely that they were involved in the home religion, which was the personal religion of the people of the tribe. The home religion was very likely led by the eldest male of each household, and was focused on the local spirits that dwelt near the home and with the fertility of the fields where crops were grown. There may have been another component of this religion that was led by the eldest female and dealt more with the spirits that resided "within" the home and focused on domestic concerns. The Druids may have helped with the home religion by answering questions such as "What is the best form of sacrifice to give to an individual spirit?" or "When should this sacrifice be given?"

The Celts believed that each person could act on their own to talk with and receive answers from the Mighty Kindred. There are many examples from the archaeological record, of small personal shrines in homes that demonstrate this. Some of these shrines included small representations of the deities or spirits and places to leave offerings for them.

As the local intelligentsia, the Wise Ones, Druids were the advisors to kings, doctors, judges, law speakers, and the *Aes Dána* (men of special gifts or arts). The Druids were one of the few groups of people who could travel freely between the tribes, the others being the chieftains and the traders, and receive the hospitality of each group they visited. The Greek author Strabo claimed that the Druids could step between two Celtic armies about to engage in battle and stop it with their words. Besides acting as advisors, lawgivers, and priests, the Druids were the repository of the tribes' histories and genealogy.

According to the Roman author and Emperor Julius Caesar, they could recite the lineage of any person in the tribe they lived with, as well as those of the chieftains of other Celtic tribes, as far back as twenty generations or more. They also had a vast repertoire of stories for any occasion.

To see where the Druids came from, we turn first to the Book of Invasions, from the mythological cycle of tales from Ireland. This cycle purports to record the founding of Ireland as written down by Christian monks, but more likely the accounts derive from the oral records of a much earlier time.

The tale starts out by telling us of the first man to come to Ireland, as part of the first wave of the invasion. His name was Cessair and he brought a small group of people with him. He was followed in the second wave by Partholon, who was accompanied by four chieftains and all their people, who worked to clear the land. In the third wave of invasions, Nemed brought his people on forty-four large boats to take the land away from the people of Partholon. The fourth wave of invasion introduced the tribes of the Fir Bolgs, which included five chieftains and their followers. After a great battle with the people of Nemed, they spread over the land and established many villages.

The Druids make their first appearance in the tale as they arrive in Ireland, during the fifth wave of invasions with the *Tuatha Dé Danann*, the people whom many NeoPagans today worship as deities. Scholars still debate their origins. Originally, they may have been a tribe of real people, but stories about them were repeated so often that they became elevated to the status of deities. It is said that they had "come from the North," and flew onto the island in magical ships.

The tale goes on to tell of the arrival of the Sons of Mil (the Celts from Gaul, the area of modern day France and Spain and the continent) during the sixth wave of invasions, and that they brought their own Druids with them.

Turning to other sources, the first mention of Druids is by the Classical Greek writer Posidonius, who lived from about 135 to 51 BCE (Before Current Era), in his work *The Histories*, written at the end of the second century, beginning of the first century BCE. As the work itself is lost, we have only references to it in the writings of later Greek philosophers and historians, such as Diodorus, Athenaeus, and Strabo. (And possibly from Julius Caesar as well; scholars continue to argue about the influence of Posidonius on Caesar's writings.) Earlier references to the Celts were made by the Greek author Herodotus in the fifth century BCE, but Posidonius was the first to write about the Druids. Later references, made by monks, Christian missionaries in Ireland who lived at the same time as the Druids they were writing about, are from the seventh century CE, and are found in the annals, the law texts, and the lives of the saints manuscripts.

Both Strabo and Pliny the Elder thought that the word "Druid" was a cognate of the Greek *drus*, which means "an oak." However, in Ireland, *druí* means "sorcerer" or "magician," and in Wales, *derwydd* means "body of the oak." Modern scholars have suggested that "Druid" derives from the Old Irish *deru*, an oak, and *hud*, an enchantment.

For many people today, the idea of whom and what a Druid is reflects a renewed interest in Druids that started in the British Isles and on the continent in the mid-sixteenth century. It began with all things old and Celtic, the ancient monuments, the Classical writers and, foremost, the idea that primitive man lived as a "noble savage."

With the discovery of the American Indians in the New World, whom Europeans saw as living in harmony with the world around them, the British wanted to look back to their own primitive ancestors in the hope that they had lived the same type of life.

The Druids came quickly to mind as leading lives of similar harmony. It is at this time that many important historic figures, such as Winston Churchill, joined the Druid movement. Unfortunately, it is from the early periods of this revival of interest in Druids that they were proclaimed the builders of Stonehenge and other megalithic monuments; something we now know is untrue. The idea that the Druids were a class of society that had reached a near perfect state was enough to drive some people to want to bring that perfect state into their own lives. This led to forgeries of written material, mainly of spurious Welsh manuscripts, that alleged that the Druids had never died out, but had gone into hiding with the advent of the Christians.

In the late 1770s, a Welsh stonemason by the name of Edward Williams, writing under the pen name Iolo Morganwg, created "translations" of supposedly lost Welsh manuscripts showing that bards in the region had survived until recent times and had preserved the "lost knowledge of the Druids." Williams was fluent in medieval Welsh and was a good enough scholar to fool many of his colleagues. This has led to many problems for modern-day investigators, who have been painstakingly trying to determine which translations are real and which are Williams's fabrications.

Today, many ideas about the Druids abound that are pure fantasy, much like those created by Williams. If you look up the term "Druid" in a Google search, you will find numerous examples of imaginings about Druids in the web sites listed, including fanciful notions that Druids:

- Came from Atlantis or were taught their skills by Atlantean masters. Not much evidence has come forth to prove the existence of Atlantis, let alone Atlantean masters.

- Built Stonehenge and similar megaliths. In fact, Stonehenge was built from about 2900 to 1600 BCE, well before the time of Druids.

- There is an unbroken line of knowledge going all the way back to the ancient Druids. No evidence of this has ever been found.

- Are the descendants of and carry the genetic material of a group of extraterrestrials that crashed in the British Isles during the Bronze Age. This argument has been presented for many civilizations but never proved.

Druids Today

Fortunately, many people walking the "Path of Druidry" base their knowledge on facts, not fantasy. We share a common love for learning, a reverence for the Earth and knowledge that the Mighty Kindred — the Spirits of Nature, the Ancestors, and the Gods and Goddesses, are all around us and will interact with us on a daily basis when we learn to slow down and listen.

Thanks to the Internet, there are many ways to learn more about us and to find out if the Path of Druidry is for you. We know, for example, that the number of Druids has been growing in the British Isles for many years and that this interest is now spreading to the U.S.

In an ongoing study done by the Graduate Center of the City University of New York, the number of people in the U.S. describing themselves as following the Druid religion rose from none in 1990 to 33,000 in 2001![3] Many people are finding groves of trees to tend or are joining with like-minded people to form groves of worshipers. If the path is right for you, then be welcome!

---

[3] "The Graduate Center, CUNY - ARIS 2001: Key Findings," accessed January 19, 2012, *http:// www.gc.cuny.edu/Faculty/GC-Faculty-Activities/ARIS--American-Religious-Identification-Survey/Key-findings*.

Chapter 2
The World
of the Druids

How did the ancient Druids view the world around them? What did they think of the Spirits around them in the land, and of their Gods and Goddesses? What was the philosophy practiced by the Druids? How did the Druids—and to a large extent the rest of the Celts—deal with matters of sexuality? In this chapter, we will explore each of these questions and consider whether the lessons learned can be applied to our lives as modern Druids.

The World Around Them

When many people think of the ancient peoples of Europe, they picture a tree-filled forest, with tribes living in small communities in harmony with the land. In reality, archaeological evidence points to a very different picture. In order to have enough room to plant crops and feed their herds, the ancients would clear large areas of land. Over many years, Europe, including the British Isles, came to be deforested. Even in the Book of Invasions, the early manuscript detailing the settling of Ireland, several passages describe "clearing plains" to tame the land. By the end of the tales most of Ireland had been "tamed."

In many ways, however, our ancestors were more in tune with the land than we are today. You can see this by looking at areas where people still work the land today. Not on large scale "factory farms," but where families work the land on a small scale for their livelihood. By working it on a daily basis, people knew the smell and the taste of the land through the seasons. They felt the pains of the earth during times of drought as well as the choking effect of the water during times of flood. People felt the comfort and restfulness of the land as it lay fallow in the winter. Most of us nowadays have lost this connection.

Along with working the land on a daily basis, our ancestors knew of sacred places where people could go to worship the Spirits that dwelt there. This is something that is not lost to us today; it can be rediscovered. Everywhere, one can find such special places where the sacredness and the power of the land can be felt. We will talk more about such areas, still worthy of our worship and love, in chapter 5 under "Contacting the Land."

The Mighty Kindred

To our ancestors, the world of Spirit surrounded them. They understood that bushes and trees had Spirits that resided in them, and that in the marshes and moors there were creatures that were "different" from humans and other animals. From the archaeological record, we know that they worshiped Spirits and more—the first among those honored and revered being their Ancestors, the first of the Mighty Kindred. An example of this worship can be found in the remains of meals left at burial mounds.

We can see also where they honored and worshiped the Spirits of the land around them, the second of the Mighty Kindred. Examples of this worship have come down to us in the tales that describe encounters with "beings" of the forest. Moreover, we can see from the accounts of Greek and Roman authors where they honored and worshiped the Gods and Goddesses that their tribe knew, the third and last of the Mighty Kindred.

Ancestor worship is still practiced in many parts of the world, as evidenced by the number of floral arrangements left on graves in memory of departed loved ones. In a more extreme example of tribute, stories handed down from the Romans tell of people taking picnic lunches to the graves of their Ancestors and eating with them. They even placed shafts leading down into the tombs so that food and drink could be deposited there, and literally be shared with their Ancestors.

Many a hero would spend the night on the tomb of a brave Ancestor to gather the wisdom the Ancestor would provide. In the tales of the Druids, one of the methods of divination practiced was to go to a tomb, sleep on it overnight, and absorb necessary information from the dead. Professor Eugene O'Curry, Dean of Celtic Studies at Trinity College in Dublin in the late 1800s, wrote:

While Murgén [an early Irish Druid] was thus seated, he composed and spoke a laidh, or lay [a poem for the dead], for the gravestone of Fergus, as if it had been Fergus himself he was addressing. Suddenly, as the story runs, there came a great mist which enveloped him so that he could not be discovered for three days; and during that time Fergus himself appeared to him in a beautiful form, for he is described as adorned with brown hair, clad in a green cloak, and wearing a collared gold-ribbed shirt, a gold-hilted sword, and sandals of bronze; and it is said that this apparition related to Murgén the whole of the Tain, from beginning to end, the tale which he was sent to seek in foreign land.[4]

Today, we can show respect and honor for our Ancestors in many ways. We can remember them in our rituals, we can have pictures and mementos of them on our altars, or we can invoke them privately in our prayers and thoughts. All are valid methods of showing respect and keeping their memory alive.

As our Ancestors worshiped and honored the Spirits of the land, so can we. These Spirits come in many forms. They are the creatures that walk and crawl upon the land, the mammals, reptiles, and insects. They are the creatures that fly in the sky and swim in the waters, the birds, fish, and amphibians. They are the creatures that burrow in the land itself, the insects, and other microorganisms. Such are the first class of Spirits of the land.

Next are the actual "Spirits" that reside in the trees, plants, stones, and other land features. It is this class of beings that help make "special" our special places. Finally, there are the members of the tribes of faeries, or Fair Folk, the otherworldly creatures that are known by many names, such as elves, brownies, and the like. Many of the European faerie tribes, each area with its own tribe, have traveled with human beings coming to the U.S. (This is discussed in more detail in chapter 4.) All of these classes of beings deserve to be honored in our rituals and our daily practice, just as our ancestors would have done.

The last of the Mighty Kindred are the Gods and Goddesses that our Ancestors worshipped. Many people who follow the Path of Druidry worship and give honor to the members of the *Tuatha Dé Danann*, the people of the Goddess Danu. These deities include the Mórrígan, the Dagda, Lúgh, Brigit, and many others. Good descriptions of them, along

---

[4]Eugene O'Curry, *Lectures on the Manuscript Materials of Ancient Irish History* (Portland, OR: Four Courts Press, 1995), 30.

with many stories of their lives, are found in the *Book of Invasions*, the *Second Battle of Maige Tuired*, the *Wooing of Étaíne*, and dozens of other tales.

By reading these stories, you can find Gods and Goddesses that resonate with you, that hold a special feeling for you and in return, you for them. Once this is done, you can meditate on them and invite them to become a stronger influence in your life. Over time, you will develop a special relationship with them and through meditation begin to learn lessons from them. They should be included in your rituals and daily worship, and the more time you spend thinking about them, worshiping them, and learning about them, the better the relationships will become.

The Druids' Place in the Cosmos

The ancient Druids were known to many as philosophers, people who studied and knew about the natural world and the use of logic. They were also people who studied the stars and heavens. Diogenes Laertius, a Greek writing in the first half of the third century CE, says in his *Vitae*, Intro 1:

> *Some say that the study of philosophy first developed among the barbarians. For the Persians had their Magi [the name given to their magicians/ philosophers], the Babylonians or Assyrians their Chaldeans [the name given to their philosophers], the Indians their Gymnosophists [the name given to their philosophers], while the Celts had those called Druids and Semnotheoi, according to Aristotle in the Agicus and Sotion in the 23rd book of his work Successions.*

He goes on to tell us:

> *They say the gymnosophists and Druids instruct by means of riddles, urging worship of the Gods, abstinence from evil and the practice of manly virtue.[5]*

We hear more of this from the Roman author Dio Chrysostom, who in the work *Orations*, 49, tells us:

> *For their part, the Celts have men called Druids, who deal with prophecy and every division of wisdom. Even kings would not be so bold as to make a decision or take action without [the Druids'] counsel. Thus in reality it was [the Druids]*

---

[5]Koch, *The Celtic Heroic Age*, 24.

who governed. The kings, who sat on golden thrones and lived luxuriously in their great residences, became mere agents of the decisions of the Druids.[6]

As the above references attest, the Druids were powerful people with a very high place in their society. Peter Berresford Ellis, a modern English historian, talks about the art of divining from the stars among the Druids in his book, *The Druids*:

...*[I]n Old Irish are found other words for philosopher; cailleóii, whose basis means auguring or star divination and which is used in Scots Gaelic in the form cáileadar to mean philosopher or star-gazer; while a further Old Irish term feallsamhacht survives in Manx as fallosgyssagh which means an astrologer.[7]*

In the Old Irish manuscript known as the *Senchus Mór*, a compilation of several older oral tales transcribed by monks working for St. Patrick in the early fifth century CE, reference is made to the ability of Druids to know about the sky and heavens, even though their estimates of the distances involved are off by a wide margin. It says:

The thickness of the earth is measured by the space from the earth to the firmament. The seven divisions from the firmament to the earth are Saturn, Jupiter, Mercury, Mars, Sol, Luna, Venus. From the moon to the sun is 244 miles; but from the firmament to the earth, 3024 miles. As the shell is about the egg, so is the firmament around the earth. The firmament is a mighty sheet of crystal. The twelve constellations [of the Zodiac] represent the year, as the sun runs through one each month.[8]

Overall, in the known world at that time, the Druids served a function similar to that of other cultures' philosophers, such as the Gymnosophists, the Chaldeans, and the Magi. Likewise, they were an elite who knew the stars and planets, knew the ways of nature, and advised the rulers of the tribes. They were people worthy of emulation today.

The Druids and Sex

The "Path of Druidry" embraces many different lifestyles. None is favored over the others. People who choose this Path can be

---

[6] Ibid

[7] Peter Ellis, *The Druids* (Grand Rapids Mich.: W.B. Eerdmans Pub. Co., 1998), 173.

[8] James Bonwick, *Irish Druids and Old Irish Religions* (New York: Dorset Press, 1986), 18-19.

comfortable in the knowledge that whatever forms their own life takes; they will be welcomed on the Path.

In my opinion through looking back in history, I feel that the Druids (and the Celts in general) had a very different view of sex than ours. They were brought up in a culture that had not been influenced by the modern monotheistic religions. Along with being polytheists, I think that they were also, in many cases, polyamorous. As well as knowing and worshiping many Gods and Goddesses, Druids had many lovers, often referred to in the old texts as many "sexual unions," often with both sexes.

We can see this in the accounts of Classical writers, the early Irish tales, and in the Brehon Laws, the native laws of Ireland, written down in the fourteenth to sixteenth centuries CE, although composed in the seventh and eighth centuries CE.

One of the best comments on Celtic sexuality that I have found is by the historian Nora Chadwick in her book *The Celts*:

> *We note the same hauteur in the reply of the Caledonian woman, attributed by Dio Cassius to the wife of Argentocoxus, when Julia Augusta, the wife of Severus, jested with her about the free intercourse of her sex with men in Britain. She replied,* **"We fulfill the demands of nature in a much better way than do you Roman women; for we consort openly with the best men, whereas you let yourselves be debauched in secret by the vilest."** [bold added] *The Celts were always and everywhere a proud people.*[9]

Looking next at the *Politics* of Aristotle (384-322 BCE), section 2.6.6, we find him talking about homosexuality and the Celts:

> *The consequence is that in such a state wealth is too highly valued, especially if the citizens fall under the dominion of their wives, after the manner of most war-like races,* **except the Celts and a few others who openly approve of male loves...**[bold added] [10]

Diodorus Siculus (circa 90-21 BCE), in the work, *Historical Library*, section 5.32, has more to say on the subject of homosexual lovers:

---

[9]Nora Chadwick, *The Celts* (London: Penguin, 1991), 55.
[10]Koch, *The Celtic Heroic Age*, 5.

...[T]he men of the Gauls pay little attention to their women, even though they are quite beautiful, but prefer unnatural intercourse with other men. They sleep on the ground on the skins of wild animals, rolling about with their sleeping companions on each side. **The oddest custom is that without any thought towards being discrete, they gladly offer their youthful bodies to others, not thinking this any disgrace, but being deeply offended when refused.** [bold added][11]

This sentiment was echoed in the work, *The Deipnosophistse* (The Learned Banquet) book XIII, section 603a, by Athenaeus (circa 295 to 373 CE):

Among barbarians the Celts also, though they have very beautiful women, enjoy boys more; so that some of them often have two lovers to sleep with on their beds of animal skins.[12]

On the topic of male lovers, *The Roman History*, Book 31, Section 9.5, by Ammianus (circa 330-391 CE), offers the following about a Gaulish tribe:

We have learned that these Taifali were a shameful folk, so sunken in a life of shame and obscenity, that in their country the boys are coupled with the men in a union of unmentionable lust, to consume the flower of their youth in the polluted intercourse of those paramours. We may add that, if any grown person alone catches a boar or kills a huge bear, he is purified thereby from the shame of unchastity.[13]

On the subject of sharing multiple wives and husbands, a passage by Julius Caesar (circa 101-32 BCE) from *The Gallic Wars*, section 5.14, comments on the lives of the Gauls, who inhabited modern-day France and parts of the British Isles:

Ten and even twelve [of the men] have wives common to them, and particularly brothers among brothers, and par-ents among their children; but if there be any issue by these wives, they are reputed to be the children of those by whom respectively each was first espoused when a virgin.[14]

---

[11]Ibid., 14. .

[12]Athenaeus of Naucratis, "Athenaeus: *Deipnosophists* - Book 13 (d)," trans. C.D.Yonge, accessed January 19, 2012, *http://www.attalus.org/old/athenaeus13d.html*.

[13]Ammianus Marcellinus, "LacusCurtius • *Ammianus Marcellinus* — Book XXXI," trans. Bill Thayer, accessed January 19, 2012, *http://penelope.uchicago.edu/Thayer/E/Roman/Texts/Ammian/31*.html*.

[14] Caesar, Julius, "The Internet Classics Archive | *The Gallic Wars* by Julius Caesar," trans. W. A. McDevitte and W. S. Bohn, accessed January 19, 2012, *http://classics.mit.edu/Caesar/gallic.5.5.html*.

From Strabo (circa 66 BCE to 32 CE), writing in *Ancient Geographies*, section 4.5.4, we find further information on, multiple partners, but only about the Irish, showing how widespread the practice was among the Celts:

> *Besides some small islands round about Britain, there is also a large island, Ierne [Ireland], which stretches parallel to Britain on the north, its breadth being greater than its length. Concerning this island I have nothing certain to tell, except that its inhabitants are more savage than the Britons, since they are man-eaters as well as heavy eaters, and since, further, they count it an honourable thing, when their fathers die, to devour them, and* **openly to have intercourse, not only with the other women, but also with their mothers and sisters...** [bold added][15]

Further evidence of multiple partners and homosexuality is found in the writings of Cassius Dio (circa 40-110 CE). In *Roman Histories*, volume 8, book 62, section 6, he quotes Boadicea (Boudica), a queen of the Iceni tribe in the early first century CE:

> *...[T]hose over whom I rule are Britons, men that know not how to till the soil or ply a trade, but are thoroughly versed in the art of war and* **hold all things in common, even children and wives, so that the latter possess the same valour as the men.** *As the queen, then, of such men and of such women, I supplicate and pray thee for victory, preservation of life, and liberty against men insolent, unjust, insatiable, impious—if, indeed, we ought to term those people men who bathe in warm water, eat artificial dainties, drink unmixed wine, anoint themselves with myrrh,* **sleep on soft couches with boys for bedfellows—boys past their prime at that**—*and are slaves to a lyre-player [the Roman Emperor Nero] and a poor one too...* [bold added][16]

Moving on to the Irish tales, we find the following reference to a male lover in the *Táin Bo Cúailnge* in the *Yellow Book of Lecan* and (more completely) in the *Book of Leinster*. These are the words from Cú Chulainn about Ferdia:

> *We were heart-companions once; We were comrades in the woods; We were men that shared a bed, When we slept the heavy sleep, After hard and weary fights. Into many lands, so strange,*

---

[15]Strabo, "LacusCurtius • Strabo's *Geography*—Book IV Chapter 5," accessed January 19, 2012, *http://penelope.uchicago.edu/Thayer/E/Roman/Texts/Strabo/4E*.html*.

[16]Cassius Dio, "Cassius Dio—Epitome of Book 62," accessed January 19, 2012, *http://penelope.uchicago.edu/Thayer/E/Roman/Texts/Cassius_Dio/62*.html*.

Side by side we sallied forth, And we ranged the woodlands through, When with Scathach we learned arms! [17]

Also in the *Tain Bo Cúailnge*, we hear of Queen Medb. It is said that with her husband's permission, she had many lovers and that "she would not take a lover without another standing in his shadow, ready to take over!" There are several references in the tale to her taking lovers for political as well as personal reasons, and she is known to have offered "the friendship of the thighs" too many.[18]

Even in Christian times, polyamory was widespread among the Celts. St. Jerome, who lived from about 340 to 420 CE, tells us that "the Irish are given to promiscuity and incest."[19] References to multiple relationships, some of which are described below, are also found in the Brehon Laws. As Fergus Kelly points out in *A Guide to Early Irish Law* (regarded by many scholars today as the best book available on the Brehon Laws):

> *The author of Brethe Crólige [an early Irish law text] frankly admits that there is dispute in Irish law as to whether it is proper to have many sexual unions or a single one. He justifies the practice of polygamy from the Old Testament, pointing out that the chosen people of God lived in plurality of unions.*[20]

The Brehon Laws are full of interesting facts about the sexual lives of the Irish. For example, the laws defined nine forms of sexual unions, called *lánamnas*, the first six of those listed below, being forms of marriage allowed in Ireland. These include:

- A union of joint property, *lánamnas comthinchuir*, where both partners contributed movable goods, their own possessions.
- A union of a woman on man-property, *lánamnas mná for ferthinchur*, where the woman contributes little, or nothing.
- A union of man on woman-property, *lánamnas fir for bantinchur*, where the man contributes little, or nothing.

---

[17]Unknown, "The Combat of Ferdiad and Cuchulain," trans. Joseph Dunn & Ernst Windisch, accessed January 19, 2012, *http://adminstaff.vassar.edu/sttaylor/Cooley/Ferdiad.html.*

[18]Jean Markale, *Women of the Celts*, 1st U.S. ed. (Rochester Vt.: Inner Traditions International, 1986), 165.

[19]David Rankin, *Celts and the Classical World* (London [etc.]: Routledge, 1996), 250.

[20]Fergus Kelly, *A Guide to Early Irish Law* (Dublin: Dublin Institute for Advanced Studies, 1988), 71.

- A union of a man visiting, *lánamnas fir for thathigtheo*, in which the man visits the woman at her house to have intercourse with her upon her kin's consent.

- A woman goes away openly with the man, but is not given to him by her kin.

- A woman "allows" herself to be abducted, *lánamnas foxail*, without her kin's consent.

- A woman is secretly visited, *lánamnas táidi*, without her kin's consent.

- A union by rape.

- The union of two insane people.[21]

Because polygamy was not only permitted but wide-spread, it was very likely that a man would have several wives from different types of unions.

Several interesting reasons for divorce are included in the Brehon Laws. A woman may divorce her husband if he is impotent or if he becomes so fat that he is incapable of intercourse; if he prefers boys to his wife; if he is sterile; or if the husband spreads "intimate details" about her.

It is important to remember that even though it is thought that the ancient Celts were very likely polyamorous—an arrangement that in Ireland endured until the fourteenth or fifteenth century— this may not be to everyone's taste today. Still, it is making a revival. Further information about the subject can be found on the following Web sites:

- *www.neopagan.net/Contents.html#PartEleven* a section about polyamory on the Web site of Isaac Bonewits.[22]

- *www.lovemore.com* devoted to the polyamorous lifestyle.[23]

- *www.polyamory.org* a site for one of the largest polyamory newsgroup.[24]

---

[21]Ibid., 70.

[22]Bonewits, Isaac, "Neopagan Net: Table of Contents / Site Map," accessed January 19, 2012, *http://www.neopagan.net/Contents.html#PartEleven*.

[23]Loving More®, "Loving More Your #1 Resource for Polyamory," accessed January 19, 2012, *http://www.lovemore.com/*.

[24]stef@polyamory.org, "Alt.polyamory Home Page," accessed January 19, 2012, *http://www.polyamory.org/*.

Chapter 3
Magic and the Ancient Druids

A s well as serving as the philosophers, astronomers, and priests of the Celts, many ancient Druids were practitioners of magic. This magic was, for the most part, a private practice, apart from the large-scale magic worked on behalf of entire tribes in times of battle. In fact, Druids and magic have **always** been connected, and we find in the literature many tales of magic involving them. These range from the transformations recounted in the Irish tale of the *Children of Lir*, in which young people were turned into swans by their stepmother, to accounts in the *Book of Invasions* of the storm-generating magic by which *Tuatha Dé Danann* repelled the fleet of the Milesians, to the story told of the *Second Battle of Maige Tuired*, where magic dried up the rivers so that the enemy could not quench its thirst. There are tales of Druid shape-shifting—changing into the form of animals or other people— and of weather magic, spells for knowledge, spells to curse, and spells to draw love. In this chapter, we will explore some descriptions of such magic as found in the Irish tales and see how they can help us in our walk along the "Path of Druidry." By learning about the Druid's magic, we can bring the use of that magic into our own lives. At the end of the chapter, I will provide some practical spells that can be used today.

Shape-Shifting

In the tale of the Children of Lir, a wicked stepmother, Aoife, changes the children into swans:

> *Aoife was a changed woman now and one day suggested that she and the children should visit their grandfather. On the journey they stopped by a lake and she encouraged the children to go for a swim. The four children played happily in the water, not noticing that their stepmother was now standing at the*

water's edge wearing her father's magic cloak. "For too long you children have stood between your father and I, but not for much longer!" she cried. "We cannot be killed by you," Aodh [the eldest of the boys] *replied. "We are the children of Lir* [a great magician and Druid] *and if you harm us our ghosts will haunt you!" "I'm not going to kill you," she shouted, "but I am going to change you!" At this she bowed her head and started an incantation. The children looked at each other in fear as they saw a red and gold circle envelop them on the water. They saw Aoife open up her cloak from which the great light of a fireball emerged and hurtled towards them, burning all in its wake. The fireball hit the water and caused masses of steam to rise about the children and they soon lost all feeling in their legs, arms, shoulders, and head. They soon regained their sight only to see Aoife laughing at them. Aodh tried to attack her and flailed his arms about furiously but nothing happened except the splashing of water. He turned to look at his brothers and sister only to see that they had all been turned into the most beautiful swans ever seen.*

Aoife scowled at them again and told them that they were to spend nine hundred years as swans, three hundred on Lough Derravaragh, three hundred on the Straits of Moyle, and three hundred on the Isle of Inish Glora. To end the spell they would have to hear the bell of the new God.[25]

This tale gives us a few pointers on how the shape-shifting magic is done. First, Aoife had on a magic cloak. We are not told that it was necessary for the magic, but the children knew that something was going to happen as soon as they saw it. Second, Aoife had to recite an incantation for the spell to work. Unfortunately, none of the literary descriptions of shape-shifting provide the texts of the incantations used.

In the *Cath Maige Tuired* which tells of the second battle between the *Tuatha Dé Danann* and the *Fomoire*, the tribe that occupied Ireland when the *Tuatha Dé Danann* arrived, we see another example of shape-shifting. In the following excerpt, Lúgh, the battle leader, asks the people what they will do in the coming battle:

"And you, Bé Chuille and Dianann," said Lúgh to his two witches, "what can you do in the battle?" "Not hard to say," they said. "We will enchant the trees and the stones and the sods of the earth so that they will be a host under arms

---

[25]Unknown, "The Children of Lir," accessed January 20, 2012, *http://www.ireland-information.com/articles/thechildrenoflir.htm.*

against them [an army of moving trees, stones, and earth]*; and they will scatter in flight terrified and trembling"*[26]

In this tale, it is the trees and rocks that are shifted in shape so that they can move. We do not find out how it was done, just that the witches had the power to do it.

Weather and the Elements

A good example of weather magic may be read in the Book of Invasions. After the Celtic bard Amergin gave the *Tuatha Dé Danann* time to prepare for battle, the Celts left the island and went out to the "ninth wave," a poetic term used to mean that they went back out to sea and waited for a bit. The tale continues:

> *"Let us trust to the powers," said the Druids* [those of the *Tuatha Dé Danann*], *"that they may never reach Ireland." With that the Druids cast Druidic winds after them, so great was the storm so that the storm took them westward in the ocean until they were weary. "A druid's wind is that," said Donn, son of Mil. "It is indeed," said Amergin, "unless it be higher than the mast* [a storm created by magic would only be near the sea, unlike a normal storm]*; find out for us if it be so." Erannan, the youngest son of Mil, went up the mast, and said that it was not over them. With that he fell on the planks of the ship from the mast, so that they shattered his limbs."*[27]

In order to get the ships back to Ireland, Amergin had to work some weather magic of his own, calling upon the land to calm the winds.

> *"No shame it shall be," said Amergin, rising up; and he said:*
> *"I invoke the land of Ireland.*
> *Much-coursed be the fertile sea,*
> *Fertile be the fruit-strewn mountain,*
> *Fruit-strewn be the showery wood,*
> *Showery be the river of waterfalls,*
> *Of waterfalls be the lake of deep pools,*
> *Deep pooled be the hilltop well,*
> *A well of the tribes be the assembly,*
> *An assembly of the kings be Tara,*

---

[26]Unknown, "Cath Maige Tuired: The Second Battle of Mag Tuired," trans. Elizabeth A. Gray, sec. 116–117, accessed January 20, 2012, *http://www.ucc.ie/celt/published/T300010/index.html*.

[27]Unknown, "The Lebor Gabala Erren - The Book of Invasions," trans. R. A. S. Macalister, accessed January 20, 2012, *http://www.ancienttexts.org/library/celtic/irish/lebor.html*.

Tara be the hill of the tribes,
The tribes of the sons of Mil,
Of Mil be the ships, the barks,
Let the lofty bark be Ireland,
Lofty Ireland darkly sung,
An incantation of great cunning;
The great cunning of the wives of Bres,
The wives of Bres of Buaigne,
The great lady Ireland,
Eremon hath conquered her,
Ir, Eber have invoked for her.
I invoke the land of Ireland."
Immediately a tranquil calm came to them on the sea.[28]

From these two tales, we see that the Druids of both the *Tuatha Dé Danann* and the Celts had the power to "raise winds" and control the storms, both starting and stopping them.

Spell Casting

While the *Tuatha Dé Danann* were preparing for battle against the *Fomoire*, the Dagda had gone out to find people to help them in the battle. He met the daughter of Indech, the king of the *Fomoire*, and after making love to her, received this promise from her:

*Then however she said, "Allow the Fomoire to enter the land, because the men of Ireland have all come together in one place [the plain of Maige Tuired]." She said that she would hinder the Fomoire, and she would **sing spells** against them, and she would practice the **deadly art of the wand** against them— and she alone would take on a ninth part of the host [one-ninth of the Fomoire army]."* [bold added][29]

In another part of the tale, we hear:

*So the aes dana [men of art] did that, and they **chanted spells** against the Fomorian hosts.* [bold added][30]

The spells could also be used for healing, as is shown in the following section from the tale:

---

[28]Ibid. Bres, Eremon, Ir, and Eber are names of Celtic leaders.
[29]Unknown, "Cath Maige Tuired," 51.
[30]Ibid., sec. 86.

Now this is what used to kindle the warriors who were wounded there so that they were more fiery the next day: Dian Cécht, his two sons Octriuil and Míach, and his daughter Airmed were **chanting spells over the well** *named Sláine. They would cast their mortally wounded men into it as they were struck down; and they were alive when they came out.* **Their mortally wounded were healed through the power of the incantation** *made by the four physicians who were around the well.* [bold added][31]

These three tales are interesting in that they tell us the spells could be sung or chanted, and they suggest that the power of the spoken word is great, but that of the sung word is even greater! Reference is made to the "art of the wand," which hints at the power of the Druid's wand in casting spells. In many such tales, the wand of the Druid is shown to be their primary magical tool. The material the wand was made from is generally yew, hazel, rowan, or ash wood.

In yet another part of the tale, Lúgh addresses Coirpre mac Étaíne, one of the Druids, and others of the *Tuatha Dé Danann:*

"And you, Coirpre mac Étaíne," said Lúgh to his poet, "what can you do in the battle?" "Not hard to say," said Coirpre. "I will make a glám dícenn [a poetic spell] *against them, and I will satirize them and shame them so that through the spell of my art they will offer no resistance to warriors."*[32]

A little more about how spells were cast is described in the following section:

Lúgh was urging the men of Ireland to fight the battle fiercely so they should not be in bondage any longer, because it was better for them to find death while protecting their fatherland than to be in bondage and under tribute as they had been. Then Lúgh chanted the spell... going around the men of Ireland on one foot and with one eye closed.[33]

All in all, there are many interesting references that fur-nish clues to follow in our search for our own magical prac-tice. The ones provided in this chapter are only the briefest hints. Many more can be found by reading the tales and looking for bits of magical workings.

---

[31]Ibid., 56.

[32]Ibid., 54.

[33]Ibid., 59.

Practical Magic for Today

Many systems of magical training are available. Not all of them are Celtic, but many can be used by people following the Path of Druidry.

The main challenge to developing a completely Celtic-based magical system is that no actual spells were recorded. We have tantalizing hints, as shown above, but not the actual steps to perform the spell. Fortunately, complete magical systems exist from some of the other Indo-European peoples. The Greeks, Romans, and Vedic peoples all left very good records of how their spells were accomplished. We know this because the Indo-European people had a common ancestor, referred to as the Proto-Indo-Europeans, (PIE's) and as a result, many of their cultures and practices were similar. Examining comparable spells from the extant records of the Greeks, Romans, and Vedic peoples, we find certain similarities emerge. By looking at the descriptions of spells used by the Celts, and comparing them to those used by other cultures, we can reconstruct how the Celts would have executed the spells.

As you can imagine, this is not an easy task, but the work is under way. If you are interested in doing some of this work yourself, I would recommend reading *Magika Hiera: Ancient Greek Magic & Religion*, edited by Christopher A. Faraone and Dirk Obbink (Oxford University Press), on the subject of Greek magic, and Arcana Mundi, by George Luck (Johns Hopkins University Press), along with *Magic in the Ancient World*, by Fritz Graf (Harvard University Press), on both Greek and Roman magic combined. To learn about Vedic magical practices, *Atharva Veda Samhita*, by William Dwight Whitney (Motilal Banarsidass Publishers), is a wonderful book that even includes the scientific names for many of the plants mentioned in the spells.

Now on to some practical spells that you can try for yourself! There are some basic rules that can be applied to all magical workings. First, plan on a time to do the spell when you can work undisturbed for at least an hour or longer if the spell is complicated or involves many repetitions of incantations. Next, before beginning the spell, spend some time cleaning the place where it will be performed. A hot bath, enhanced by pleasant bath salts or herbs, works wonders to prepare your subconscious mind to do effective magic.

Spells for Knowledge

In the ancient world, several types of spells were used to gain knowledge. One method was through divination, to be covered separately in the next chapter. Another was to sleep on the grave of a revered Ancestor—something that isn't very practical today. A third way, however, is highly practical: the use of incense to aid in studying.

This might not seem like spell work, but truly it is! Much of the magic used in past times involved the use of "physica," naturally occurring substances like plants and stones, found in gardens and woods. One incense blend that has helped me for studying and meditation uses the following herbs and oils:

  2 parts sage leaf

  2 parts anise seed

  2 parts rosemary leaf

  1 part myrrh

  1 part calendula flower petals

  A few drops sandalwood oil

I usually mix up a large batch at the start of each year and burn some while I'm doing research. In my opinion, incense allows me to retain information better and to make connections between obscure facts.

Another easy way to use herbs while studying is to keep a rosemary plant growing in your kitchen. When you reach a point in your studies where you feel tired or unable to focus, simply brush your hand over the plant and inhale the odor. It will stimulate you enough to get the focus back! (The herb also can be used for cooking.)

Spells to Curse or to Heal

Curses were one of the main reasons to work magic in the ancient work. One way to place a curse was through the use of binding spells, called *defixiones* in Latin. In this type of spell, the name of the person you want to curse, and what you want to happen to them, were written on a sheet of lead and thrown into a well or body of water. This variety of spell was widespread in both Greek and Roman territories and thousands of these lead tablets have been recovered.

You can use the binding spell format today—without actually "cursing" anyone—if you are involved in a court case. A special variety of defixiones was the defixiones judicariae, judicial spell, where the adversary in the court case was "bound" by the spell. To do this, write the name of the person opposing you in court, along with how you want them to be bound, on a piece of wood, something that will last for awhile and put it in the ground. How the object of the spell is to be bound could be something as simple as not being able to speak well, or to constantly forget what they intended to say.

This same type of binding spell has also been used for healing. In this case, the "bound" object would be the disease. A museum in the English spa town of Bath has retrieved hundreds of these lead sheets once thrown into the local mineral waters to take away disease. The format used is the same no matter which disease is named, and is followed by the preferred cure.

A Spell to Draw Love

One of the ways employed in ancient days to draw a person's love was to pray and give offerings to a deity associated with love. This spell has been reconstructed using Vedic material, where in one instance, a wife was sought by praying to the God Indra. We find something similar to this in Celtic tales, in which people would ask Angus mac Og, also known as the Young God, to aid them in drawing a lover to them.

To work this spell, begin by summoning up a mental image of the characteristics you are looking for in a lover. It works best to actually list them on paper and to refine the list over the course of a few days. While you are compiling the list, gather together items that can be given as offerings to the deity you choose to call upon. These should be items that will be well received by the deity; for example, if you are calling upon Brigit, you could give offerings of love poems, inspired by her role as patroness of poets or milk products, for her birth in a cowshed.

The formula for the spell work is as follows:

1. *Brigit, bright flame of knowledge, I call upon you this night and give you this offering of a milk. I ask that you aid me in finding my true love!*

   At this time, pour an offering of fresh milk on the ground, or, if working indoors, in a bowl that can be taken out later and placed on the ground. While the spell is being worked, visualize Brigit standing in front of you and see her, in your mind's eye, agreeing to do as you ask.

2. *Brigit, the person I seek will be* [insert the qualities you want in your lover]. *Bring them to me as I give this offering to you."*

   Then, to show the Goddess how you feel, read a love poem that expresses your feelings. As you recite, visualize the type of person you are looking for, imagining all of the characteristics you desire.

3. *Brigit, I thank you for aiding me in this quest and give you this offering of whiskey as a small token of my thanks.*

   At this time, pour a small glass of whiskey on the ground or in the bowl. At this point, visualize Brigit drinking the whiskey and thanking you for it.

The spell is started and will work its way out into the cosmos. Results should appear within a few weeks.

In this chapter, we have looked at how the Druids used magic in the ancient world, and how their magic may be used today. This brings the first section of this book, dealing with the past, to a close. Now is the time to move on to the present-day skills you can use in your journey along the Path of Druidry.

Chapter 4
Living the Life
of a Solitary Druid

I n this chapter, we will learn how to do daily devotionals to the Mighty Kindred, let others know what path you are following and how to talk to your parents about our religion. Not all of those tasks are easy, but they are all important parts of living your life by the example you set.

Walking the Talk

Now that you have learned about the ancient Druids, it is time to incorporate the beliefs of the Druids into your personal life. This can be done through setting up an altar in your home, making time for daily worship, and increasing the spirituality in your life.

We will start first by talking about setting up a home altar or shrine. One special place should be set aside in your house for use **only** as an altar. That way it becomes much easier to do the daily work of giving offerings to the Mighty Kindred. (When my altar was set up just inside the door of my office, it quickly became a repository for paperwork that needed to be filed. I have since re-arranged the office and moved my home shrine downstairs to the library.) From examples of home shrines I have observed, I believe that the best location is on a shelf or shelves in an out-of-the-way corner. A home shrine should include representations of important parts of Druid ritual such as deity images, including an Earth Mother, representations of the Ancestors and Spirits of Nature, the fire, well and tree that make up the vertical axis of our cosmos, a bowl into which offerings are made, and other items that have a spiritual significance to you.

Above is a photo of my personal altar. The image to the left is a statue that represents the Dagda. The image next to that is a representation of the Mórrígan. The framed text is a poem that reminds me of Ireland and holds a special place in my heart. Toward the back right is a sculpture holding a representation of an Earth Mother, some seasonal decorations, and a shell to hold water and represent the well. In the center of the altar is a sculpted tree and a candle to represent the fire. The small disc and the feather are tokens for the Ancestors and Spirits of Nature. Not shown in this picture is a bowl to hold offerings.

Daily Devotionals

Now we move along to daily worship. I have found that the best way to do daily devotionals, which are simply rituals done on a daily basis to honor the Mighty Kindred, is to pick a set time, for example just after getting up or just before going to bed, and to make sure that the time is always observed. If you make an excuse even once in a while, you will find that it gets easier and easier to make the excuses and the devotionals will be put off. If you do not have time one morning to do them after getting out of bed, then you should have gotten up earlier to compensate for it. It should not be put off as unimportant.

Depending on how much time you have in your daily schedule to allot for devotionals, the sequence of what is done can be adjusted. If you are pressed for time, you could have a schedule where, for example, Monday is devoted to the Earth Mother, Tuesday to the Spirits of Nature, Wednesday to the Ancestors Thursday to the Shining Ones and Friday to your patron deity or deities. Then on the weekend, you could do a full devotional to all of them. Alternatively, you might have enough time to devote to all of them daily.

As you will notice throughout this book, I firmly believe in repetition, especially repetition in form. The more often things are repeated; the easier it becomes to remember them. Even though repetition is good, the words that are spoken are better if they come from the inspiration that flows through you each day. They do not always have to be the same. Some days you will know that something special has to be said, so say it. This is your time to commune with the Kindred and that communion will work both ways!

A question that is often asked by people new to following the Path of Druidry is: Is it necessary to open a gate, an opening between the planes of reality that allows our words and actions to be observed easily by the Ancestors and Shining Ones (the deities) while doing daily devotions? There are conflicting ideas about this. Some people feel that the Mighty Kindred are powerful enough to hear what we say to them without a gate being open. Other people say that even though that may be true, by opening a gate each time you do a devotional rite, you're making it easier for them to hear. Personally, I belong with the latter group. In my opinion, opening a gate each time you do a devotional rite also has the added advantage of strengthening your connection with the Gatekeeper, the deity that helps you open the gate, on a daily basis. I know that by doing this, my connection with Manannán mac Lir has increased greatly. We'll be talking more about gates in Chapters 6 & 7.

The only times that I do not open a gate is if I am doing a rite strictly for the Earth Mother or the Spirits of Nature. It is my belief that the Earth Mother and the Spirits of Nature are with us on a daily basis and do not need a gate opened to commune with us. In fact, the best place to hold that type of ritual is outside among the trees or alongside a creek or river with the essence of the Earth Mother and the Spirits of Nature all around us.

Another question that comes up is: Do you need to speak the parts out loud? There are times when I do and times when I do not. It is more powerful to hear the words and feel the vibration of them but at times, it may not be necessary. The best answer is to do what feels right for you each day.

The example of a daily devotional ritual that follows is one that I use myself. This daily devotional ritual takes about ten minutes and includes giving honor to the Earth Mother, the Kindred and to my patrons, the Dagda and the Mórrígan. Both of the names of my patrons are actually titles, not personal names. The Dagda, An Dagda (pro-nounced "*An Doy-da*") in Irish, is really a title meaning "The Good God", so usually in the devotional, I call upon him by one of his names, either *Eochaidh Ollathair* ("*Yo-hee All-tear*" meaning "Father of All"), *Aedh* ("*Aev,*" Fire), *Deirgderc* ["*Deei-der,*" Red Eye or the Sun) or as *Ruad Rofhessa* ["*Ru-a Ra-fo -sa,*" Lord of Great Knowledge), depending on which aspect of him I feel I should talk to. Mórrígan ("*Mor-rig-ahn*") means Great Queen or Phantom Queen.

The Ritual Itself

I sit in front of my home altar, center and focus, then concentrate upon the Goddess I will be calling upon as Earth Mother. I usually work with Eriu as the Goddess personifying Ireland. For this visualization, I see her as a mature woman, standing in a heather covered meadow, with rolling hills on each side of her.

Next, I light a candle that is on the altar, focusing on re-lighting the Sacred Fire and reconnecting it to all the Sacred Fires that have been lit before.

I then fill a shell with water and sit it on the altar. I place my finger in it and focus on re-connecting it with all the Sacred Wells throughout the land.

I touch the *Bilé*, a sacred tree statue that sits on the altar. To the Irish, the word *Bilé* was used to designate any sacred tree. The representation here can be any-thing that represents the sacredness of the center and the stability of the tree to you. Next I focus on connecting that tree with the rest of the Sacred Trees throughout time.

With the center and vertical axis established by con-necting to the fire, well and tree, I call upon the Gate-keeper, Manannán mac Lir, to help me open the gate while saying something like:

Great Manannán mac Lir, I call upon you now and ask that you join your magic with mine.

And with our magic's joined, let the Well open as a gate [pointing at the shell].

And let the Fire open as a gate [pointing at the candle].

And let the Tree [pointing at the statue] *form the conduit that spreads between all the planes. Let the gates be opened!*

I then place an offering of herbs, usually sweet smelling which vary by what I have on hand, in a shell or offering bowl on the altar. As I fill the shell to give offerings to the Spirits of Nature, I say something like:

This offering is for you, Spirits of Nature. Spirits of Place, spirits of the creatures, and you of the Fair Folk, today I give you offerings and honor and my love. I ask at this time for your blessings on me and mine for this day.

I next place an offering of cornmeal or food in a shell or offering bowl on the altar. As I fill the shell to give offerings to the Ancestors, I say something like:

This offering is for you, Ancestors. Ancestors of my tribe and Ancestors of this place, today I give you offerings and honor and my love. I ask at this time for your blessings on me and mine for this day.

I then place an offering of whiskey, which is a favorite offering of many of the Shining Ones, in a shell or offering bowl on the altar. As I fill the shell to give offering to the Shining Ones, I say something like:

This offering is for you, Shining Ones. Gods and Goddesses that my people honored and called upon, today I give you offerings and honor and my love. I ask at this time for your blessings on me and mine for this day.

I next place an offering of whiskey in a shell or offering bowl on the altar. As I fill the shell to give offerings to my patrons, I say something like:

This offering is for you, Eochaidh Ollathair and Mórrígan. Father of All and Phantom Queen, today I give you offerings, honor, and my love. I ask at this time for your blessings on me and mine for this day.

I then sit and meditate on all of the Kindred and my patrons, and open myself up to receive any feelings or return messages.

After meditating, I say something like:

Eochaidh Ollathair, Mórrígan, I thank you for your aid and blessings today.

Gods and Goddesses of my people, I thank you for your aid and blessings today.

Ancestors of my tribe, Ancestors of this place, I thank you for your aid and blessings today. And Spirits of Place, spirits of the creatures, and you of the Fair Folk, I thank you for your aid and blessings today.

With the devotion finished, it is time to close the gate. This is done while saying something like:

Manannán mac Lir, once again I ask you to join your magic with mine.

With our magic's joined, let the Fire become once again a candle.

And let the Well become once more a shell filled with water.

And let the Tree be once again a statue. Let the gates be closed!

With the gate closed, I blow out the candle and empty the shell of water to bring my mind back to the mundane. This completes the daily devotional that I do; others may do it differently, of course. Any offerings of food or whiskey are then taken outside and placed on the ground to allow the offerings to be consumed by the proper Spirits.

A Rite of Self-Dedication

After having worked with the Mighty Kindred on a daily basis, it is now time to decide if you want to dedicate yourself to the "Path of Druidry." As was stated in the beginning of this book, walking the Path is a lifelong journey. Once you are sure that this Path is for you, then you can do the following ritual.

This ritual can be done at your personal altar or outdoors in a place that is special to you. You will need offerings of cornmeal, herbs and oil, and a bowl for water. If you are working inside, you will need an offering bowl that the offerings will be placed in. After the ritual, these offerings can be taken outside and poured on the ground.

Turn your attention to the earth beneath you and sprinkle an offering of cornmeal on the ground or into an offering bowl if you are working inside while saying:

Earth Mother, this offering is for you. I vow to you now that I have placed my feet upon the "Path of Druidry" and will walk this Path to the best of my ability. Earth Mother, guide my steps!

If working outdoors, kindle a fire near the center of the space you will be working in. If you are working indoors, light a candle on your altar. While starting the fire, you can say something like the following:

> *Sacred Fire, once again I kindle you and vow to you that I am prepared to walk the Path of the Old Ones. May I pray with a good fire!*

Place the bowl of water near the fire or candle, place your fingers in it and say the following:

> *Sacred Well, again I call to you and invite you to fill this bowl. In your presence, I vow that I am prepared to walk the Path of the Old Ones. Sacred Well, flow in me!*

With your sacred center established, it is time to call upon the Mighty Kindred so that they can hear your vow. Pour some of the cornmeal on the ground or into the offer-ing bowl while saying:

> *Ancestors, I call you forth today to witness my oath. Standing here before you I vow that I am prepared to walk the path of the Old Ones. Ancestors, hear my vow!*

Next sprinkle some of the herbs on the ground or into the offering bowl while saying:

> *Spirits of Nature and of this Place, I call you forth today to witness my oath. Standing here before you I vow that I am prepared to walk the Path of the Old Ones. Spirits of Nature and of this Place, hear my vow!*

Now give some oil to the fire or into the offering bowl while saying:

> *Shining Ones, I call you forth today to witness my oath. Standing here before you I vow that I am prepared to walk the Path of the Old Ones. Shining Ones, hear my vow!*
>
> *Mighty Kindred, you have heard my vow and now I ask for your aid. Guide my steps and give me the strength to follow this Path where it leads. When my steps falter, I ask that you push me in the necessary direction. And finally, I ask that you come to me during my meditations to show me what needs to be learned.*
>
> *Be it so!*

Sit for a while and meditate on what the Mighty Kindred want you to learn, and then close the ritual by saying,

> *Mighty Ones, I have listened to you and thank you. This rite has ended!*

Bringing More Spirituality into Your Life

One of the best ways to bring more spirituality into your life is by taking the time to get outside and walk in the woods or otherwise spend time in nature. Even city dwellers have a park near them where they can get out and spend time in nature.

Our ancient Ancestors were able to understand the role of the Kindred in their lives better than we do because even for the cosmopolitan Romans and Greeks, just about everyone spent time in the countryside as often as they could. Even the large landowners would pack up their households, including all their slaves, and get away from the cities during the summer.

Most of us do not have that luxury today, but we can make sure that we at least spend vacations somewhere to allow us to refresh ourselves in nature. You can go to some of the national or state parks and spend time walking the trails or camping out. Wake up to the alarm clock of the birds instead of the ringing or musical sound of the man-made alarms. Spend some time lying in a field away from the cities at night to remember how bright the stars can be.

Another way to bring spirituality into your life is by studying. Read the tales from the ancient cultures, you can find a good starting place for them in chapter 8, to see how the people lived then. Find out what they considered important. Look to see if there are virtues that you can incorporate into your life.

Druids have their own "Nine Virtues," a modern invention but helpful nonetheless. They are, from the first function—wisdom, piety, and vision; from the second function—courage, integrity, and perseverance; and from the third function—hospitality, moderation, and fertility.

When I speak of "function," I am referring to the division of society among the Indo-Europeans, as first expressed by Georges Dumézil, who lived from 1898 to 1988. He was a French scholar who is considered the father of modern comparative mythology. Dumézil is best known for his theory of the three types of functions: the first, encompassing those functions performed by kings and priests; the second, those performed by warriors; and the third, those performed by workers. He claimed this division was the foundation of all Indo-European mythologies.[34]

---

[34]Wikipedia, "Georges Dumézil - Wikipedia," accessed December 22, 2011, *http:// en.wikipedia.org/wiki/Georges_Dum%C3%A9zil.*

Yet another way to bring spirituality into your life is through prayer. Speaking with the Kindred is the main point of the daily devotionals. Your time communing with them does not have to be limited to just the time spent before your personal altar.

- **When you see something in nature that strikes you, thank the Spirits of Nature.**
- When you remember one of your Ancestors, thank them for giving you their wisdom.
- When you feel the presence of one of the deities, thank them for being with you, and ask if there is a special lesson you should be learning from this moment.
- Last, by opening yourself up to what is really happening around you, you will find it easier every day to understand this communion with the Mighty Kindred.

Letting Others Know Who You Are

When you first start telling others what you believe, you will start to get questions about your new ways. Following are some of the questions I have heard and how I would answer them.

"Will I burn in Hell?" Druids don't typically believe in the Christian version of Hell. If you do, that's fine, but I believe that after we die, we spend time in the Summer Lands resting and contemplating our past life before choosing to be reborn again. If the person is at all open in their thinking, this can lead to a nice discussion about what the Summer Lands are and where the idea comes from.

"Do you sacrifice babies or virgins?" The answer to this is an emphatic and resounding NO! In fact, most if not all Druid groups have policies that no animal or blood sacrifices are allowed in their rituals.

"Are there naked people there?" The answer to this question has to be that in large group rituals done at festivals, sometimes there are naked people. It depends on where the ritual is taking place. For a personal ritual, it does not matter if you are robed in special clothes or nude. The choice is yours. If it is a group ritual done at a large festival, some of the festivals are clothing-optional, so people may be nude. Many people on the Path of Druidry do not have the same problems dealing with nudity that many American Christians do. I have noticed in my travels, that it appears mainly to be American monotheists who have the attitude that the body is something that needs to be hidden all the time. Most Europeans I have seen do not have this problem at all and their countries are very open about nude beaches and nudity on television.

"Do you believe in the Devil?" I usually respond to this question with something like "No, he's one of your Gods, not one of mine." I then usually follow up by reminding them that Satan and the Devil are only referred to in the Bible or in the work of the Satanists, and that the Satanists are just a Christian sect with the position of the Gods reversed. Either this starts an interesting discussion about Satanism or the person will walk away.

"Are you a good witch or a bad witch?" This question could easily be rephrased, as "Are you a good Druid or a bad Druid?" I usually would respond with something like "It depends on the mood I'm in. Are you a good [insert their faith here] or a bad one?" Either this can lead to a discussion on our respective religions or they just get mad and walk away. It appears that most people really do not understand how a question like this can be offensive until it has been turned around on them; then they do not see any humor in it at all.

"Why are you wearing that thing?" This may refer to a triskele, a three-lobed symbol many Druids wear; a pentacle, a five-pointed star that many Wiccans wear; a Thor's Hammer, a hammer-shaped symbol that many Asatru and Heathens wear; or something else, and is similar to the last question. The usual response is "It's a symbol of the religion I believe in. Why do you wear that cross?" If they are open in their thinking, it will lead to a discussion about religious symbols and how we feel about them. If not then they will walk away and it is their loss.

"What is the difference between a Witch and a Druid?" While both Wicca and Druidry are NeoPagan religions, they are not the same. Wiccans meet in groups called covens, while Druid groups are called groves. Many Wiccan groups are designed for small, closed-group rituals, while most Druid groves are designed to meet the needs of the community in large-scale rituals open to anyone. Many Wiccan practitioners are duotheistic and believe in a God and a Goddess, while most followers of the Path of Druidry are polytheistic, and believe in many deities and see them as individuals. These are just a few of the differences and in many cases, depending on the tradition a person comes from; there can be more similarities than differences! Many people follow both paths at the same time.

Talking to Your Family

Talking to your family about your beliefs can lead to many of the same questions as talking with your friends. Nevertheless, some questions are very family specific. One of those questions is "Why do you want to quit the church?" Many people's parents ask this as the first question, when they are told that you want to join or that you already belong to a Druid organization or that you have started to follow the "Path of Druidry." They usually have a problem understanding why you would reject the religion that has given them comfort through their lives. There are several good responses for this question, but I think the best, and what I would have told my parents if I had been asked, is "[your religion] isn't right for me. Religion has to be the choice of the individual and just as we are all different people, no one religion is right for everyone."

Small family gatherings can be a good time to talk to your family about your beliefs. You are not trying to convince people to join with you in those beliefs, just to get them to understand what they are all about and to answer some of the common questions about them. In this setting, there is usually time to get people in a small group and tell them a little about how you feel.

The hardest part is usually finding a way to broach the subject. One way is to start telling them that you have been doing some comparative religion studies. This will open up the subject that you may not be happy with the religion that you have been following. Once the discussion is open, you can explain that you have been looking for a religion that strikes a more resonant chord within you, a religion that makes more sense to you, or however you truly feel about the question. With that out of the way, it should be easy to bring in Druidry or NeoPaganism in general. With that dialogue open, you can start to focus on the positive aspects of Druidry.

Holidays can be one of the good times to explain about your beliefs with, more people there, people will be less inclined to make a scene, and it gives you a wider audience so that you do not have to tell the same things to them individually. It also provides for more opportunity for questions, which make it easier to have a real dialogue, rather than just having you talk to them.

Thanksgiving can be a time where you ask to do the blessing of the food. You can then use the blessing to explain a little about our ways. For example, you could start out by saying something like:

We give thanks for this food first to the Earth Mother. The Earth Mother, the living Earth we live on, is the source of all the food that we eat. It is fitting that the first offerings go to her.

While saying this, you can place a small portion of the food on a plate to leave outside later on as an offering. Then you could say:

Next, it is important to remember our other Kindred. Our thanks go to the Spirits of Nature that gave their lives so that we could eat, to the turkey and the potatoes and the other meats and vegetables. These were all living creatures that were sacrificed for us. And so it is right to give some of that sacrifice back to them.

Again, while you are saying this, place a small portion on the offering plate. You could continue with something like:

And it is also fitting to give thanks to our Ancestors. They are the ones that taught us about coming together as family, about celebrating this time together. This offering is for them.

While you say this, place a portion on the offering plate. You could then finish with:

And last, we give thanks to the Shining Ones, the Gods, and Goddesses our people honor. Even though we follow different paths, all the Gods and Goddesses we honor have a place here as we gather at this time of Thanksgiving.

You can then place the final offering on the offering plate and set it aside to take outside later.

After the blessing, questions will probably arise about the form used. This is a great time to begin answering them and to start explaining about what you believe in.

Christmas is another good time if your family gathers for a large family meal. Christmas is also an excellent time to explain to people about the Pagan origins of the holiday and about how many of the Christian holidays came from earlier Pagan ones.

A one-on-one talk might be the hardest way to explain your beliefs to your parents. Very likely, several of the common questions we have discussed earlier will come up here. How the conversation will go depends on how open your parents are to new ideas. If they are willing to listen and think about what they hear, then there should not be too many problems. If they are closed to new ideas and their way is "*the only way*" then you might have to agree to disagree about religion. That brings us right into the next topic.

What can you do if they will not accept our religion? Many people in this world have very closed minds on the subject of religion. If you have to deal with them, I have found that the best thing to do is to let them know that everyone is entitled to their own opinion and that you simply do not agree with theirs. If they cannot understand this, then they have a problem they need to learn to deal with. If it is a parent, then the best way I have seen is to explain to them that you are an adult and as such, you have the right to make up your own mind. You can then explain to them that they did not do anything wrong raising you, in fact, they did a wonderful job and taught you to examine things critically, and to make decisions based on that examination. Your decision on religion is based on just such a critical examination, not on a spur of the moment whim.

We are at a time in history when people's ideas about religion are changing. NeoPaganism is the fastest growing religion today based on a survey done in 1999 by the World's Council of Religions and one done in 2001 by the Graduate Center of the University of New York.[35] People are learning from many sources today—magazines, newspapers, TV, and so on—that there are alternative religions available. As more and more people become involved in these religions and talk to others, then the idea of tolerance will grow. Slowly it seems, but at least as fast as a speeding oak!

---

[35]"The Graduate Center, CUNY - ARIS 2001: Key Findings."

Chapter 5
Learning the Skills of the Modern Druids

N ow that we have learned what a druid is and how the ancient druids viewed the world, it is time to start learning the skills of a modern Druid. Just as the ancient Druids practiced divination, you can learn similar skills today. As the ancient Druids worked with the land Spirits, so can you today. You can find the Spirits in your local land and find allies, friends and helpers, among all three classes of the Mighty Kindred. And we start this section of the "Path of Druidry" with divination.

Divination

Divination is a way of obtaining information. That information or knowledge can come from the Kindred, from the subconscious mind of the person doing the divination, or from some unknown place. However it comes through, the information is useful and over time, a druid will come to trust it, although that may be hard in the beginning. The more the art of divination is practiced, the better the diviner becomes!

Through the ages, there have been many methods used to divine and tell the future. We will now look at some of them because it's interesting to see methods from the past that are still used today. In the list that follows, the definitions given for the words are from *www.dictionary.com*, originally from Webster's Revised Unabridged Dictionary, unless otherwise noted.[36]

Aeiomancy—divination from the state of the air or from atmospheric substances; also, forecasting changes in the weather. A

---

[36]Dictionary.com, "Meanings and Definitions of Words," Dictionary.com, accessed January 23, 2012, *http://dictionary.reference.com/*.

modern example of this is found in the folk saying, "Red sky at night, sailor's delight; red sky at morning, sailors take warning."

Alectiyomancy—divination by means of a rooster and grains of corn placed on the letters of the alphabet, the letters being put together in the order in which the grains were eaten.

Chiromancy—the art or practice of foretelling events, or of telling the fortunes or the disposition of persons by inspecting the hand; palmistry.

Gastiomancy—(a) a kind of divination, by means of words seemingly uttered from the stomach; (b) a species of divination, by means of glasses or other round, transparent vessels (crystal balls) in the center of which figures are supposed to appear by magic art.

Gyiomancy—a kind of divination performed by drawing a ring or circle, and walking in or around it. For this method, the answer to any question asked would have appeared after the person was dizzy enough to fall down.

Lecanomancy—divination practiced with water in a basin, by throwing three stones into it, and invoking the demon whose aid was sought.

Omithomancy—divination by means of birds, their flight, etc. This is one of the methods of augury that the Romans were famous for using.

Scapulomancy—divination by examining the patterns or cracks and fissures on the burned (after being roasted over an open fire) shoulder-blade (scapula) bones of an animal.[37]

Tuphramancy or **Tephramancy**—divination by the ashes of the altar on which a victim had been consumed in sacrifice.

If you are interested in finding out more information on divination, there are several good sites on the Internet. One Web site is located at *http://en.wikipedia.org/wiki/Methods_of_divination*. The very best site I have found so far is located at *http://www.occultopedia.com/d/divination.htm*. This site not only has the name, but also includes some of the history of the method and examples of how to do it. Many of the types have further links to other sites that specialize in that one particular form of divination or to books or videos about each one.

---

[37]Occultopedia, "Scapulomancy - Scapulomancy, Divination by Shoulder-blade Bones - Occultopedia, the Occult and Unexplained Encyclopedia," accessed January 23, 2012, *http://www.occultopedia.com/s/scapulomancy.htm*.

Divination should be done in the same manner all the time; you are allowing your subconscious mind to open up to the message you are receiving. By repeating the same form of actions each time, you let your subconscious know that it is being called upon to do the work.

We know how the ancient Germans practiced divination from the works of the Roman writer, Tacitus, who wrote about the end of the first century CE. In chapter 10 of his work *Germania*, he writes:

> *Augury and divination by lot no people practise more diligently. The use of the lots is simple. A little bough is lopped off a fruit-bearing tree, and cut into small pieces; these are distinguished by certain marks, and thrown carelessly and at random over a white garment. In public questions the priest of the particular state, in private the father of the family, invokes the gods, and, with his eyes toward heaven, takes up each piece three times, and finds in them a meaning according to the mark previously impressed on them. If they prove unfavourable, there is no further consultation that day about the matter; if they sanction it, the confirmation of augury is still required. For they are also familiar with the practice of consulting the notes and flight of birds. It is peculiar to this people to seek omens and monitions from horses. Kept at the public expense, in these same woods and groves, are white horses, pure from the taint of earthly labour; these are yoked to a sacred car, and accompanied by the priest and the king, or chief of the tribe, who note their neighings and snortings. No species of augury is more trusted, not only by the people and by the nobility, but also by the priests, who regard themselves as the ministers of the gods, and the horses as acquainted with their will. They have also another method of observing auspices, by which they seek to learn the result of an important war. Having taken, by whatever means, a prisoner from the tribe with whom they are at war, they pit him against a picked man of their own tribe, each combatant using the weapons of their country. The victory of the one or the other is accepted as an indication of the issue.[38]*

From this, we see that lots, no one is sure if they were actually talking about runes, the divination system and alphabet most associated with the Germanic tribes or oghams, the divination system and alphabet most associated with the Celtic tribes, in this paragraph, were made of wood from trees that bear fruit. For the ancients, fruiting trees also included nut trees, seeing the nuts as the "fruit," so there is a wide range of material that could be used to make the lots. We also see that

---

[38]Tacitus, "Medieval Sourcebook: Tacitus: Germania," accessed January 23, 2012, *http://www.fordham.edu/halsall/source/tacitus1.html*.

divinations were done after turning the face up to the Gods and praying for a good omen. Last, they only took one omen per day on any affair, without supplementing it by further divination to amplify the reading, to understand it better.

I have found that divination tools, be they runes, ogham discs, crystal balls, tarot cards—whatever—all work best if they are kept in a special darkened place. For the runes, ogham discs, and tarot cards, a special bag works well. For a crystal ball, a special stand with a pretty cover to keep over the ball is usually chosen.

When collecting the tools, it helps to develop a connection with them by sleeping with them under your mattress or near your bed. This special connect should be continued even after working with the tools on a daily basis. They also work best if used on a regular basis. If runes are put away for six months, do not expect to be able to pick them up and get accurate answers right away! The interplay and connections need to be kept up between the divination tools and the user and when it is not; the connections need to be remade.

The best way, by far, to improve divination skill is practice. The more often they are used, the closer the connection grows and the better able you are to understand what they are trying to show you. Many people firmly believe in keeping a close physical connection to their tools, even when they are not being used. This can be done by carrying them with you at all times or by sleeping with the tools in close proximity.

Another way to improve skill is by reading and studying a favorite method. The more you learn about them, the greater the pool of useful "information bits" your subconscious mind will be able to tap into during a reading. You do not have to try and consciously memorize all the material; having read it once, the mind will be able to use it as needed.

A third way to improve divination skill is by meditating with your divination set. Once a week, try to spend time in a meditation involving them. One way to do this is by spreading the discs or cards before you on a table. With your eyes closed, allow your hand to move slowly over them, noting any "odd" or "different" perceptions you may feel, such as warmth, coldness, or a tingling sensation. Do not hesitate to linger over one or two if it feels right.

This is not an exercise to memorize the tools or to learn the different symbols; it is simply to allow your subconscious to tap into them better, to develop the connections needed for an accurate reading. The visual clues we receive from the tools are important, but what your subconscious "feels" from them is just as important. This "feeling" is one that really cannot be described, but it is one that you will know when it occurs and it is usually the first thing that pops into your mind when looking at the omen!

Oghams

One of the most popular divination systems used by people following the Path of Druidry is the oghams. Historically, there are very few references to oghams being used in this manner. Damian McManus describes one instance of divination using the oghams that comes from *Tochmarc Étaíne*, 'The Wooing of Étaíne' (quoting Windisch, 1880 [Irische Texte mit Wörterbuch], 129, § 18). He gives the quote as:

> *After Midir's abduction of Étaíne, Eochaidh sends forth his messengers to search for her and he himself seeks her out for a year and a day, but to no avail. He then gives his druid Dallan the task of finding her. Dallan is troubled by her disappearance for over a year and 'he makes four rods of yew and writes Ogam (oghumm) in them and it is revealed to him through his keys of science (triana eochraib ecsi) and through his Ogam (ocus triana oghumm)' that Étaíne is in the sid of Brí Leith, having been carried there by Midir.[39]*

It appears from looking at the ogham inscriptions in Ireland that the ogham alphabet originated a century or two before the first ogham stones appeared. This would have placed its origin about the second century CE. This is about the same time as the runic alphabet appeared. Almost all of the surviving inscriptions date from the fourth to the eighth centuries. Most scholars today believe that the inscriptions are some form of markers, such as boundary markers, grave inscriptions, or memorial stones.

The Tree Ogham is the best known of all the oghams and is what most people think of as the *only* ogham, while in actuality there are really 150 types. The table on pages 54-55 gives an overview of all the tree oghams, including the most common meanings I use in divinations.

---

[39]Damian McManus, *A Guide to Ogam* (Maynooth: An Sagart, 1997), 157.

To do an actual divination, I have designed a set of ogham discs that are used. Descriptions with pictures can be found on my Web site.[40] The order of the oghams given on the web site varies slightly from some of the other listings of the Tree Ogham. It is the one used in a magical training system I developed, called the Way of the Trees, and was developed from my research into the original manuscripts dealing with the oghams. Further information about many of the types of oghams can be found in my book, *Ogham: The Secret Language of the Druids* published in 2007 by ADF Publishing, ISBN 9780976568117.

I suggest downloading the pages, printing them out and then copying the discs onto small 1-inch diameter wooden discs from a craft store. This will give the best results and the pictures are set up to print out at the correct size. The ogham chart on the next page is handy to copy and keep at hand while you are learning the oghams.

The fews (individual oghams) in the first aicme (grouping) can be found pointing either to the right or down, and the fews for the second aicme can be found pointing either left or up.

When I am doing a divination, I start by spreading a white rabbit's fur on the table or ground where I am doing the divination. White is a traditional color for a divining cloth and when I passed the rabbit fur in a shop in New Mexico, it called out to me. A piece of cloth could be used as a substitute for the rabbit fur if desired.

Next, I hold my bag of oghams up in the air and say a short prayer that my reading will be true. The prayer would be something like: "*Mighty Kindred, I ask that my hand be guided truly to answer this question.*" Then I would state the question I want answered. I shake the bag while saying the prayer to allow the "proper" oghams to come to the top. I then put my hand in and pick the first three discs I touch, unless something tells me to dig deeper. That does sometimes happen. This is why it is important to be open to your feelings at this time.

With the three oghams drawn, I lay them out and read them from left to right. My usual method is the one on the left represents an answer from the Ancestors, the center one is from the Nature Spirits, and the one on the right is from the Shining Ones. I may also use past, present, and

---

[40]Ellison, Skip, "Divination Books & Tools by Rev. Skip Ellison," accessed January 25, 2012, *http://www.skipellison.us/dk/Divination_Main.html.*

Symbol	*Aicme-Few*	Tree	Standard Name	Other Names	Letter	Divinatory Meaning
T	1-1	Birch	*Beith*	*Beth* [1,2] *Beithe* [3] *Beith* [4]	B	new beginnings
⊤	1-2	Rowan	*Luis*		L	protection & control of senses
⊤	1-3	Alder	*Fern*		F	guidance, associated with Bran
⊤	1-4	Willow	*Sail*	*Saille* [1,2]	S	mysteries and water related subjects, feminine attributes
⊤	1-5	Ash	*Nion*	*Nin* [3] *Nuin* [4]	N	ancient knowledge, the weaver's beam
⊥	2-1	Hawthorn	*Uath*	*Huath* [2,3] *Huath* [4]	H	counseling, protection & cleansing
⊥	2-2	Oak	*Dair*	*Duir* [1,2,3]	D	wisdom & strength
⊥	2-3	Holly	*Tinne*		T	justice & balance
⊥	2-4	Hazel	*Coll*		C	wisdom & intuition
⊥	2-5	Apple	*Ceirt*	*Quert* [1,2] *Queirt* [3] *Cert* [4]	Q	otherworld & choice
+	3-1	Vine	*Muin*		M	prophecy & inhibition
#	3-2	Ivy	*Gort*		G	search for yourself & inner wisdom
#	3-3	Broom	*nGéadal*	*Ngetal* [1,2,3]	NG	working & tools
#	3-4	Blackthorn	*Straif*	*Straiph* [3]	ST STR	trouble & negativity
#	3-5	Elder	*Ruis*		R	entrance to the Otherworld & the Fairfolk

[1]As used by Robert Graves in the *White Goddess*
[2]As used by Nigel Pennick in the *Celtic Oracle*
[3]As used by Eadred Thorsson (Stephen Flowers)
[4]As used by Michael Everson
[5]The 4th *aicme*, or vowels, are sometimes shown as dots on the line as well as the full line across.
[6]This figure is drawn facing both to the left and to the right.
[7]This figure is shown drawn with between 2 and 4 cross lines.

Symbol	Aicme-Few	Tree	Standard Name	Other Names	Letter	Divinatory Meaning
+ [5]	4-1	Silver Fir	*Ailm*	*Ailim* [2]	A	far seeing & knowing the future
‖	4-2	Gorse	*Onn*		O	collecting things to you
‖‖	4-3	Heather	*Úr*	*Ura* [1] *Ur* [2,3]	U	healing & homelands
‖‖‖	4-4	Aspen	*Eadhadh*	*Eadha* [1,2] *Edad* [3,4]	E	communication
‖‖‖‖	4-5	Yew	*Iodhadh*	*Idho* [1] *Iodho* [2] *Idad* [3,4]	I	death & rebirth
✳	5-1*	White Poplar	*Éabhadh*	*Ebad* [3] *Ébad* [4]	EA, CH or K	buoyancy, floating above problems
◈	5-2	Spindle	*Ór*	*Oir* [3]	OI or CH	community, working within the home
⊙ [6]	5-3	Honeysuckle	*Uilleann*	*Uileand* [3] *Uilen* [4]	UI, IO or PH	drawing things together & binding
✖ [7]	5-4	Gooseberry	*Ifín*	*Iphin* [3]	IO, IA, P or PE	The Kindreds, especially of Nature
≖ [8]	5-5	Witchhazel	*Eamhancholl*	*Phagos* [3] *Emancholl* [4]	AE, X or XI	magic & hidden knowledge
⎺w⎺	6-1**	Norway Maple	*Mailp*			modifier for the land
⎺ẅ⎺	6-2	Rush (Reed)	*Brobh*			modifier for the sea
⎺ᴧᴧ⎺	6-3	Bird Cherry	*Craobh Fhiodhag*			modifier for the sky
⊱			*Eite*	*Saighead* [4]		feather/arrow – used to show direction to be read
—			*Spas*	*Bearna* [4]		space–also seen as • or :

[8]This figure is shown drawn from both above and below the line.

*The 5th *aicme*, also known as the dipthongs, is not used in some divination systems because they were not part of the original Oghams. They were added at a later time. Most systems do not associate trees with them, but in my system I have.

**I've added the 6th *aicme* in my system as well to be used as modifiers. This is not found normally in Ogham systems.

future if I feel that the answer may be more time related, rather than coming directly from the Kindred.

Further resources for the Oghams are:

Calder, George (ed). *Auiaicept Na N-Eces: The Scholars Primer.* Four Courts Press, Portland, OR. 1995. ISBN 9781851821815.

I believe that this is the best book available today for anyone with a serious interest in learning the oghams.

Ellison, Robert Lee (Skip). *Ogham: The Secret Language of the Druids.* ADF Publishing, Tucson, AZ. 2007. ISBN 9780976568117.

In my book, I have brought good digital copies of the ogham pictures from the Book of Ballymote out to the public, along with much of the latest research into the original meanings for the names used for the Tree Oghams.

Macalister, R.A.S. *Corpus Inscriptionum Insularum Celticarum.* Four Courts Press, Dublin, Ireland. 1996. ISBN 9781851822423.

This is considered one of the master works on ogham. It lists and shows all of the ogham inscriptions found in the British Isles.

McManus, Damien. *A Guide to Ogham.* Leinster Leader Ltd., Kildare, Ireland. 1991. ISBN 9781870684750.

This book was written to correct errors and update the findings of R.A.S. Macalister. As such, it really needs to refer to Corpus Inscriptionum Insularum Celticarum. *In fact, this book and the Macalister book should be used together.*

Jackson, Nigel and Pennick, Nigel. *The New Celtic Oracle.* Aquarian Press, London. 1997. ISBN 1-898307-56-3.

This is a fairly good book with lots of information on the Oghams.

Information on the Web includes:

Clark, Curtis, *http://www.csupomona.edu/~jcclark/ogham/ogh-tree.html.* 1998. *A natural history of the trees of the Ogham compiled in 1995.*

Everson, Michael, *http://www.evertype.com/standards/og/ogmharc.html.* *Everything Ogham on the Web. Just what the name says, it has it all!*

Everson, Michael, *http://www.evertype.com/standards/og/leabhair.html.* *This site maintains a bibliography of books useful to the study of the Oghams.*

Runes

Another very popular method of divination used by people on the Path of Druidry is the runes. The runic alphabet was designed for writing as we use the term. When we think of writing, we usually think of some type of flowing script to be used on paper. The runic alphabet was designed to be inscribed on something hard, like stone or metal, usually. This was the primary divination system of the early Germanic people, the tribes who spoke the Germanic language, the ancestor of many of our modern languages such as: High German, Low German, Norwegian, Swedish, Danish and that had a great influence on the development of English.

The earliest inscriptions date from the late second century CE, but researchers are not sure how much earlier it was developed. Because most of the early writing was on wood, none of the early material has survived.

The runes are divided into three sets known as *Aett*. The first *Aett* is composed of the runes *Fehu* to *Wunjo*. The second *Aett* is composed of the runes *Hagalaz* to *Sowila* The last *Aett* is composed of the runes *Tiwaz* to *Dagaz*. The table on pages 58-59 gives a good overview of the runes with the most common divinatory meanings I use.

To do a divination, I start in the same way as when using oghams. I use the same rabbit skin to lay out the drawn runes and shake the bag over my head while saying the same type prayer to the Mighty Kindred. The order drawn may be the same as when using oghams—Ancestors, Nature Spirits and Shining Ones or past, present and future; but the runes can be used in other layouts that can give more information. One way is a seven rune draw that is a variation of a tarot [another, more modern method of divination] spread called the Celtic Cross.

In this method, the first rune drawn is laid in the center. It is the person the reading is for and tells about who they are. The second rune drawn is laid immediately to the right, of the first and shows what is currently influencing the person. The third rune drawn is placed below the center two and shows what is behind the person, in the past. The fourth rune drawn is placed to the far left of the center two and signifies what problems there are, on the "sinister" side. The fifth rune drawn is placed on the far right side of the center two and shows what help is available to the person. The sixth rune drawn is laid above the first two and signifies

Symbol	Aett-Position	Standard Name[1]	Other Names	Letter	Divinatory Meaning
			Freyr's Aett		
ᚠ	F-1	Fehu	Feoh[3]	F	wealth, cattle & luck
ᚢ	F-2	Uruz	Uruz[2] Ur[3]	U	strength, ox & power
ᚦ	F-3	Þurizaz	Thurisaz[2] Thorn[3]	Th	giant, defense & Thor
ᚨ	F-4	Ansuz	As[3]	A	words, answers & god (Odin)
ᚱ	F-5	Raid--ō	Raidho[2] Rad[3]	R	journey & travel
ᚲ	F-6	Kenaz	Ken[3] Cen[4] Kaun[5]	K	opening, fire & ulcer
ᚷ	F-7	Geb--ō	Gebo[2] Gyfu[3]	G	gift & partnership
ᚹ	F-8	Wunj--ō	Wunjo[2] Wyn[3]	W	joy & happiness
			Hail's Aett		
ᚺ	H-1	Hagalaz	Hagal[3]	H	hail & destruction
ᚾ	H-2	Naudiz	Naudhiz[2] Nyd[3]	N	need, constraint & destiny
ᛁ	H-3	Isa	Is[3]	I	ice & stability
ᛃ	H-4	Jēra	Jera[2,3]	Yuh/J	year, harvest & summer

[1] as used by R.I. Paige

[2] as used by Diana Paxson

[3] as used by Nigel Pennick

Symbol	Aett-Position	Standard Name[1]	Other Names	Letter	Divinatory Meaning
		[Hail's Aett continued]			
↑	H-5	Eihwaz	I(h)waz[1] Eoh[3]	Ei/Eo/Z	yew & change
K	H-6	Perþ	Perthro[2] Peorth[3]	P	luck, dice cup & fate
⅄	H-7	Algiz	Elhaz[2,3]	Z/X	elk & protection
⟨	H-8	S--ōwil--ō	Sowilo[2] Sigil[3]	S	sun, progress & wholeness
		Tyr's Aett			
↑	T-1	Tíwaz	Teiwaz[1] Tiwaz[2] Tyr[3]	T	justice, will & Tyr/Twi
ß	T-2	Berkanan	Berkano[2] Beorc[3]	B	birch & new growth
M	T-3	Ehwaz		E	movement, change & horse
M	T-4	Mannaz	Man[3]	M	man, self & mastery
↑	T-5	Laguz	Lagu[3]	L	water, flow & womb
◇	T-6	Ingwaz	Ing[3]	Ng	Ing, fertility, Freyr
⋈	T-7	Dagaz	Dag[3]	D	day, growth & enlightenment
⊗	T-8	Ōþila	Ōþala[1] Othalo[2] Odal[3]	O	home & inheritance

---

[4] Old English, as used on *http://en.wikipedia.org/wiki/Kaunan*

[5] Old Norse, as used on *http://en.wikipedia.org/wiki/Kaunan*

Note: you will often see Dagaz and Ōþila (T-7 & T-8) reversed in some systems.

the conditions before the person, in the future. And the seventh and last rune drawn is placed immediately to the left of the center two and shows the final outcome. Many other methods of laying out the runes can be found in the books listed in the resource section for the runes.

Further resources for the Runes are:

Baushcatz, Paul. *The Well and the Tree: World and Time in Early Germanic Culture.* University of Massachusetts Press, Amherst. ISBN 9780870233524.

> *This is an out-of-print book that is very expensive ($400 to $4000 range), but is very good if you can get a copy from a university library.*

Halvorsen, Ingrid, *http://www.sunnyway.com/runes/*.

> *An interesting site on the Futhark runes. She has very good commentary and many links to other sites.*

Paige, R. I. *Reading the Runes.* British Museum Press, London. 1987. ISBN 0714180653.

> *This book is very informative and is a good scholarly source. It runs about $12 new and $6 used.*

Paxson, Diana. *Taking Up the Runes: a complete guide to using runes in spells, rituals, divination, and magic.* Weiser Books, Boston, MA. 2005. ISBN 9781578633258.

> *By far, the best book on the runes and rune work available today.*

Pennick, Nigel. *Secrets of the Runes.* Thorsons: Harper Collins Press, London. 1992. ISBN 9780722537848.

> *This is a very good book for a beginner. He goes into good detail on many aspects of divination and rune magic. It runs about $16 new or $7 used.*

Thorsson, Eldred.

> *Any of the books written by him on runes or Germanic magic are good. He also writes under his real name, Dr. Stephen Flowers, and those books are much more academic based.*

Contacting the Land

Historically, we have records from many cultures whose people immigrated to new lands. The best information that we have concerning how religions were transposed to new lands come from two sources, the Norse, moving to Iceland and the Celts, as they moved into the British Isles.

In my opinion, the best source regarding how a tribe found the Spirits of the new place comes to us from the Icelandic Eddas and Sagas written about the Vikings' move westward. Several stories in the Eddas and Sagas, the main telling of the tales of the Norse, speak of both taking the land and meeting the Spirits of the land. One good source is *Egil's Saga*, the story of the great skald (poet) and rune-master, Egil Skallagrimsson. An online version of this tale can be found on the Northvegr Foundation Web site under "Sagas & Epics," then "Icelandic Family Saga's."[41] The book, *Icelandic Folktales and Legends* by Jacqueline Simpson and Magnus Magnuson, ISBN 9780520038356, is also very good in that it deals with the stories of what Spirits the Norse met and the sacred areas they found when they came to Iceland. It can be found on *www.amazon.com* fairly cheaply. In addition, one of the best sources for this subject is *The Book of Settlements: Landnámabók* [Land Taking] which is an Icelandic compilation of information about individual settlers from Scandinavia and their families and their stories. An online edition of this book can be found on the Northvegr Foundation website.[42] Hermann Palsson and Paul Edward translated the best print version and it was published in 1972 by the University of Manitoba Press, ISBN 978-0887556982, but it is fairly expensive, in the $50 to $150 range.

Land Taking

One of the primary themes that appear in Land Taking, making a new land their own, was the transport of objects from the old home to the new. Usually the most important object to bring from the old home was the high-seat pillars, the poles that supported the chief's chair. The high-seat was the special chair that was reserved for the chief alone and it stood taller than the other chairs in the house. These high-seat pillars were thrown overboard as the ship approached land, and where they washed ashore, the new homestead was established.

Today, we usually do not approach our new home by water, but the idea of bringing something important to a new home from an old is worth

---

[41] Egil Skallagrimsson, "Egil's Saga," trans. Rev. W. C. Green, accessed January 25, 2012, *http:// www.northvegr.org/sagas%20annd%20epics/icelandic%20family%20sagas/egils%20saga/Index.html.*

[42] Ari The Learned, "Landnámabók: The Book of The Settlement of Iceland," trans. Rev. T Ellwood, accessed January 25, 2012, *http://www.northvegr.org/sagas%20annd%20epics/ miscellaneous/landnamabok/index.html.*

doing if possible. One idea mentioned in the story of Thorhadd, in *The Book of Settlements* was that he was told to bring some of the earth from beneath his old homestead with him. This idea could be used when you first move to a new location. Even for an apartment dweller, a flowerpot full of dirt could continue the ties that were established at an old home. We do not use high-seats anymore, but an altar that had been in your old home could ceremonially be set up in the new as well.

Claiming and Hallowing

One way the Icelandic settlers used to establish their land holdings was by establishing boundary markers. *The Book of Settlements* mentions four methods: first, using a tall pole; second, using a freshly cut birch tree; third, by an arrow shot; and fourth, by cairns to mark the four corners. Both the tall pole and the fresh cut birch tree were set in the center of the land, and as far as you could see from the top of the pole or tree was land that you claimed. With the arrow-shot method, you would stand in the center and shoot an arrow in each direction. Where the arrows fell were the boundary lines. Yet another way to claim the land was either by building fires at every boundary point or by carrying fire around the perimeters. Because fire was so important to the ancients, for both warmth and food preparation, carrying the fire around appears to be the primary method used.

Holding Sacred

When the Norse came to Iceland, they found several special places that they considered holy, and therefore held sacred. These included a grove, a waterfall, a mountain, and individual boulders. It appears from reading the tales that they were not trying to *make* these special sites holy, but that they were recognizing what was inherent in them. These were special areas were the tales talk about the people going to hold rituals and to give sacrifices.

When moving into a new home, a good first step is to do as the Vikings did. Walk around the land and see if there are any places that feel special, where you feel a sense of awe, or where you get the feeling that offering to the Mighty Kindred should be made. If there are, try to give them a special look, maybe with a circle of stones around them or with ribbons decorating a tree.

Once the local land Spirits find out that they will be given honor, they will work to help make improvements on the property. It's important to remember that all the improvements you want to make might not be accepted by them as well, so it's a good idea to meditate on what you want to do, in the place you want to do it, to see if it is acceptable to the land. If it is acceptable to the local land Spirits, a feeling of joy or acceptance will come through.

Moving on to the Celtic material regarding moves to new lands, we find that most of the tales we have are found in *The Book of Invasions*, the book dealing with how the invading tribes came to Ireland.[43] Another very good source, but much harder to come by, is the *Metrical Dindshenchas*. This book is a five part series dealing with the place names in Ireland and the stories about each place. My copy is translated by Edward Gwynn and was published by the School of Celtic Studies at the Dublin Institute for Advanced Studies. It has the advantage of having the Old Irish on one side with English on the facing page, which allows you to check the translation yourself if a question arises. Selections from this book can now be found online at *http://www.ucc.ie/celt/published/T106500A/index.html*.[44]

What we see in the histories that have come down to us is that, at least for the Celtic peoples—and very likely for others—that they would adopt the Land or River Goddess they found through meditation and listening to the land of the area they were in, and "marry" her to the Father God, the primary male deity, of their tribe. We can see examples of Father Gods in Bilé, who married Danu, of the river Danube in central Europe, and Dagda and his mate, Boann, of the river Boyne in Ireland.

It is important to stress that each of the many different tribes of the Celts—we know that about 50BCE, there were twenty-one separate tribes in what is now Britain alone— really had their own pantheon of deities. That is why so many God and Goddess names have been found among the insular Celts, the Celts from the British Isles. We see many people today claiming that because the name of a deity was found in one place, it meant that they were worshipped in all the Celtic lands. Scholars like Ann Ross, Miranda Green and many others believe today that this is completely wrong.

---

[43]"Lebor Gabala Erenn," accessed April 8, 2013, *http://www.maryjones.us/ctexts/leborgabala.html*.

[44]Unknown, "The Metrical Dindshenchas," trans. Edward Gwynn, accessed January 31, 2012, *http://www.ucc.ie/celt/published/T106500A/index.html*.

Although typically tied to a specific people or location, there are, however, a few notable exceptions, one such being Atargatis, also known as the "Syrian Goddess." Not very much is known about her worship, but she was one of the Mother Goddesses that were so universal in the ancient world. Her worship started out in the Middle East, moved through Greece to Rome, and finally into the British Isles where a third century CE creed, author unknown, acknowledges her in the form of *"dea Syria,"* a universal Goddess.[45]

But this is a rarity. One problem seen today is that people often believe that because two Goddesses, or Gods, have similar characteristics, that they are the same. For example, many people say that the Gaulish Goddess Epona is the same as the Irish Goddess Macha. They do share a similarity because horses are involved with both, so they are cognate, but they are not the same Goddess. They are both individuals with their own separate characteristics. Macha is a warrior goddess, who along with her "sisters," the Mórrígan and Badb, make up the Battle Furies know as the Morrígna.[46] Epona does not share these martial connections.

Not only modern day people make the mistake of equating the deities. This problem goes back at least to the Romans, who did the very same in all the lands they conquered. In most of the Roman inscriptions in the Celtic countries, you will see a native deity paired with a Roman deity, for example, Sulis Minerva at Bath. In this example, Sulis is the Celtic deity of the springs in Bath, and Minerva is a Roman goddess of springs and healing.

Sovereignty and the Land

To the Celts, sovereignty, the ability to rule well, was thought to be reflected in the land itself. If a king or chief ruled badly, the land would wither and crops would fail. If he or she was a just ruler, crops would thrive and the land would prosper.

Usually when the king was selected by the other chiefs, he would have to go through a ceremony in which he was "married" to the land. This ceremony took several forms, usually with the ruler having intercourse with a Priestess who represented the land; or in a few recorded instances

---

[45]Simon Hornblower, *The Oxford Classical Dictionary*, 3rd ed. (Oxford; New York: Oxford University Press, 1996), 199; Wikipedia, "Atargatis - Wikipedia, the Free Encyclopedia," accessed January 31, 2012, *http://en.wikipedia.org/wiki/Atargatis*.

[46]Wikipedia, "Badb - Wikipedia, the Free Encyclopedia," accessed January 31, 2012, *http://en.wikipedia.org/wiki/Badb*.

with a mare that represented the land. In the cases involving the mare, the mare was then killed and the meat placed in a large pot of water where it was cooked. The king would then be placed into the pot with the meat after it cooled, to drink the soup he was sitting in. After this, the soup was shared with the people, allowing them to partake in the essence of both the land and the king. This type of kingship inauguration is also found among the Vedic people of India in a very similar ritual

A very good example of how the land chooses the king and the relationship between them can be found in the story of Niall and the nine hostages, which was written sometime between 200 and 475CE and tells about Niall Noígíallach, the founder of the Uí Néill dynasty. Here is one version of the story:

Niall and his four stepbrothers, Brian, Fiachrae, Ailill, and Fergus were given weapons by a smith and sent into the woods hunting. As night approached, they set up camp and Fergus went looking for water. He came to a well guarded by a large old woman. She told him that he could have some water in exchange for a kiss. He refused and went back to his brothers. They each in turn went to try to get water, but Brian and Ailill each refused to kiss her. Fiachrae said that he would give her "the bare touch of a kiss." For that she later prophesied that his descendants would get "the barest touch of Tara," meaning that only two of his sons would be kings. When it was Niall's turn, he not only gave the old woman a kiss, but also embraced her and "laid her down" as they say in the Christian versions. At this, she turned into a beautiful young woman and told Niall that his descendants would rule Ireland for a long time. After the woman had turned into a young woman, Niall asked her who she was and her reply was "King of Tara, I am Sovereignty." Sovereignty, meaning that she was the land itself, and therefore the only one who could grant kingship to Niall. She also told Niall to take the water back to his brothers but not to give them any until they had granted him seniority over them and had agreed that he might raise his weapon a hand's breathe over theirs.[47]

The Three Queens

Another example of sovereignty appearing as women is the story of Amergin we touched briefly upon earlier in the *Book of Invasions* where

---

[47]Charles Squire, *Celtic Myth and Legend: Poetry & Romance* (Hollywood Calif.: Newcastle Pub. Co., 1975), 73–74; Wikipedia, "Niall of the Nine Hostages - Wikipedia, the Free Encyclopedia," accessed January 31, 2012, *http://en.wikipedia.org/wiki/Niall_of_the_Nine_Hostages*

the Sons of Mil came to Ireland, When Amergin came ashore with the rest of the Sons of Mil, he met a succession of three women, Banba, Fódla, and Érie. They each ask him the same question, "If I give the Celts [the sons of Mil] victory, will the land be named after me?" He tells all three that it will, and Ireland is still known poetically by all three names, as anyone who does crossword puzzles can tell you.

Find the River Source and Research the River

With regard to a river that runs close to your home or land and finding the local goddess connected to it, gathering information about it is a very important part. The more research done up front, the easier it will be to get in touch with the local River Goddess. In areas where the rivers do not run year-round, you may wish to work with a land feature instead. We will be covering that in the next section.

We are going to spend just a moment here to talk about "liminal" places, places that are "in the middle" and truly "undefined." To the Celts, and to many people on the "Path of Druidry" today, liminal space and times are very important and sacred due to their being at an edge point. Fords of a river, shores of the sea, swamps, and any place that is neither one thing nor another are all liminal spaces. Dusk and dawn, times that are neither day nor night, are liminal times.[48]

You can use old survey maps of the area to find the old Indian trails. This will lead you to finding the river fords, which were and still are liminal spaces, neither fully land nor fully water.

As part of your research on the river, it is important to find the headwaters of the river. Topographical maps will be a big help in finding this. The best way to find the headwater is to trace the river back to the highest point around you. It has to flow downhill from there. Most rivers today really have more than one headwater. Any spring that flows year-round into the stream can be considered a headwater. The headwater is the best place to contact the local River Goddess for it is her source of power as well.

Finding a Land Goddess

In the desert or certain other areas, it might be hard to find a year-round river or spring. In this case, it may be easier to work with a Land

---

[48]Wikipedia, "Liminality - Wikipedia, the Free Encyclopedia," accessed January 31, 2012, *http://en.wikipedia.org/wiki/Liminality*.

Goddess. Alternatively, you may know of a special land feature that resonates with you more than a river or lake. Look at local legends and at local aboriginal stories to find places that were held sacred. Many times, smaller bookstores will have a section for Local History, and this is a good first place to look. Visit those places and see if a special feeling is there for you, a feeling of "coming home" or of a sense of awe. If you find this sacred space, then you can use it to allow you to get in touch with the local Land Goddess.

Meditate at the Headwaters or Sacred Space

After you have done the work on finding the headwaters, or sacred space, the next step is to go there for meditation. Start by making offerings to the spring, lake, or stones, singing an Earth Mother chant (several examples can be found in the ritual section, chapters 6 and 7), and then asking for guidance on how to best worship the resident goddess. Next, find a comfortable spot where you can sit for an extended period. Once you have found it, open yourself up to the impressions you feel. After a set period, about an hour or so, write down what you felt, and saw and heard. After you have done this several times, compare the notes. Look for similarities in impressions. They will give you clues as to how the Goddess wants to be addressed and how she appears. If you are fortunate, you might get her name. If not, more work can be done later to know this.

The next step is to set up an offering place, a place designed to leave small offerings to her and start holding small rituals there. The daily devotionals discussed in the previous chapter are good examples of this type of ritual.

After you have meditated several times at your head-waters or sacred space, begin making more small offerings, such as flower, ale, songs or poetry and rituals, such as the daily devotionals addressed, but specifically to her. This can be done each time you go to this place and at high days, the eight most important times of the year to people on the Path of Druidry, if you wish. More information on the high days will be given in chapters 6 and 7. The more offerings that are given and the more rituals held there, the easier it becomes to work with the River or Land Goddess.

What to Do When You Find Your Local Goddess

You will know that you have found your local Goddess when you start to receive impressions of her in your meditations. But finding her is only the first step to the process. It is important to work on your relationship with her as well. The best way to grow this relationship is to start giving her regular offerings at your main rituals, the rituals you do on a regular basis at other places. These can be either daily rituals or rituals for special occasions. After you have found her name, call to her at each ritual you do. She is the Earth Mother, the local representation of the living Earth itself, for you, and can be called anytime you would call upon an Earth Mother deity in your rites. In ADF rituals, this is usually the first step.

Remember, once you have started including her in your rituals, keep it up! The more she is called upon and included, the better the connections between you and her, and the easier it will be to hear and understand her. Make sure that the rituals at the headwaters or sacred space are kept up as well. As more and more meditations are done at these places, your picture of the River or Land Goddess will expand. You will find more and more small details of her appearance and her preferred methods of being worshipped appearing to you in your meditations.

Finding Allies

The River or Land Goddess is only the first of the deities that can be found. Most Celtic tribes had several archetypal deities in their pantheons.

Archetypal Deities

One of the primary archetypal deities, as mentioned previously, is the Father God. He is frequently seen as the head of the tribe. He is usually, but not always, seen as a Sky God. Usually the Celtic tribes would bring the Father God with them as they traveled to a new home. For the modem people trying to reestablish the connections, this poses a problem. We do not know who the Father God of our Ancestors was, or there may have been several as our Ancestors came from different tribes. One way to find your Father God is to do a meditation to get him to adopt you. Give offerings and read about the different male deities before the meditation, and do a divination afterwards to see which God name comes through.

One of the main parts of an ADF ritual is the opening of the gates. Within ADF, "opening the gates" allows our words, actions and thoughts to move through all the planes to wherever the Gods and Goddesses and the Ancestors may be. Typically the deity called upon at this time to aid us is a transporter of souls. The transporter of souls, also called a psychopomp figure, was the deity of, and was usually seen and worshipped at, a liminal place. If they lived across the sea, they were worshipped by the shore, for example Manannán mac Lir among the Irish, or Seonaidh (anglicized as Shony or Shoney) among the Britons; if they were underground deities, such as Gofannon among the Welsh, or Goibniu among the Irish, they were worshipped in a cave.

The Celts usually included a hero of some kind in their pantheons. For us, this could be a local hero, someone who has lived the kind of life that we aspire to. You can find that person or persons, who are heroes for you and include them in your devotions by naming them during part of it. They may be either living or dead and if they are dead, they may be included in the Ancestor portion of your daily devotional or high day rites as well.

Another archetypal deity for many of the Indo-European peoples was the guardian of the forest, the Green Man. One way to get in touch with this figure is by going into the woods and doing a "hunt," or walking meditation, to get in touch with him. The hunt should be done in silence and you should wait to see what auguries or signs you see from him. The hunt should not be done to find any specific animal or place, just to give you a chance to be in the woods and allow you to open up and meditate on what the woods and the guardian of the forest has to say to you.

Spirits of Place

The next step in our process is to establish a relationship with the "Spirits of Place," the local Nature and Land Spirits. These are the Spirits that live in the trees, lakes, and earth of your area. They are also the animals, birds, and insects that live above, on, and in the land. And they are also the tribes of Faeries that reside on the land. An important step in this is to learn as much as you can about the ecosystem you live in, what should and what should not be there, what changes occur with the seasons and what can be done to protect it. Spend time out in the woods and green areas near you. Learn what trees, plants, and animals live around there. Spend time with individual trees and plants and listen to what they have to tell you. For example, is there enough water in the area or are they overcrowded?

A question has been raised about imposing the Nature Spirits that the Celts were used to on the Spirits that live on your land. A good first step is to do a ritual to acknowledge the local Spirits and the Ancestors of the people who were there first. Tell them what you plan to do and ask their permission. See what kind of impression is received in a divination and work from there. For example, if you were using oghams to take the divination and the response drawn was Blackthorn, an ogham that signifies strife and troubles, ask them what needs to be done to have them work with you. This can be done by pulling another ogham and seeing what comes up. If for example it was Birch, then you would know they are looking for new growth in the area. You could plant some new trees or shrubs for them.

I believe that when the Irish came to America they brought members of the Fair Folk, the tribes of Faeries also known as the Sidhe, with them. Once the troops of the Fair Folk were here, they warred with the local troops of Land Spirits. In some areas, the Fair Folk, the European tribes won and in other areas, the local Land Spirits did. This belief was arrived at by talking to people following the "Path of Druidry" across the United States and listening to the stories of their interactions with the local Spirits of Place.

In my home grove, a local congregation within ADF, we worship the local Spirits of Place as the Spirits of Nature as well as the Fair Folk, and they always join enthusiastically at our rites. Many times during rituals, you can hear animals and other creatures moving in the woods around us and the offerings that are left are usually consumed within a few days. Our usual call during ritual goes something like this:

We call to the Spirits of this Land, creatures of land, you who walk, crawl, and flow, creatures of the waters, who swim, float and cleanse, creatures of the sky, who fly, glide and soar, and to those that reside in the land itself, you beings of rock and earth and trees, and to those of the Fair Folk who live with us here, to all of you, we ask that you join your might with ours for this rite.

In England, the house Spirits are called the "brownies." They are usually seen as small beings that are naked or wearing shaggy brown clothes.

They are very helpful beings that will do many small chores around the house as long as the family does not anger them. They are displeased if they are offered food or clothes *as payment* for the work they do. It is fine if you leave food or whiskey out for them, you just have to be very careful not to give it in thanks of the work they do. You also need to be careful not to insult them or take their work for granted. Their favorite offerings are water, milk, bread, and cheese. The house elf in the Harry Potter series is based on the folklore of the brownies, including the scene where he no longer is bound to the house after having received clothing from his master.

With all the benefits associated with having an elf or Spirit living in the house, what can be done to attract one to it? The first step to attract a Spirit to your home is to prepare a place for it to live. Find a special stone, especially one with a hole in it if you can and wash it thoroughly. If you have a fireplace, clean it and lay a new fire, if not, clean a place near the stove for the stone and clean the stove.

In the evening when the family is gathered, put the rock near the fireplace or stove and put flowers around it. Set a cup or plate filled with an offering near it. Offerings that work well for brownies and other small Spirits are milk, cider, food, or whiskey, but only in small amounts because you do not want a drunken Spirit in your house. Then say something like:

> *Brownie, be welcome to this house!*
> *In this house let there be good cheer,*
> *A welcome for friend and stranger,*
> *Mirth and music, cleanliness and good order.*
> *In this house let there be food and drink in plenty,*
> *In this house let there be prosperity, harmony and health, love and luck for all.*
> *Honored One, for thy help we thank thee.*[49]

Then light the fire and put sweet smelling incense on it. Leave the offering in place overnight. In the morning, burn whatever is left. Make offerings to the house elf whenever there is a family gathering or if you need to get a lost object returned. When you are getting ready to do spring cleaning, make sure to let the house Spirit know in advance and then give their stone a good washing as well. If you do not let the Spirit

---

[49]Paxson, Diana, "Lares and Landwights" (presented at the Wiccan Fest, Ontario, Canada, June 6, 2001) Used with permission.

know in advance, you might very well make it mad at you and find your house without a Spirit!

As well as the Spirits inside the house, it is a good idea to keep the other Spirits of nature happy near you. Put out bird feeders, or place leftovers outside where the local animals can get to them, as long as there is not a rabies problem in your area. Perhaps providing birdhouses or piling up leftover Yule trees in a field to provide cover can act as housing. Keeping **all** the Spirits of Nature happy is beneficial in many ways! It gives you the enjoyment of their company, the help from them to keep harmony in a household, and the knowledge that they will be there for you if you need them. But do keep it up—it's important to maintain relationships with the faerie folk and all the other spirits. If you have to be away for a long period of time, say more than a week, arrange with someone else to leave the offerings for you, or at least let the Spirits know that you are going away temporarily and will be leaving the offerings out again as soon as you get back. By doing this, the house Spirits will keep a better watch on your home, knowing that no one is supposed to be in it.

Ancestors

The third triad of our Kindred is the Ancestors. At my home grove, when we call upon the Ancestors, we call to the Ancestors of our tribe, the Ancestors of the people gathered there, and the Ancestors of the people who lived on our land before. This relationship seems to work well for us. We have a shrine set up for the Ancestors where people from the grove place pictures of their Ancestors and an Ancestors' box where members of the grove can place mementos of their deceased loved ones. This box has a special place in our Samhain ritual. During the ritual, the box is opened, the only time during the year this happens, and grove members place objects in it to allow the memory of their loved ones to live on.

On a personal level, you can keep a small altar in one part of your home with mementos of your deceased loved ones. Having pictures, favorite items and maybe even letters from them in one place keep their memories alive. This can become a special place in your house where you can daily give honor to them.

The Next Step

Having started to work with your local pantheon, what is the next step? What techniques have been used to expand the relationships that have been built? Once you have found your local deities, include them in your regular worship. Within ADF, we have found that the more the deities are offered to and called upon, the stronger the connections are to the people and the more pronounced the effects seen from them. Many of our groves have reported stories of their members having personal experiences with the local deities. To us, the deities are not some abstract figures far away and unapproachable, but are real and very willing to communicate with us. The hardest part is learning to listen to them, to open yourself up during meditations and when in a ritual setting.

There are many people following the "Path of Druidry" that are establishing Sacred Wells, found wells where a local Goddess resides, and covering willows with prayer flags at Imbolc, February 1, as is still done in Ireland today. Others are leaving out "Brigit's blankets," blankets for healing work blessed by Brigit herself at Imbolc, and of course bringing the fertility to the land at Beltane, May 1, with Maypole dances and other "bringing in the May" customs. As a Druid, I feel that the relationships developed with the deities, the Nature Spirits and the Ancestors should be part of your daily life and worship. I strongly advise people to begin some form of daily communion and/or worship of them.

Chapter 6
Rituals for the Solitary Druid

We start out in this chapter by exploring some of the High Day holidays. I want you to be able to understand the history behind the holidays as well as the many ways rituals can be created or crafted. One day you will hopefully create your own rituals and see the need for this. For those new to Druidry, you will find information on and a personal ritual for each holiday.

High Day rituals can be performed in a sacred space, usually referred to as a *Nemeton* or grove, within a room where you can be undisturbed for about an hour or in a special location in the woods or along the shore of a lake or other body of water. Although they can be done indoors if necessary, being outdoors always seems to work best with High Day rituals. They can also be performed at the personal altar where you do your daily devotionals, but they seem to have more meaning, at least to me, if they are done in a "special," rather than an everyday place.

I will be dividing this discussion of rituals into two chapters because of the amount of material involved. In this chapter, we will cover the Fire Festivals, the four festivals we can historically trace to the Celts which involved the use of large bonfires, and in the next, the festivals for solstices and equinoxes, which we cannot prove were celebrated by the Celts, along with some other rituals I have created.

Many people on the "Path of Druidry" follow the NeoPagan tradition of scheduling the Fire Festivals on the first day of the month in which they are given. Others use the actual "crossing day" between the solstice and the equinox. The "crossing day" varies from year to year, but can easily be determined by counting the days between the actual solstice date and the actual equinox date and dividing by two. It usually falls on the sixth or seventh of the month, rather than the first.

The traditional dates for the festivals are:

Samhain—November 1

Winter Solstice—December 21 or actual date of the solstice

Imbolc—February 1

Spring Equinox—March 21 or actual date of the equinox

Beltane—May 1

Summer Solstice—June 21 or actual date of the solstice

Lúghnasadh—August 1

Fall Equinox—September 21 or actual date of the equinox

The chants used in the rituals are traditional NeoPagan or Druid chants. As such, they are written mainly to be used by groups of people, but I have included them in these solitary rituals to give the reader a chance to learn them and to feel a connectedness with followers of the Path of Druidry who do similar rituals. The tunes for these chants are available on my Web site, located at *www.skipellison.us/chants.html*.

First, a Little About My Form of Druid Rites

Because of my longtime involvement with ADF, I usually use the ADF liturgical format in all my rituals. This outline has been evolving over the almost thirty years that ADF has been in existence, and has proven to be a very workable format, easily adaptable for almost any ritual use. Further information about the ADF Core Order of Ritual (COoR) can be found here: *http://www.adf.org/rituals/explanations/core-order.html*.

Before we proceed much further, it is important to talk a little about purification. *www.dictionary.com* defines the word to mean:[50]

1. to make pure; free from anything that debases, pollutes, adulterates, or contaminates: to purify metals.

2. to free from foreign, extraneous, or objectionable elements: to purify a language.

3. to free from guilt or evil.

---

[50]"Purification | Define Purification at Dictionary.com," accessed November 28, 2012, *http://dictionary.reference.com/browse/purification?s=t*.

4. to clear or purge (usually followed by 'of' or 'from').
5. to make clean for ceremonial or ritual use.

It is the last meaning that we are mainly talking about here, but all apply. Before beginning the rite, it is good to make sure that you are clean "of body and mind," as the old books of magic said. In other words, take a bath before starting, and meditate to free your mind of all distractions of the day. It is also important to clean the space you will be using. If it is indoors, make sure it is swept and the area around it is uncluttered. The same applies if you will be doing the ritual outside. While you probably won't be able to sweep the area, make sure that nothing clutters the area or will interfere with you walking in the area. During the rite, you can also magically purify the space and yourself. In both this chapter and the next, I'll be giving you several examples of how this can be done.

Customarily these rituals begin by giving a musical signal, such as ringing a bell or giving three beats on a drum. This is also an excellent place to put an opening prayer. After that, I meditate to connect myself to the powers of Earth and Sky, which may be thought of as above and below, warmth and cold, or order and chaos. In the rituals given in this chapter, I have phrased this meditation, called the "Two-Power Meditation," to be recorded into a tape recorder and played back during this section of the ritual. Once you have gone through the rituals a few times and feel comfortable speaking the parts from memory or extemporizing, you can change the phrasing to the first person. For the next chapter, I will have them phrased to be read during the ritual to demonstrate how this can be done.

Next, we give an offering of some kind to an Earth Mother, or honor her in some other way, such as a song or spoken piece. Throughout history there have been many Earth Mothers, so this part is very likely historically accurate. Even if it is not, as part of an Earth-centered religion, I feel that honoring and protecting the Earth should be of primary importance to all NeoPagans. I then call to one of the bards of old, such as Taliesin or Brigit, to help me make my words and actions pleasing to the Mighty Kindred.

After this, I remind myself, while in a sacred space, why I am celebrating the holiday. This is the section called the "historical precedent," or "statement of purpose." Then I move on to connecting with the horizontal plane, the physical boundaries around the sacred space, or the land, sea, and sky that surrounds us all, and the vertical plane, the fire, well, and tree that make up the path to carry our words and actions, both up and down, through all of the worlds to the Mighty Kindred. The fire, well, and tree make up the central elements of the gate that is opened later, and they need to be magically established at this point of the ritual. This is often done through chanting. In the rituals that follow, I will show how this is accomplished. If you are working inside, a candle can be used for the fire, even if it is only a flickering candle light if no flames are allowed; if you are outdoors, a nice, roaring *fire* (if it is allowed in your area) gives a special feel to the ritual.

After the horizontal and vertical axes are developed, as will be shown in the individual rituals, I "open a gate" to allow the words and actions easier passage to the Ancestors and the Deities, both of which are categories of beings that reside outside our normal plane of existence. Working with the Gatekeeper deity, to help open the gate, allows you to build strong connections with them and makes creating the gate easier. Creating the gate is a magical act and by drawing more of the magic from the deity, it is easier to do. The gate is not necessary for the Spirits of Nature because they exist with us on this plane.

After the gate is opened, offerings are given to the Mighty Kindred: the Ancestors, the Spirits of Nature, and the Deities. Offerings can be flowers, food, ale, wine, whiskey, song, stories, poems, or artworks. People following the "Path of Druidry" do not give blood or living creatures as offerings, no matter what the ancients may have done. These offering are usually given to the Deity of the Occasion, but may also be given to other beings if the ritual is geared toward them, for example to the Ancestors at Samhain, or to the Nature Spirits at Spring Equinox.

After the rest of the offerings are given, there is a final "Prayer of Sacrifice" and final "key offering" which is the main offering of the rite, to focus all that was given, both in your mind and to the Kindred.

Then an omen, a divination using either oghams, runes, or some other method you favor, is taken to see how the offerings were received, or to ask what blessings the Kindred are giving you in return. In the early days of ADF, the omen was taken to make sure the Kindred approved of the gifts we had given them. If it was favorable, and the ogham or rune showed increase or happiness, the ritual wound down in reverse fashion. If it was unfavorable, and the ogham or rune indicated standstill or problems, more offerings were given and another omen was taken. This was done for a total of three omens and if all three were unfavorable, the ritual was stopped. Over the years, many ADF members have learned that the Kindred are very happy to receive our offerings, and ask instead what lessons the Kindred want us to work on.

After the omen is taken, it is time to receive a blessing from the Kindred called upon. This blessing is usually in the form of a glass of water, or beer, or mead that is "magically" charged with the blessings the Kindred give us in exchange for the offerings we have given them.

A very important concept to the ancient Indo-Europeans was *ghosti*. This concept deals with the guest-host relationship, and our modern word for quest comes from it. A simple way to understand it is found in the phrase "a gift calls for a gift." In the rituals, we give gifts, offerings, to the Kindred and we know that they will in return give us gifts back. Since the Kindred are so much more powerful that us, we can expect their gifts to be much more than ours. After the blessings are drank, the ritual is closed down in the reverse order to what it was began.

Cross-Quarter Days or Fire Festivals

The first of the High Day holidays we will discuss are the cross-quarter days, also known as the Celtic Fire Festivals. They are called the cross-quarter days because they fall opposite, or "across" the solstices and equinoxes, which are con-sidered the "quarter days." Current scholarship suggests that the ancient Celts celebrated only four holidays: Samhain, the beginning of the dark half of the year and summer's end; Imbolc, sacred to the goddess Brigit; Beltane, the beginning of the light half of the year and summer's beginning; and Lúghnasadh, a summer festival of games and the principal time for gatherings and marriages.

Samhain

We start our year with Samhain, a time when the veil between the worlds is thin and the dead can move easily in both directions. Samhain, also known as "Samain," "Hallowe'en," "All Hallows Eve," "Mallowmas," "All Saint's Eve," "All Soul's Eve," "*Sauin*" on the Isle of Man, "*Samhuinn*" in Scots Gaelic, "*Nos Galan-gaeof*" (the Night of the

Winter Calends) in Wales, and the "Witches' New Year" in modern times, is traditionally celebrated on the night of October 31.

Samhain (pronounced "Sow-en") is one of the original four Celtic Fire Festivals and means "summer's end"— when the sun's power wanes and the strength of the gods of darkness, winter, and the underworld grows great. The activities of the year have come to fruition in the harvest and the warmth of summer has ended. The days grow shorter and the nights stretch longer. The earth falls into a winter sleep and reawakens in the spring when life renews itself. As Beltane marks the beginning of summer, Samhain records its end.[51]

The Holiday

From the Coligny calendar, the first-century BCE Gaulish calendar found in 1897 in Coligny, France, that likely was used by the Druids, we see that Samhain is the only one of the Fire Festivals listed. According to Alexei Kondratiev, the name given to the festival was *Trinouxtion Samonii*, which implies that the festival was three days long,[52] although other authors tell us that it lasted seven days with the actual feast held in the middle.[53] Anne Ross and James MacKillop state that the name given in the calendar was *Samonios*. The calendar also tells us that the Gauls believed that the period of dark proceeds the period of light. This supports the idea that Samhain was a time of beginnings, being the start of the dark half, and thus the beginning of the year.[54]

Reflecting the reverence with which Celts treated liminal spaces, Samhain was thought to be a special time. It was believed easy to move from one "space" to another, from the world of the humans to the world of the Faeries for example. The laws of time and space were thought to be suspended at Samhain—and so too were the laws of the tribe. People could not kill each other, but during this time, certain lesser rules were relaxed. Tradition tells us that people would dress up as members of the opposite sex and go among their neighbors asking for treats. If the treats were not given, then tricks, such as stopping up

---

[51] Kia Marie Wolfe, *The Wheel of the Year*, n.d.

[52] Alexei Kondratiev, *The Apple Branch: a Path to Celtic Ritual* (Cork [Ireland]: Collins Press, 1998), 105.

[53] Nigel Pennick, *The Sacred World of the Celts: An Illustrated Guide to Celtic Spirituality and Mythology*, 1st U.S. ed. (Rochester Vt.: Inner Traditions, 1997), 105.

[54] James MacKillop, *Dictionary of Celtic Mythology* (Oxford; New York: Oxford university press, 1998), 333.

the chimney with peat or scattering the piles of hay, would be played on the homeowner.[55]

In the Irish romance *The Boyhood Deeds of Fiona*, part of the *Tales of the Fianna Cycle* written down by Irish monks in the 1600s but based on earlier oral legends, mention is made of the mystical nature of Samhain. There is a reference to the *Bean-Sidhe* (woman of the hill), who would wail in prophetic anticipation whenever anyone of royal blood was about to die and her shrieks would be heard this night. Elsewhere, the tale notes that the entrances to the burial caves were open at Samhain, to allow the spirits of the heroes to come out for an airing, and the interiors were illuminated until the following cockcrow. The spirits of the sacred kings of Bronze Age Ireland, which also appeared on this night, were believed to have gone to *Cáer Sidi*, the castle of Arianrhod (also referred to as the Spiral Castle), where the cauldron of inspiration was housed. There was a revolving wheel before the door of the castle, and no one could enter or exit until it had stopped.[56]

The spiritual significance of Samhain is its most important aspect. This festival is regarded as a celebration of the New Year and as the "festival of the dead." As death is seen to be merely a door that opens to another life, it is believed that at this time of year the souls of the dead can walk among the living. Samhain is also the time when those souls still wandering this plane after departing from life can be called to the cauldron of rebirth, the place that in many of the tales is an entrance into the Summer Lands, a place of rest and learning.

One practice among the modern Celts, those living within the past few hundred years, was to set a place at the table for those who had passed over during the preceding year. This offering was usually a plate of food assembled from all the foods present before anyone else was served. In Wales, it was the custom to leave the food outside for the wandering dead. The offering, called *bwyd cennad y* was made in the hope that the dead would be satisfied and leave the living in peace. Along with the offering of food, Celts would make sure that the doors of the house remained unbolted so that the dead could enter the house if they desired. Special care was taken to prepare the hearth for the visit of the dead before going to bed.[57]

---

[55]Rees, Alwin and Rees, Brinley, *Celtic Heritage: Ancient Tradition in Ireland and Wales* (London: Thames and Hudson, 1973), 90.

[56]Kia Marie Wolfe, *The Wheel of the Year.*

On Samhain, as on the other three Fire Festivals, bonfires were lit on the highest hills and the hearth fires were solemnly rekindled from the community bonfires after the hearths had been extinguished the preceding night. The Druid priests oversaw the ritual lighting of the fires in pre-Christian times. The main fire in ancient Ireland was kindled on the hill of Tlachtga, the modern-day Ward Hill, located northwest of Tara. This fire had to be lit by a spindle of oak turned on an oaken block by a wheel spun only in a sunwise direction.[58] This is a very old method of creating fire, similar to using a "fire drill," and is hard to learn but fairly easy to do, once you know how. On this night and throughout the first week of November, ritual fires remained ablaze. Some modern NeoPagans believe that through these fires the early Celts symbolically burned away all the frustrations and anxieties of the preceding year.

Samhain was also the time of the year when the *Fomorians*, the tribe the *Tuatha Dé Danann* fought against when they came to Ireland, extracted their tribute from them. Each year, the people were forced to give them two thirds of their corn, milk, and children. There is a poem in the *Dindshenchas*, the early tale that talks about place names, that tells us how at this time of year children were sacrificed to *Corm Cruet*—one of the many god names about which we have little information—at *Mag Sleuth* in Ireland.[59] The purpose of this sacrifice was to ensure the supply of milk and corn from the gods of the land. This action may be a remnant of the culling of the herds of animals that could not be kept through the winter months, interpreted by Christian writers as a sacrifice of children.

Another interesting aspect of the sacrificial aspect of the holiday can be found on the Isle of Lewis in the Hebrides. Until modern times, on Samhain people would gather on the shore and one of them would wade out to give an offering of ale to Shoney, the god of the sea, to enrich their fishing grounds for the coming year.[60]

Other pieces of Samhain lore include the belief that any fruit remaining on the trees was not to be eaten, but was to be left for the *pucas*, or Land Spirits. In Cork, one can see the procession of the "White Mare," a

---

[57]"Rees, Alwin and Rees, Brinley, Celtic Heritage: Ancient Tradition in Ireland and Wales, 90.

[58]Bonwick, Irish Druids and Old Irish Religions, 206.

[59]Rutherford, Ward, Celtic Lore: The History of the Druids and Their Timeless Traditions (London: Thorsons, 1995), 96.

[60]MacKillop, James. *Dictionary of Celtic Mythology*. (Oxford: Oxford University Press, 1998), p. 333.

group of young men walking the countryside, led by a man wearing white robes and a horse's head. His followers would blow horns and visit houses to obtain provisions for the celebrations.

Divination is prominently featured in the tales that take place at Samhain, most often to see who a future husband or wife might be, but it could be done for any reason. One way to look into the future was to pour hot lead or wax onto water and divine from the shapes formed. Unfortunately, those meanings have not come down to us. Other methods featured apples, nuts (usually hazelnuts), beans, snails, and candles. Bobbing for apples is a vestige of this form of divination, using the method but not putting it to interpretive uses. The Roman Catholic Church tried to Christianize Samhain in the seventh century by making November 1 All Saints' Day and the night of October 31 All Hallow's Eve in tribute to the saints of the past. The holiday, thus, retained its veneration of the dead. The Church encountered difficulties assimilating these celebrations into its religious calendar, thanks to prevailing Pagan influences at the time, and they were removed from its calendar altogether in the mid-1100s, not to be reinstated until 1928, when the Church felt confident that the Pagan belief systems were no longer a threat.

An ancient ritual practiced to this day by some groups involves calling on those who have recently died, to help them resolve whatever concerns hold them to the lower astral plane, and to aid them to find solace and guidance along their trek toward reincarnation. This is done by lighting lights and calling out for any spirits that may still be lingering to "come to the light and move on to the Summer Lands." To this end, the jack-o-lantern was used in times past as a beacon to light the way for the dead. Originally carved from a turnip in the British Isles, or what we in the U.S. call a rutabaga, today a pumpkin is most familiar.

If you are interested in carving a jack-o-lantern from a rutabaga, it is easy. Simply cut off the top and hollow out the inside with a spoon. Then cut a circle out of the bottom and place it over the top of a flashlight. When you turn the flashlight on, the rutabaga takes on a spooky look, similar to the pumpkin version, but slightly different. A candle can be used, but the flashlight is safer when doing this with children.

In today's group rituals, restless souls are summoned to "come to the light" by participants in the ceremony. Everyone wears black to represent the fragile veil between the dusk and the dawn, the living and the dead. An apple is passed slowly around the circle and cloves are inserted into the fruit to represent each departed spirit being guided to the light and to allow the ritual participants a chance to put to rest anything that troubles them. The ritual itself is very beautiful, loving, and emotionally spellbinding. To add this to your personal ritual, set up a candle or jack-o-lantern in the center of your sacred space and make the calling. You too can use the apple and pierce it with cloves for everyone you know who has "passed over" in the past year. When the ritual is finished, bury the apple in the ground to allow it to decay naturally, symbolizing the natural process the souls of the dead will take.

A recommended Web site that lists many Samhain customs, including several good recipes for Samhain foods, games, folklore, is located at *http://en.wikipedia.org/wiki/Samhain#Historic_Samhain_customs*. A quick search on *www.google.com* will find many others as well.

A Personal Ritual for Samhain

As Isaac Bonewits points out in his book *Rites of Worship: A Neopagan Approach*, there are five phases to any Druid ritual:

Phase One. Consecrating space and time and getting the people purified, centered, grounded, and unified into a group mind. This makes them ready for...

Phase Two. Recreating the cosmos by defining a ritual center and/or opening "gates between the worlds," enumerating the various parts of existence [individual sections of the cosmos] and (usually) evoking or invok-ing entities from them, thus starting a back and forth flow of manna [personal power or energy] through the gates, culminating with...

Phase Three. Giving the major part of the congrega-tion's manna to the primary Deity(ies) being worshipped on the occasion. This is followed by...

Phase Four. Receiving and causing a return flow of manna from the primary Deity(ies) of the occasion, and finally...

Phase Five. Reversing the beginnings of the rite (unwinding the various manna fields woven) and closing down the ceremony."[61]

Obviously, not all of these phases need be applied to create a ritual for a solitary, but keep them in mind. Another thing that is helpful in designing rituals is repetition. If you use the same line for common events, it makes it easier to extemporize when needed. The ritual given below is an example of one you can use in designing your own.

The area is prepared in advance with the offerings and other objects needed nearby for easy access. A bath is taken and mediation is completed. The primary deities honored in this ritual are *An Dagda* (pronounced "An Doy-da") and the *Mórrígan* (pronounced "Mor-rig-ahn"). In one of the stories about the preparations for the second battle of *Mag Tuired* (pronounced "moy tura"), the second battle between the *Tuatha Dé Danann* and the *Fomorians*, the Dagda comes upon the *Mórrígan* on a Samhain eve, straddling the river Unis, in the province of Connacht, "washing herself," as they say in the Victorian translations. The Dagda is excited by what he sees and after talking to her, they make love by the river. It is through this story that the Dagda and the *Mórrígan* have come to be associated with Samhain.

Phase One. As Isaac describes it above: consecrating space and time and getting the people purified, centered, grounded, and unified into a group mind.[62]

Musical Signal

A bell is struck nine times in three groups of three rings.

Opening Prayer

A short declaration of why the ritual is happening is spoken:

I am here tonight to give praise to the great Ones, to the Ancestors to my friends in nature. I am here on this Samhain night to help the souls of those who have passed in the last year to move into the next world. I can feel the magic on this night!

(Forcefully) *I am here to honor the Gods!*

---

[61]Isaac Bonewits, Rites of Worship: a Neopagan Approach (Miami Florida: Earth Religions Press, 2003), 57–58.
[62]Ibid.

Two-Power Meditation—Earth and Sky

This meditation incorporates the subtle energy difference between the Earth and the Sky. To start, slow down your breathing, take deep, full breaths, and clear your mind. Then, start using your "inner vision," that is found in your mind's eye. This part of the ritual works well if it is recorded on tape and played back, so you can concentrate on what the words are telling you to do:

Close your eyes. Take slow, full breaths and allow your mind to settle and focus on the work to be done. Feel the wind on your face, the sounds of the trees, and the smell of the fire. Allow these sensations to fill your mind.

Now, using your inner vision let your being move out of your body and flow down into the ground. As you move down, you can smell the warm, clean smells of the Earth; hear the sound of sweet water as it passes by you. You can feel the movement of energies around you. Follow those energies down until they join with the currents of molten lava flowing around and though the earth. These currents are the source of the power in the Earth. They flow around and under the skin of your Earth Mother. They change the shape of the continents and allow new earth to form. As you flow with these energies, allow your being to fill with them. Filled with the warmth of these energies, allow your being to start moving back up toward the surface, toward your body.

As you move upward, you know that you are bringing these energies with you— not just what's within you, but the totality of these energies. As you reenter your body, let these energies flow out from you and move around the sacred space. As the energy moves around this place, you can feel the warmth around you.

As you feel that warmth around you let your being again move out of your body. This time, allow it to move upward. As you move up, you can hear the wind around you, smell the clouds as you pass through them, and feel the water in them. Above you, you can see a star brighter than the others. This star is your special star, the source of the power from the Sky. Allow your being to move up until it merges with this star. The energy here is different from the energy of the Earth, colder but still very powerful. Let this energy fill you till your being feels full. Now start back down toward the sacred space and your body, bringing the energies with you. Again, you're bringing not just the energies within your being, but the totality of those energies. As you come back into your body, let these energies flow out from you and move around the sacred space and the energies from the Earth.

With the powers and energies of Earth and Sky joined together here with you tonight, be filled with the power and love that is here. Be at peace with yourself. Now, open your eyes and let your vision return to your mortal eyes as your work continues.

Purifying the Space

While there are many ways to purify a space, most involve water and incense. The water "washes" the space clean, and then the incense "purifies" it by helping to raise the body's or space's vibrational rate. One way it can be done in Solitary work is to have a shell full of water and a lit incense stick or three, we are Druids after all. As you sprinkle yourself with the water, you can say something like:

I stand here prepared to begin this work. As this water touches me, may it wash away all earthly cares.

Then as you wave the incense around yourself, you can say something like:

May the Spirit rise within me.

After you are purified, you can carry the water and incense around the space you will be working in and repeat the same lines to purify it.

Honoring an Earth Mother

Honoring an Earth Mother can be done by making an offering to the earth or into an offering bowl, using offerings such as flowers, cornmeal, or some other natural object, while speaking words of honor: If you are doing your ritual inside, offerings can be placed in a bowl and taken outside after the working is done. They can be spread out for the local Nature Sirits to find, or spread into a garden or composting area to go back into the Earth.

I give honor first to the mother of us all, the Earth Mother. Earth Mother, you support me in my work and in my very life.
(Forcefully) *Earth Mother, I honor you!*

Then kiss the Earth.

Honoring the Bardic Deities

One form of honoring the bardic deities, those Gods or Goddesses involved strongly with poetry, singing, storytelling, and the spoken word, is a calling upon of the spirit of the bards of old to join with you during this ritual and to give your words the sweetness and inspiration needed:

I call now upon all the bards of old. I ask that I receive your inspiration to allow my words to flow with honeyed sweetness. May the fire of inspiration burn within me, not only for this sacred time, but whenever I call upon it.

Historical Precedent

This section is included to allow yourself to be reminded a little of the history of the holiday.

Samhain is one of the original Celtic fire festivals and means "summer's end"— when the sun's power wanes, and the strength of the gods of darkness, winter, and the underworld grows great. As Beltane marks the beginning of summer, Samhain records its end.

Samhain is regarded as the Celtic New Year and also the "Festival of the Dead." It is believed that at this time of year the souls of the dead can walk amongst the living. On the night of Samhain, the door to realms beyond mortal comprehension is opened, the veil between life and death is at its thinnest, and the revolving wheel guarding the gates of the Spiral Castle has stopped for a brief moment.

This night and all of the first week of November once blazed with ritual fires— upon which the early Celts symbolically burned all the frustrations and anxieties of the preceding year.

Phase Two. As Bonewits describes it: recreating the cosmos by defining a ritual center and/or opening "Gates Between the Worlds/' enumerating the various parts of existence [individual sections of the cosmos] and (usually) evoking or invoking entities from them, thus starting a *back and forth* flow of manna [personal power or energy] through the Gates.[63]

Establishing the horizontal Axis

We all live in the Middle Realm, with the Upper and Lower Realms being the other two planes of existence. But this Middle Realm is divided itself. It can be thought of as consisting of Land, Sea and Sky, which was a common element among the Celts. When the Celts first met Alexander the Great, they formed a treaty and bound themselves to it with this oath:

---

[63]Ibid.

"If we observe not this engagement," they said, "may the sky fall on us and crush us, may the earth gape and swallow us up, may the sea burst out and overwhelm us."[64]

In my home ADF Grove, we have always used the following to establish the horizontal boundaries, but many other wordings are possible. Walk around the boundary of your space sprinkling cornmeal while saying:

I ask that the Earth not open up and swallow me.

Next walk around the space sprinkling water while saying:

I ask that the Seas not rise up and drown me.

And walk around the area one more time waving a stick on incense while saying:

I ask that the Sky not fall down upon me.

Establishing the Vertical Axis

One way to establish the vertical axis is by reconnecting the Well, Fire, and Tree with their roots to all the other sacred wells, fire, and trees in the cosmos. At this time, offerings can be given to each of the three in the sacred center as they are addressed. Customary offerings include silver to the well, olive oil to the fire if using an actual fire (if using an offering bowl indoors, place the oil in the bowl or burn stick incense), and incense and/or water to the tree. These offerings can be made by holding your hand near the objects and saying:

Sacred Well, let your waters flow down, down to all the sweet waters beneath the earth. Once again I ask you to become the mouth of the earth, the eye of the earth, the opening of the earth.

Sacred Fire, become once again all the fires that have burned and that ever will. And may you carry my words, praise, and love to the Gods and Goddesses, Ancestors, and Nature Spirits.

Sacred Tree, roots going into the Mother below and with your crown stretching to the heavens above. I ask that you connect this world with all the other worlds.

---

[64]"Myths and Legends of the Celtic Race: Chapter I: The Celts in Ancient History," accessed November 29, 2012, *http://www.sacred-texts.com/neu/celt/mlcr/mlcr01.htm*.

Calling Upon the Gatekeeper

This calling is usually done while giving an offering of olive oil to the fire. The more you work with a gatekeeper deity, the stronger your ties with him will become. As was briefly discussed in the section on daily devotionals, a gatekeeper deity is one that helps transport the dead to the Summer Lands, that is, a deity of the underworld or a psychopomp. I personally call upon Manannán mac Lir as a gatekeeper, but I suggest that you find the deity that works best for you through experimentation. The calling could be something like:

> *Manannán mac Lir, rider of the waves, guide to the land of eternal youth, I call you to come to me now in your coracle, your magic boat, the Wavesweeper. Manannán, I ask that once again, you join your magic to mine and let the Well open as a Gate* [pointing to the Well and visualizing a gate, or ring of fire, opening over it].

> *And let the Fire open as a Gate* [pointing to the Fire and visualizing a gate, or ring of fire, opening over it].

> *And let the Tree extend through the gate* [pointing to the Bile and visualizing it growing through the gates over the Fire and Well, both up and down, to all the planes of existence], *to carry my voice to the Gods.*

> (Forcefully) *O Manannán let the gates be opened!"*

Phase Three. As Isaac said, giving the major part of the congregation's manna to the primary Deity(ies) being worshipped on the occasion.[65]

Kindred Callings

First, we call to the Kindred. An offering of cornmeal (or some other type of food, but cornmeal works best) is sprinkled around the inside of the sacred space or into the offering bowl. A calling is spoken at this time as the offering is sprin-kled. In the calling below, the Ancestors of the tribe are those Ancestors of the people around you, not necessarily your family, but your friends. The Ancestors of your people are your direct Ancestors and the Ancestors of the place are the people who lived where you are holding the ritual in days long past.

---

[65]Bonewits, *Rites of Worship*, 57–58.

I call now to you who have come before, Ancestors of my tribe, my people, and of the tribes that were in this place before me. This offering is for you. I ask that you give me your aid and your blessings in my work tonight.

(Forcefully) *Ancestors, be with me tonight and accept my sacrifice!"*

Next, an offering to the Nature Spirits of a sweet-smelling herbal mix (or incense stick if working indoors) is sprinkled around the inside of the sacred space. A calling is spoken as the offering is made:

I call to the Spirits of Earth, creatures of land, you who walk, crawl, and grow, creatures of the waters, who swim, float, and cleanse, creatures of the sky, who fly, glide and soar, and to those of the Fair Folk who live with me here, to all of you, I ask that you join your might with mine for this rite.

(Forcefully) *Spirits of the Earth, be with me tonight and accept my sacrifice!"*

Finally, an offering to the Shining Ones (the Deities) of olive oil is sprinkled on the fire or into the offering bowl. A calling is spoken at this time:

I call now to all the Gods and Goddesses not specifically named in this rite. I ask that you join with me tonight and give me your aid and your blessings in this working.

(Forcefully) *Shining Ones, be with me tonight and accept my sacrifice!*

Calling upon the Deities of the Occasion

A calling is made to the primary deities, *An Dagda* and the *Mórrígan*. As each calling is spoken, an offering of olive oil is poured into the fire or offering bowl:

I call to you, An Dagda, father of tribes, protector, and provider. Come to me now with your great club that takes life with one end, and bestows life with the other. Come to me with your great cauldron of bounty and rebirth. Come to me now with your wisdom and knowledge to help and bless me in this work.

(Forcefully) *An Dagda, accept my sacrifice!*

I call to you, Mórrígan, Queen of darkness and death. Come to me covered in the wings of a raven. Come to me swift as the winds. Come to me now with your wisdom and knowledge to help and bless in this work.

(Forcefully) *Mórrígan, accept my sacrifice!*

Praise Offering

This can be done through offers of song, poetry, story, dance, artwork, etc. You should prepare what you will be offering in advance of the ritual and make sure that it is a worthy offering. It is a good idea to have on hand extra olive oil, more songs, and so forth, in case you feel that additional offerings are needed.

Prayer of Sacrifice and Key Offering

This final offering is given as the words of the prayer are said. It should be something special, and is usually a physical offering rather than a song or story. For this example, I will be using a full bottle of whiskey as the offering. If an offering such as this is poured into a real fire, be very careful how it is poured, as the fire can travel back up the stream of liquor and explode the bottle! It is best poured in small amounts and "around" the fire rather than directly into it.

> *An Dagda and Mórrígan, you have seen the offerings I have given you and know how much I honor you. Now I give my final offering to you this night. This bottle of fine whiskey is for you. My you drink well and enjoy it!*
>
> (Forcefully) *An Dagda and Mórrígan, accept my sacrifice!*

Phase Four. Receiving and causing a return flow of manna from the primary Deity(ies) of the occasion.[66]

Omen

The omen is usually done with either runes or ogham cards/sticks. It used to be the belief within ADF and other Druid groups that if the omen turns out badly, the Kindred aren't happy with the offerings given and we need to give more. If, after giving supplemental offerings, three bad omens in one ritual are drawn, the ritual stops and extra parting gifts would be given to the Kindred. This has never happened in my own ADF grove but it has happened in other ADF groves. Whether or not you follow this practice in your personal work is up to you. An alternative is to ask what lessons the Kindred want you to work on, or what blessings do they give you.

After the omen is drawn, feel free to use a book to help you interpret the omen. Take time to reflect upon how the omen is relevant to your

---

[66]Ibid.

personal life. It is also helpful to take the meanings of that omen and "infuse" it into the return flow.

Return Flow

Many people following the "Path of Druidry" believe that, having given offerings to the Kindred, blessings will flow back to us, magnified many times. This belief is based on the stories of hospitality, both given and returned, in the tales of the Celts, as well as of the Indo-European peoples. The "Return Flow" is started by holding up a cup of water, juice, beer, or ale. Energize the beverage by visualizing while saying something like:

I close my eyes and let my inner vision look upward. Looking through the gate, I can see the crowd of people and spirits looking down upon me. The Shining Ones, Ancestors, and Spirits of Nature have been given sacrifices of honor, love, and praise. Now is the time when I ask them to return the blessings to me magnified by their greatness! Shining Ones, let your blessings flow into this cup! Spirits of Nature, let your blessings flow into this cup! Ancestors, let your blessings flow into this cup! As this cup fills with the energy and blessings of the Kindred, I can watch it with my inner vision. I can see how it glows and sparkles as the blessings flow into it. I can see how it is glowing with the blessings received. I can see the blessing that the omen told me about in here.

(Forcefully) *Behold, the Waters of Life!*

The waters are now drunk while contemplating everything that has gone on so far.

Phase Five. Reversing the beginnings of the rite (unwinding the various manna fields woven) and clos-ing down the ceremony.[67]

Thanking the Deities

A gift of olive oil is poured into the fire or into the offering bowl, as the parting is spoken:

Mórrígan, great lady, I thank you for your aid and your blessings tonight. As this rite is ending, I give you this gift in parting, given out of love, with nothing asked in return.

(Forcefully) *Mórrígan, I thank you!*

A gift of olive oil is poured into the fire or into the offering bowl, as the parting is spoken:

---

[67]Ibid.

An Dagda Father of all, I thank you for your aid and your blessings tonight. As this rite is ending, I give you this gift in parting, given out of love, with nothing asked in return.

(Forcefully) An Dagda I thank you!

Thanking the Kindred

Similarly, a gift of olive oil is poured into the fire or into the offering bowl, as the parting is spoken:

To all of the Gods and Goddesses who were here but not named, I thank you for joining with me and giving me your blessings. As this rite is ending, I give you this gift in parting, given out of love with nothing asked in return.

(Forcefully) Gods and Goddesses, I thank you!"

The gift of olive oil is repeated as the next parting is spoken:

To all of the Spirits of Nature, I know you are around me every day and are always in my life. I thank you for joining with me and giving me your blessings. As this rite is ending, I give you this gift in parting, given out of love, with nothing asked in return.

(Forcefully) Spirits of Nature, I thank you!

A gift of olive oil is repeated as the parting is spoken:

Ancestors, without you I wouldn't be here. I thank you for joining with me and giving me your blessings. As this rite is ending, I give you this gift in parting, given out of love, with nothing asked in return.

(Forcefully) Ancestors, I thank you!

Thanking the Gatekeeper and Closing the Gates

The gates are now closed by saying something like:

Manannán mac Lir, I ask you once again to join your magic with mine, and let the Tree be again a tree [pointing at the Tree and visualizing it shrinking back down to normal size].

And let the Fire be again a fire [pointing at the Fire and visualizing it simply as a candle or small fire],

And let the Well be once again a well [pointing at the Well and visualizing it as simply a bowl of water].

(Forcefully) O Manannán mac Lir, let the gates be closed!

A gift of olive oil is poured as this parting is spoken:

Manannán mac Lir, rider of the waves, you have been my guide to the Land of Eternal Youth tonight. As this rite is ending, I give you this gift in parting, given out of love, with nothing asked in return.

Thanking the Bards and Earth Mother

Parting gifts of olive oil are poured to both the Earth Mother and the Bards that were called upon while saying something like:

Bards of old, I thank you for giving me a honeyed tongue, and as this rite is ending, I give you this gift in parting, given out of love, with nothing asked in return.

Mother of us All, I think you for upholding this work and as this rite comes to a close, I give you this gift in parting, given out of love, with nothing asked in return.

Reversing the Two-Power Meditation

This meditation is reversed at the end of the ritual by allowing the energies to move back to their source. Again, this works best if instruction for it has been recorded on tape and played during this part of the ritual:

Once again close your eyes. Using your inner vision, look at the sacred space filled with bright swirls of energies— energies that have come from above and below and from within yourself. Take those energies from the Sky above and bring them back into yourself. Now, let your being expand upward, back toward your special star. Bring those energies with you and guide them on their way back to the star. As the energies leave your being, keep what you need for yourself, and let the rest go. Let your being return to your body as you continue.

Now, as you look around you, you see that the energies of the Earth are still swirling around you. Take those energies into yourself and start transferring them back into the Earth. Let your being flow with them, down into the Earth. When you've gone far enough, allow the ener-gies to flow back to where they came from, keeping as much as you need for yourself. Let your being return to your body. As this phase of the work draws to a close, allow your body to be energized by the forces that have gone through it. Open your eyes and look around you at the sacred space. Be at peace with yourself.

Conclusion

Some type of formal closing must be spoken aloud, even if it is as simple as: *This rite has ended!* And then the bell is rung once again in the same way it was done to start the ritual.

Imbolc

Imbolc is a Fire Festival sacred to women and especially to Brigit. It is the point in the cycle of seasons when new life is beginning, a time when the first stirrings can be felt in the natural world.

Occurring at the midpoint between the winter solstice and spring equinox, this spoke on the "wheel of the year" celebrates the female mystery of the germination of the seed, the spark of life, symbolic of fertility, impregnation, and the start of new spiritual life for the Earth and her inhabitants. For in the womb of the Earth, hidden from our mundane sight but sensed by a keener vision, there are stirrings. The seed that was planted in her womb at the Winter Solstice is quickening and the New Year grows.[68]

The Holiday

Imbolc means "in the belly"—that is, *im*, within; *bolc*, belly—but it has many variant names. One possible source for the name is from the Irish *imb fholc*, "washing oneself," a reflection of the purification aspect of the holiday.[69] The Irish called it *Óimelc* (Middle Irish) or *Ouimelko* (Old Irish), meaning "ewe's milk" (*oi*, sheep; *melc*, milk). Other spellings include *Imbolg*, *Oimelk*, and *Óimelg*. In Scots Gaelic, the holiday is called *Là Féill Bhride* (holiday of Brid or Brigit). Another Irish name for the holiday is *Lá 'il Bríde* (day of Brid or Brigit). In modern Irish and Manx, the holiday is commonly called Candlemas Day, after the candles associated with it.[70]

Traditionally, this festival was celebrated when the first sign of milk was observed in the ewes, and the newborn lambs, harbingers of spring, were ready to suckle. It was a "floating" holiday, fixed not on the calendar, but on signs observed in nature, that represented the agricultural awakening of the Earth.

---

[68]Kia Marie Wolfe, *The Wheel of the Year*.

[69]Kondratiev, *The Apple Branch: a Path to Celtic Ritual*, 139.

[70]MacKillop, *Dictionary of Celtic Mythology*, 239–240.

The three months of winter between Samhain and Imbolc are associated with the Cailleach, a Goddess (also known as the "Carline of *Mag-Moullack*" by the Scots) who was pictured as an old woman who embodied the forces of contraction and was the enemy of growth. Each year, on the Eve of Brid, as the first glimmer of dawn touches the sky, the Cailleach drinks of the Well of Youth and is magically transformed into the fair young Goddess Brighid. By this action, the never-ending cycle of birth, life, death, and regeneration continues each year.[71]

Brigit's Day, or Brigantia, as the feast of Brid was known among the ancient Celts, honored Brigit. Although she went by many names, variations on the term "Exalted One," she bestows her special patronage on any woman about to be married or handfasted (a NeoPagan form of marriage), and hence the word "bride."[72]

Brigit is also a Goddess of poetry, the patroness of the smiths and the Goddess of healing (especially the healing touch of midwifery). According to the *Book of Invasions*, she was the daughter of the *Dagda*, and her mother was Boann [*Bófhionn* in Old Irish). Her special animal is the white cow with red ears, - her flower is the dandelion (*caiseanbhán* in Irish), a medicinal (healing) plant with white milky juice; and her bird is the oystercatcher [*giollabride* in Irish, meaning "Bride's servant").[73]

The Church could not very easily call the great Goddess of Ireland a demon. Instead, they canonized her and she became Saint Brigit, patron saint of smithcraft, poetry, and healing. Irish peasants were told that Brigit was really an early Christian missionary sent to the Emerald Isle, and that the miracles she performed there misled the common people into believing that she was a Goddess. In the early sixth century, the Christian Saint Bride of Kildare did in fact found many women's religious communities through-out Ireland. The Church also changed the name of the holiday Brigantia to Candlemas—the "Feast of Waxing Light" or the "Festival of the Purification of the Virgin." The notion of purification may seem a little obscure to us today, but it has to do with the old custom of "churching women." It was believed that women were impure for six weeks after giving birth. Since Mary allegedly gave birth at the winter solstice, she would not be purified until February 2.

---

[71]Kia Marie Wolfe, *The Wheel of the Year.*

[72]John Adlemann, "Brigit, Behind the Veil," *Oak Leaves*, January 1998, 8–12.

[73]Kondratiev, *The Apple Branch: a Path to Celtic Ritual*, 137–138.

The theme of purification carried over to several folk customs associated with the holiday. One was the cleaning that was traditionally done at this time of year, when the mistletoe, evergreen boughs, and holly that had been brought into the house for the winter solstice had to be removed, lest bad luck befall those who dwelled there. Other customs were for the head of the house to wash the hands and feet of people entering the house on Candlemas, and for people to pass newborn lambs and babies between torches to be purified and blessed.

The kindling of sacred fires marked Brigit's holiday, as she symbolized the fires of birth and healing, the fire of the forge, and the fire of poetic inspiration. One of the most important aspects of this festival was the lighting of candles and torches at midnight. Bonfires were lit on the beacon tors (hilltops), and masses of candles celebrated this special holiday. The Church was quick to claim this symbolism, declaring Candlemas the day to bless all the church candles to be used during the coming liturgical year. (Catholics will remember that the following day, St. Blaise's Day, is the occasion on which newly blessed candles are used to bless the throats of parishioners, protecting them from colds, flu, sore throats, etc.)[74]

At her shrine, located near the ancient city of Kildare, a group of nineteen priestesses (no men were allowed) kept a perpetual flame burning in her honor. This fire burned until the beginning of the nineteenth century, when it was abandoned. It has since been rekindled by a group of nuns called the Sisters of Bride, who have revived the former traditions again and welcome the NeoPagans who celebrate with them.

We may hesitate to describe early February as spring because at this time of year in many parts of America we see a blanket of snow and the days are filled with drizzle, slush, and steel-gray skies—the dreariest weather of the year. However, the early Pagans, living in a milder climate in the British Isles, perceived the forces of spring working at this time and were preparing spiritually for the germination and regrowth of the months to come. As such, Imbolc is the perfect time for a Pagan festival of lights! Although spring may seem nebulous and far off, distinct beginnings of growth will arrive on schedule long before spring has run its course to Beltane. With emphasis placed more on light rather

[74]"St. Blaise - Saints & Angels - Catholic Online," accessed November 29, 2012, http://www.catholic.org/saints/saint.php?saint_id=28.

than on fire, Imbolc signifies the return of light after dark winter days, as days grow gradually brighter and longer.

One traditional ritual, usually done by the men of the village, involved making an effigy of Brid out of straw saved from the harvest, and is still enacted in Ireland and the Scottish Highlands. This effigy is believed to come to life during the night with the spirit of Brid. The straw dollies, called *brídeóg* or Bride's doll, are carried around the community while gifts of food and drink are collected for the feast.[75] They are then placed in another object made of straw, usually made by the women of the village, called *leaba Bride*, the bed of Bride. Some of the offerings are left out overnight for Brigit to partake of as she journeys across the land.[76]

Customs of the holiday also include the weaving from straw or wheat of *cros-Bríde* or "Brigit's crosses" that are hung throughout one's house for protection, and other rites of spiritual cleansing and purification. It is said that a house will be protected from fire if a Brigit's cross is hanging above the door.[77]

Still carried out today is the making and blessing of the *Brat Bríde*, "Bride's Mantle," and the *Bratach Bríde*, "Bride's Banner." Both are pieces of cloth left outdoors on the eve of Imbolc to receive the blessings of Brigit and to be imbued with her healing power when she makes her tour of the countryside to visit her followers. The smaller *Brat Bríde* can be divided up the following day to give to family members, while the larger *Bratach Bríde* is usually kept whole and re-blessed year after year to gain in healing power.[78]

Women followed yet another custom, that of "smooring the fire." Prior to going to bed on the evening before Imbolc, the oldest woman in a household would very carefully smooth out the fire in the hearth. If marks were found in the ash come morning, the women would know that Brigit had visited with them.

---

[75]"Brídeóg," accessed November 29, 2012, http://www.djibnet.com/photo/brideog/brideog-5415130689.html.

[76]"Carmina Gadelica Vol. 1: II. Aimsire: Seasons: 70 (notes). Genealogy of Bride. Sloinntireachd Bhride," accessed November 29, 2012, *http://www.sacred-texts.com/neu/celt/cg1/cg1074.htm.*

[77]"Brigid's Cross - Wikipedia, the Free Encyclopedia," accessed November 29, 2012, *http:// en.wikipedia.org/wiki/Brigid%27s_cross.*

[78]John Adlemann, "Brigit, Behind the Veil," 13–16.

As Imbolc was a festival of lights, Crowns of Light (i.e., of candles), similar to those worn on St. Lucy's Day in Scandinavian countries, were made to be worn in celebration of Brigit. Overall, this festival, dedicated to the regeneration of the Earth, is one of the most beautiful and poetic holidays celebrated in the NeoPagan calendar.

A Personal Ritual for Imbolc

The ritual site is prepared in the customary fashion, with all offerings and other items needed readily available. A bath is taken and mediation is completed. The primary deity honored in this rite is Brigit, and she is called upon using the older form of her name, Brid.

Musical Signal

A bell is struck nine times in three groups of three rings.

Opening Prayer

A short declaration of why the ritual is happening is spoken:

I am here to honor the Gods, Ancestors and Spirits of the Earth. As my Ancestors celebrated this time, so too do I celebrate tonight.

(Forcefully) *I am here to honor the Gods!*

Two-Power Meditation—Earth and Sky

Like the meditation used for our Samhain ritual, this part may be recorded on tape and played back, while you can concentrate:

Close your eyes. Take slow, full breaths, deep breaths, in and out. Allow your mind to settle and focus on the work to be done. As you stand here tonight in this grove of trees, remember the ancient days, remember the old ways. Let your vision turn inward. Use the eye that looks into and behind your normal eyes and allow that vision to flow down through your body. Down through the land that you stand on, down past the sweet waters that flow through the Earth, down to the hot lava that makes up the magma of the Earth. As your vision travels, so too can your other senses. You can feel the coolness of the Earth. You can smell the cool dampness of the Earth. And when you get down to the magma, your can smell the heat. You can feel the heat. You can feel the energies that flow through the Earth. Feel those energies. Savor those energies and allow those energies to move up, up through the conduit that you make through your senses. And allow that energy to flow through you. Fill your body till it glows with the energies of the earth and allow that energy to spill out all around you.

And feel the wonders of the sky, that which only your spirit can feel, that your inner eyes can glimpse. Watch the twinkling of the stars as they dance back and forth. Feel that spirit, that knowing, that life, rise up like the smoke of this fire. To dance in the arms of the trees. To dance on the embrace of the winds. And up even further until it's among the light of the stars, where cool, cleansing, and clean energy fills your soul. That song, that celestial being that surrounds you, that is you, sings you back and forth, back and forth. Let that energy-like song go back into the wind, and down into the tops of the trees. Down like the smoke of this fire and the flames. And into the coals, to the ground. Be at peace, be at peace, be at peace.

Purifying the Space

Another way to purify the space that has become very common in ADF Groves is again by using water and incense together while saying:

By the might of the Waters and the Light of the Fires, this Grove is made whole and holy.

Honoring an Earth Mother

Honoring an Earth Mother can be done by giving an offering to the Earth while singing a chant or by giving an offering to a specific Earth Mother. The offering could be flowers, cornmeal, or some other natural item. One example of a chant follows. The tunes for all the chants in this book are available on my Web site at *http://www.skipellison.us/chants.html*. And as with any chant, if you feel that you cannot sing, just say the words in a rhythmic pattern.

Chant – "Earth Mother" (author unknown)

Earth Mother, we honor your body
Earth Mother, we honor your bones
Earth Mother, we sing to your spirit
Earth Mother, we sing to your stones.
(Forcefully) Earth Mother, I honor you!
Kiss the earth or ground.
Honoring the Bardic Deities

One way to honor the Bardic deities is through song. Here is a chant that honors one of the Irish deities, Brigid:

Chant – "Lady Brigid" (words by Peggy Kaan)

Lady Brigid of the bards
Blessed fire of inspiration
Spark the flames within our hearts
Lead our creative exploration
Lady Brigid hear our song
As we give offerings of praise"

Historical Precedent

Here you can say something like:

> *This is the night of Imbolc, the spoke on the Wheel of the Year that celebrates the revival of life for the Earth Mother and the beginning of spiritual re-growth for her inhabitants. I watch as the waxing light basks and warms the Earth, awakening her from long winter hibernation. Seeds planted begin to take root. I plant myself firmly like the Cosmic Tree, the pillar of the World, and feel newborn life replenishing my soul. I look to the sky, so that my aspirations may reach up like limbs to touch the pinnacles of my devotion. May I be refreshed and renewed as I rejoice in ritual and song in honor of the Goddess Brigit, bringer of Light, the Goddess of healing, poetry, fertility, and inspiration.*

Establishing the Horizontal Axis

Walk around the boundary of your space sprinkling cornmeal while saying:

> *I ask that the Earth not open up and swallow me.*

Next walk around the space sprinkling water while saying:

> *I ask that the Seas not rise up and drown me.*

And walk around the area one more time waving a stick on incense while saying:

> *I ask that the Sky not fall down upon me.*

Establishing the Vertical Axis

One way to establish the vertical axis is by reconnecting the Well, Fire, and Tree with their roots to all the other sacred wells, fires and trees in the cosmos. At this time, offerings can be given to each of the three in the sacred center as the words are sung about each. Usual offerings include silver jewelry to the well, olive oil to the tree or into the offering bowl, and incense or water to the tree.

Chant— "Portal Song" (words and music by Ian Corrigan)

Chorus: *By fire and by water, between the earth and sky*
We stand like the world tree, rooted deep, crowned high
By fire and by water, between the earth and sky
We stand like the world tree, rooted deep, crowned high

Come we now to the well, the eye and the mouth of earth
Come we now to the well, and silver we bring
Come we now to the well, the waters of rebirth
Come we now to the well, together we sing

[Chorus]

We will kindle a fire, bless all and with harm to none
We will kindle a fire, and offerings pour
We will kindle a fire, a light 'neath the moon and sun
We will kindle a fire, our spirits will soar

[Chorus]

Gather we at the tree, the root and the crown of all
Gather we at the tree, below and above
Gather we at the tree, together we make our call
Gather we at the tree, in wisdom and love

[Chorus]

Calling upon the Gatekeeper

This calling is usually done while placing an offering of olive oil to the fire or into the offering bowl.

The snow melts from the Earth ... feeding it with the waters of life. The Earth's womb contains the seeds of rebirth. They are our foundation. Let the light shine forth, to nourish what has been planted. All you who keep the boundaries, who walk the borders, I ask that you open the way for me that I may tread the secret paths.

Manannán mac Lir, Gatekeeper, opener of the ways between, I ask that you open the gates that I may commune with the Goddess Brid. [During this calling, you can visualize the gates opening above the Well and Fire and see the Tree growing through them.]

(Forcefully) *Manannán mac Lir let the gates be opened!*

Kindred Callings

The offering to the Ancestors, such as cornmeal, is sprinkled around the inside of the sacred space or placed in the offering bowl. A calling is spoken while the offering is sprinkled:

> *Ancestors I give you offerings of cornmeal* [or whatever offering is given] *and my love tonight. I know how much you've given to bring me to where I am and I thank you for it. I ask you now to join with me in this ritual, to lend your strength to mine.*
>
> (Forcefully) *Ancestors, be with me tonight and accept my sacrifice!"*

The offering to the Nature Spirits of a sweet-smelling herbal mix is sprinkled around the inside of the sacred space. If you are working indoors, walking around with a lit stick incense will work. A calling is spoken at this time as the offering is sprinkled or carried.

> *Spirits of this place, you who live on, swim through, or fly over the lands and waters, I give you offerings of these sweet smelling herbs* [or whatever offering is given] *and my love tonight. I see and hear you around me all the time and I know that you are never really far from me. I ask you now to join me in this ritual, to lend your strength to mine.*
>
> (Forcefully) *Spirits of the Earth, be with me tonight and accept my sacrifice!*

The offering of olive oil to the Gods and Goddesses is sprinkled on the fire or into the offering bowl. A calling is spoken while the offering is sprinkled:

> *Shining Ones, Gods and Goddesses of all my people, I give you offerings of oil and my love tonight. I listen to your stories and tales with wonder at what you have done. I ask you now to join with me in this ritual, and to lend your strength to mine.*
>
> (Forcefully) *Shining Ones, be with me tonight and accept my sacrifice!*

Calling of the Primary Deity, Brid

An offering of olive oil is poured on the fire or into the offering bowl, as the calling is spoken:

> *Come, daughter of eternity*
> *Come, Brid of the flame*
> *Come, sister of infinity bring healing to the lame*
> *Come, mother of the waters*

Come, Brid of the well
Come, muse of many daughters ring inspiration's bell
Come, lover of the anvil
Come, Brid of the hammers
Come, artisan, crafter, most able sing of sparks and glimmers.
Brid, I invoke thee Known to many ages
Healer, bard, and artisan she
Many names to call her own
Midwife, war chief, Goddess
Come into this Nemeton
My heart I offer guileless
Come into this Nemeton.

Praise Offering

This can be done through offers of song, poetry, story; dance, artwork, etc. You should prepare what you will be offering in advance of the ritual and make sure that it is a worthy offering.

Prayer of sacrifice and key offering

A large offering is given to the fire while the following is spoken:

Lady Brid, I have called you tonight and shown you my love. I ask that you take this final sacrifice and know that I will always love you!

(Forcefully) *Lady Brid, accept my sacrifice!*

Omen

The omen is usually done with either runes or ogham cards or sticks and the meaning to you can be incorporated into the return flow.

Return Flow

Having given offerings to the Kindred, you hope that blessings will flow back to you, magnified many times. The Return Flow is started by holding up a cup of water, juice, beer, or ale. Energize the beverage by visualizing while saying something like:

As I have given love and sacrifices and praise to the Shining Ones, the Ancestors and the Nature Spirits, I know that you all will return that love and honor to me, magnified by your greatness. And so, I turn once again to my inner vision and look within myself to that place where I can see all. As I look up to the gate above me, I can see the Shining Ones, the Ancestors and the Spirits of

Nature looking down on me with love. You are all pouring forth your radiance, pouring forth the energies that I have given up to you, magnified many times by your greatness. I can see it descending upon me. I can see the energy fill this cup. I can see how the cup shimmers and glows with the energy.

(Forcefully) *Behold, the waters of life!*

The waters are now drunk while contemplating everything that has gone on so far.

Thanking the Deity, Brid

A gift of olive oil is poured on the fire or into the offering bowl, as the patting is spoken:

> *Brid, I thank you for your aid and your blessings tonight. As this rite is ending, I make this gift in parting, given out of love, with nothing asked in return.* (Forcefully) *Brid, I thank you!"*

Thanking the Kindred

A gift to the Gods and Goddesses of olive oil is poured on the fire or into the offering bowl, as the parting is spoken:

> *To all the Shining Ones, I thank you for joining with me tonight. As this rite is ending, I give you this gift in parting, given out of love, with nothing asked in return.*
> (Forcefully) *Gods and Goddesses, I thank you!*

Another gift to the Spirits of Nature of olive oil is poured on the fire or into the offering bowl, as the parting is spoken:

> *To all the Spirits of the Earth, I thank you for joining with me tonight. As this rite is ending, I give you this gift in parting, given out of love, with nothing asked in return.*
> (Forcefully) *Spirits of Nature, I thank you!*

One more gift to the Ancestors of olive oil is poured on the fire or into the offering bowl, as the parting is spoken:

> *To all of the Ancestors, I thank you for joining with me tonight. As this rite is ending, I give you this gift in part-ing, given out of love, with nothing asked in return.*
> (Forcefully) *Ancestors, I thank you!*

Thanking the Gatekeeper and Closing the Gates

The parting is spoken as the Gates are being closed:

As the Earth awakens from her long winter sleep and life flourishes below, upon, and above the Earth, I will remain firmly rooted with my knowledge—a light that shines from within and offers warmth, solace, and protection to all who wish to drink from its cup. Even though the gate is now being closed, I will remember that each time it is opened on this plane, it will be easier to open it again. The key to the gate exists within.

I thank Manannán mac Lir for being in my rite as I celebrate this new life. As this ritual is ending, I ask that the Well be once again a well [pointing to the Well and visualizing it as simply a bowl of water],

And let the Fire be once again fire [pointing to the Fire and visualizing it simply as a candle or small fire].

And let the Tree be once again a tree [pointing at the Tree and visualizing it shrinking back down to normal size]

(Forcefully) *O Manannán mac Lir let the gates be closed!"*

One last time, a gift of olive oil is poured as the following is said:

Manannán mac Lir, I thank you for working with me tonight, and give you this gift of oil, given out of love with nothing asked in return.

(Forcefully) *Manannán, I thank you!*

Thanking the Bards and Earth Mother

Parting gifts of olive oil are poured to both the Earth Mother and the Bards that were called upon while saying something like:

Bards of old, I thank you for hearing my song and joining with me. As this rite is ending, I give you this gift in parting, given out of love, with nothing asked in return.

Earth Mother, even though I called to you in song, I close this work with just the simple words, I thank you! I give you this gift in parting, given out of love, with nothing asked in return.

Reversing the Two-Power Meditation

This meditation is reversed at the end of the ritual by allowing the energies that you brought into yourself at the beginning to return to their source. Again, this works best if you record the following and play it during this part of the ritual:

Now it is time once again to begin using your inner vision. Look around you with your inner vision, and you can see the energies within this Nemeton. See the

energies that you brought down with you from the sky. Allow that energy to move back into your being and to fill you with all that you need. When you are filled, allow that energy to return to where it came from.

And with the energy from the sky moved back to where it came from, look about to the energies from the earth. Allow that energy to move back into your being and to fill you with all that you need. When you are filled, allow that energy to return to where it came from. You now have all the energy within you that you need. See how relaxed and energized you feel. As this ritual comes to a close, be at peace and relaxed and energized!

Conclusion

Some type of formal closing must be spoken aloud, even if it is as simple as: *For tonight this work is over. The rite has ended!* And then the bell is rung once again in the same way it was done to start the ritual.

Beltane

Beltane is the start of the light or *samos* half of the year. Nowadays, it usually starts at dusk on April 30 and continues through May 1. For the ancient Celts though, the holiday depended on nature for its timing. Traditionally, it was celebrated when the hawthorn trees began to bloom in late April or early May. The date was not fixed until modern times.

The Holiday

Variously spelled Beltaine, Belltaine, Beltain, Beltine, Beltane, Bealtaine, Bealteine, *Boaldyn* (in Manx) or *Bealtuinn* (in Scots Gaelic), the holiday is also called May Eve or May Day, and also was known by various other names: *Cetshamain* (from the Old Celtic) *Kentu-saminos*, "first of summer") in Ireland; *Shenn do Boaldyn* on the Isle of Man; *Calan Mai*, *Dydd Calen Mai*, or *Cyntefrm* in Wales; *Calá Mé* in Cornwall; and *Kala-Hañv* in Brittany.[79] It is not specifically mentioned in the Coligny calendar, but the ninth century Irish commentator Cormac refers to *Beloteniá*, "bon fire of Belos (the bright)."[80]

Judging from the multitude of stories about events, invasions, and appearance of "monsters" that have occurred on Beltane, this is one of the most important festivals of the year. The main feast in Ireland would be held at Uisnech, on the plain of Meath, near Tara.

---

[79]MacKillop, *Dictionary of Celtic Mythology*, 35.

[80]Kondratiev, *The Apple Branch: a Path to Celtic Ritual*, 155.

Originally, the Celts had two seasons—the light half and the dark half of the year—not four; subtler divisions concerned crop raisers, rather than cattle raisers, as the earlier Celts were. Beltane gave way to its counterpart Samhain, on the last night of October, which as we have discussed signaled the start of the dark half of the year. Of primary importance to pastoral people was that Beltane marked the first day of taking cattle to the summer pastures (or *booleys*). The cattle would then graze on those pastures until Samhain.

To the ancient Celts, this time of the year—the greening time, when crops began to sprout, flowers bloomed, vegetation became lush, animals bore their young, and the earth spirits returned—was anticipated with great delight. The coming of fair weather and longer daylight hours was most welcome after the long months of inclement conditions in the British Isles. It is no wonder that Beltane was the holiday of dancing, contests, frolicking in the woods, young love, and passion![81]

The original meaning of the name may be derived from "Bel-fire"—the fire of the proto-Celtic god variously known as Bel, Beli, Balor, Bile, or, in Latinized form, Belenus. These are names traceable back to the Middle Eastern Ball, which simply means "lord." Bel was the "Bright One," God of the light of fire, and associated with the rising sun. A pastoral God, he watches over the cattle and the fields. His reign continues through the summer solstice. Throughout Celtic and British folklore the two themes that dominate the May Eve/Beltane festival are fertility and fire.

Fertility rites are ceremonies of a magic-religious nature performed to ensure the perpetuation of mankind and to control the environment. Expressed as invocations, incantations, prayers, hymns, processions, dances, and sacred dramas, these liturgical endeavors were, and still are, believed to be closely connected with the mechanisms of nature. The basis for such rites is usually a belief in sympathetic magic—that is, magic worked on one level to have an effect on a different level, and based on the assumption that life and fertility, whether animal or vegetable, are one and indivisible. If such fertility rites could induce fertility in the animal and human worlds, then the vegetable world would also be stimulated to reproduction, resulting in an abundant harvest.

One Irish custom that comes down to us from the ancients is "planting the May." Around this time of year, young men try to place

---

[81]Kia Marie Wolfe, *The Wheel of the Year.*

branches of blooming hawthorn in the bedrooms of girls they like. If they are successful, the girls would go with them to "bring in the May," and make love.

Traditionally, starting near midnight on May Eve, the people of the villages and towns would spend the night in the fields and forests in an effort to bring fertility and blessings to their lives and fields through lovemaking. As the first rays of the sun would appear, the people would bathe in the dew from the grasses and dry themselves in the warming sun. This dew was also bottled and kept through the year to use in healings, a practice that many NeoPagans still follow. Flowers were then gathered with which to bedeck themselves, their families, and their homes.[82] In couples or in groups, the townspeople would then return to their villages, stopping at each home to leave flowers, and to receive the best of food and drink that the home had to offer. This custom is somewhat similar to "trick or treat" at Samhain, except that there would be no tricking, which was very significant to the ancients. John Williamson, in his book *The Oak King, the Holly King, and the Unicorn: The Myths and Symbolism of the Unicorn Tapestries*, writes:

> *These revelers were messengers of the renewal of vegetation, and they assumed the right to punish the selfish, because avarice (as opposed to generosity) was dangerous to the community's hope for the abundance of nature. At an important time like the coming of summer, food, the substance of life must be ritually circulated generously within the community in order that the cosmic circuit of life's substance must be kept in motion (trees, flocks, harvests, etc.). These revelers would bless the fields and flocks of those who were generous and wish ill harvests on those who withheld their bounty.[83]*

In some Indo-European societies, such as the Roman and Vedic ones, ritual prostitution and displays of phallic symbols were believed to stimulate agricultural fertility. In a number of preliterate societies, among them Ireland and India, the role of the vegetative God was combined with that of the king, and the fertility of the land and people was linked to the king's state of perfection and purification. (Accordingly, in old folk tales, when a king received a "blemish," such as the loss of a limb, he could no longer be king.)

---

[82]Kondratiev, *The Apple Branch: a Path to Celtic Ritual*, 161.

[83]John Williamson, *The Oak King, the Holly King, and the Unicorn: The Myths and Symbolism of the Unicorn Tapestries* (Olympic Marketing Corp., 1986).

Remnants of this tradition may be seen today in the "sacred marriages" held during Beltane in many NeoPagan groups, in which a "King and Queen of the May" are appointed to rule over the holiday festivities, symbolizing the fertility of their "subjects" through their own fertility and in the strength of their lovemaking. These sacred marriages often formed a major part of the fertility rituals and lovemaking taking place at Beltane; the effectiveness of this symbolic union at times depended on the fertility of the participants. Beltane is the time of many mundane marriages or handfastings as well. For the ancient Celts, it was the first day of the year that marriages were permitted. During the dark half of the year, from Samhain to Beltane, marriages were prohibited.

The May Queen also features in another custom from the Isle of Man. There, on Beltane, the May Queen fights with the Queen of Winter (actually a man dressed in fur and wool), for the possession of the land.[84] The May Queen always wins, and, afterward, the people would start to wear the green of summer instead of the straw of winter.

As in all Celtic Fire Festivals, a bonfire is often present, and the traditional jumping over the fire, said to bring fertility, or driving the cattle (their most important domesticated animal) between two fires was done to bring luck, to aid in finding husbands or wives, to ensure good journeys, and, in the case of cattle, to increase the milk yield. It is believed that certain herbs (though exactly which ones are not known) were burnt in the fires to produce smoke that would help destroy parasites that could sicken cattle and other livestock.

On the eve of Beltane, all fires in the community were extinguished, so that the element of fire for that night was completely absent. At sunrise, the community gathered on their sacred hill to join those who had spent the night in the woods and fields and ritually took a burning branch from the main fire back to their homes to re-light their hearths. The Beltane fires in Wales and Scotland were kindled with nine different woods (again not specified) gathered on Beltane morning by nine men. These men would then dig out a square of eight turfs, leaving the ninth turf in the center. As on Samhain, the need fire, fire from which the main fire was lit, would be kindled on this center turf.[85] It was started by the use of either a hawthorn or oak fire wheel turned against an oak plank. This wheel was turned only in a sunwise direction.

---

[84]Rutherford, Ward, *Celtic Lore*, 92.

[85]Pennick, *The Sacred World of the Celts*, 105..

Beltane was a busy night and day for the people but one that was important to keep the community strong. When Christianity came to the British Isles, most of the ancient holy sites and customs were appropriated by the new religion. Old Gods and Goddesses often became Christian saints. In Celtic Myth and Legend, Charles Squire says:

> *An ingenious theory was invented after the introduction of Christianity, with the purpose of allowing such ancient rites to continue with a changed meaning. The passing of persons and cattle through flame or smoke was explained as a practice which interposed a magic protection between them and the powers of evil.*[86]

This is precisely what the original festival was intended to do—to offer magical protection. Only the definition of "evil" had changed. Older customs continued to be practiced in many areas for centuries. One that has continued is the making of rowan crosses, tied together in the shape of an "X" with yellow flowers and hidden in the tails of cattle and placed on barns and in houses. These crosses were supposed to protect the cattle and the buildings from fairies and witches.

Another custom that still exists today is the practice of making Beltane or bannock cakes, large round, flat cakes made out of oats or barley. These cakes are used in several ways. One use is to break off a small piece and throw it over your left shoulder with an invocation to spare and protect your livestock. When a sacrificial victim was offered to the Gods in pre-Christian times, the person who picked out the cake that had been burned or bore a charcoal mark on the bottom, was the chosen one. "Lindow Man," a corpse found in 1983 in an English bog called Lindow Moss, is believed by some to be a sacrificial victim. A piece of burned cake was found in his stomach. Large versions of these cakes were also rolled down a hill and if your cake broke on the way down, it was a sign that you would die, during the coming year.[87]

The recipe on the following page can be found on a website of Scottish recipes located at:

http://www.rampantscotland.com/recipes/blrecipe_bannocks.htm[88]

---

[86]Squire, *Celtic Myth and Legend*, 441.

[87]Rutherford, Ward, *Celtic Lore*, 93.

[88]"Traditional Scottish Recipes - Oatcakes/Bannocks," accessed December 5, 2012, *http://www.rampantscotland.com/recipes/blrecipe_bannocks.htm*.

Bannock Cakes

Ingredients

4 oz (125g) medium oatmeal
2 teaspoons melted fat (bacon fat, if available)
2 pinches of bicarbonate of soda
Pinch of salt
3/4 tablespoons hot water
Additional oatmeal for kneading

Method

Mix the oatmeal, salt and bicarbonate and pour in the melted fat into the centre of the mixture. Stir well, using a porridge stick if you have one and add enough water to make into a stiff paste. Cover a surface in oatmeal and turn the mixture onto this. Work quickly as the paste is difficult to work if it cools. Divide into two and roll one half into a ball and knead with hands covered in oatmeal to stop it sticking. Roll out to around quarter inch thick. Put a plate which is slightly smaller than the size of your pan over the flattened mixture and cut round to leave a circular oatcake. Cut into quarters (also called farls) and place in a heated pan which has been lightly greased. Cook for about 3 minutes until the edges curl slightly, turn, and cook the other side. Get ready with another oatcake while the first is being cooked.

An alternative method of cooking is to bake them in an oven at Gas 5/375°F/190°C for about 30 minutes or until brown at the edges. The quantities above will be enough for two bannocks about the size of a dessert plate. If you want more, do them in batches rather than making larger quantities of mixture. Store in a tin and reheat in a moderate oven when required.

Food, drink, and sex are the order of the holiday. In a few of the smaller NeoPagan groups around the U.S., the celebration of Beltane can become one large orgy, as the participants are encouraged to enact their own unions of love. Clothing is optional at some of the large modern festivals on this holiday, and if worn it is usually sensual and colorful. Even those groups that are prudish about nudity and sex tend to be more liberal on this day, as it is the holiday of free love. It is said that a child conceived on Beltane will grow up to wield great power and knowledge and to be healthier than those conceived on any other day of the year.

A Personal Ritual for Beltane

We start our ritual in the same format as previously described. As well as giving honor to the Kindred, we honor the primary deities Angus Mac Óg (pronounced Angus mac *Óg*) and Bláithíne (pronounced *Bla*-heane, which means "flower face"). Angus Mac Óg, a fertility God, is the son of the *Dagda*, and is one of the Celtic Gods that help young lovers. As such, he is very appropriate for this holiday. Bláithíne was the wife of Cú Roí(pronounced *Coo* Roy), a Fennian warrior, and one of the lovers of Cú Chulainn (pronounced *Coo* Hoolan), a great Irish hero. In addition to her reputation as a wonderful lover, Bláithíne is known as a Goddess of the fields.

Musical Signal

A bell or drum is struck nine times in three groups of three rings.

Opening Prayer

A short declaration is made about the reason for the ritual:

As I stand here under the stars, I can see all of creation around me. I come here to give honor and love to the Shining Ones, the Spirits of Nature and the Ancestors.

(Forcefully) *I am here to honor the Gods!*

Two-Power Meditation—Earth and Sky

Again, instructions for the meditation can be recorded on tape and played back during the ritual:

Close your eyes and find that quiet, still place. Breathe deeply. Listen to the sounds of spring around you. Listen as the Earth comes alive again. Feel your toes wiggle down into the soil. Reach down deep into the Earth Mother. Let your toes become roots, seeking the quiet, warm waters beneath the Earth and then drawing it up, up like the sap in spring. Up, into your roots, up further still into your legs. Let it pool in your groin. Draw it up your spine, and let it pool in your heart. Up further, to pool in your mind. And still it comes until it flows down, and out, and back into the Earth.

And with that energy of the Earth flowing in you, look now with your inner vision. Look up to the Sky. Look above. Look all the way to the stars above. You can see the cool energy of the stars. You can see it flowing down from the stars. Down, down to you. And as that energy of the stars flows into you, you can feel it fill you. Fill you to overflowing. And as that energy of the stars mingles with the energies of the Earth moving through you, feel those energies combining, filling you to overflowing. And as that energy moves out, feel it mixing and moving around and around the sacred space. Be at peace.

Purifying the Space

Purifying the space is again done by using water and incense together while saying:

By the might of the Waters and the Light of the Fires, this Grove is made whole and holy.

Honoring an Earth Mother

Honoring an Earth Mother can be done by giving an offering (flowers, cornmeal or some other natural object) to the Earth while singing a chant:

Chant—"As One" (Words and Music by Denean)
As One we join with Her, our Mother.
As One we sing to Her our song.
As One we touch Her
As One we heal Her
Her heart beats with our own as One.
(Forcefully) *Earth Mother, I honor you!*

Bestow a kiss upon the Earth.

Honoring the Bardic Deities

The following is a prayer to honor one of the bardic deities, in this case Brigit:

As the flame, you enter my being with your spirit. Your presence is with me at all times. You have taught me to know my voice and the power it has over others. You have shown me the powers within myself. Brigit, you are the voice of the bards. You are the words of the poet. I call to you now to be with me. I ask you to show me the words, the phrases that are the best, to let me send my thoughts sweetly to the Kindred. Brigit, I call upon you now to give me the powers of inspiration. Brigit, I call upon you now![89]

Historical Precedent

This could be followed by telling a little about why you are doing the ritual:

This is the time when sweet desire weds wild delight. Beltane celebrates the beginning of a bold and virile season, when the God of Nature lustily impregnates the Earth Mother. Life springs eternal, with joy and beauty. Now is the time for the celebration of the powers of life, sensuousness, and newness. For richness and plenty now bless the land. This is the time for all things to grow, a time to build, a time to explore. I exult in the glory of the earth, and celebrate my own strengths.[90]

Establishing the horizontal Axis

Walk around the boundary of your space sprinkling cornmeal while saying:

I ask that the Earth not open up and swallow me.

Next walk around the space sprinkling water while saying:

I ask that the Seas not rise up and drown me.

And walk around the area one more time waving a stick on incense while saying:

I ask that the Sky not fall down upon me.

Establishing the Vertical Axis

One way to establish the vertical axis is by reconnecting the Well, Fire, and Tree with their roots to all the other sacred fires, wells and trees in the cosmos. At this time, offerings can be given to each of the three in the sacred cen-ter as the words are sung about each. Usual offerings include silver to the well, oil to the fire, and incense or water to the tree.

Chant—"Portal Song" (words and music by Ian Corrigan)
Chorus: *By fire and by water, between the earth and sky*
We stand like the world tree, rooted deep, crowned high
By fire and by water, between the earth and sky
We stand like the world tree, rooted deep, crowned high

---

[89]Prayer written by Phoenix, a bard belonging to Muin Mound Grove. ADF. Used with permission.
[90]Written by Gloria, a member of Muin Mound Grove, ADF. Used with permission.

Come we now to the well, the eye and the mouth of earth
Come we now to the well, and silver we bring
Come we now to the well, the waters of rebirth
Come we now to the well, together we sing

[chorus]

We will kindle a fire, bless all and with harm to none
We will kindle a fire, and offerings pour
We will kindle a fire, a light 'neath the moon and sun
We will kindle a fire, our spirits will soar Chorus

[chorus]

Gather we at the tree, the root and the crown of all
Gather we at the tree, below and above
Gather we at the tree, together we make our call
Gather we at the tree, in wisdom and love

[chorus]

Calling Upon the Gatekeeper

This calling is usually done while placing an offering of olive oil to the fire or into the offering bowl.

Manannán mac Lir, once again I call upon you. I ask you to be my Gatekeeper. I ask you to come across the waves in your magical coracle, the Wavesweeper. Come across the waves and open the ways for me. Manannán, I ask you to be my magician, my Druid, and I ask you to hold the ways open for me tonight. Manannán, I give you this offering of fine oil in praise of your wonders and in love of you.

Manannán, once again I ask, let the well open as a gate [pointing to the Well and visualizing a gate, or ring of fire, opening over it].

Let the fire open as a gate [pointing to the Fire and visualizing a gate, or ring of fire, opening over it]

And let the tree open as the connection between all the planes [pointing to the Tree and visualizing it growing through the gates over the Fire and Well, both up and down, to all the planes of existence].

(Forcefully) *Manannán mac Lir, let the gates be opened!*

Kindred Callings

An offering to the Ancestors of cornmeal is sprinkled around the inside of the sacred space or into the offering bowl. A calling is spoken while the offering is sprinkled:

> *Ancestors, I ask that you be with me tonight. Mothers and Fathers of all, not just of me, but of the earlier inhabitants of this land as well. I call to you tonight and ask you to join with me and lend me your wisdom.*
>
> (Forcefully) *Ancestors, be with me tonight and accept my sacrifice!*

An offering to the Spirits of Nature of a sweet-smelling herbal mix is sprinkled around the inside of the sacred space or into the offering bowl. A calling is spoken while the offering is sprinkled:

> *Spirits of Nature, I ask that you accept this sacrifice of sweet-smelling herbs and join in this ritual. Spirits of this land and all the lands around it, Spirits of the waters and of the air and skies above it, I call to you now. I ask that you join with me and lend me your strength.*
>
> (Forcefully) *Spirits of Nature, be with me tonight and accept my sacrifice!*

An offering of olive oil to the Gods and Goddesses is sprinkled on the fire or into the offering bowl. A calling is spoken while the offering is sprinkled:

> *I call now to all the Gods and Goddesses that have not been named. I give you this offering of fine oil and ask that you join with me for this ritual tonight. I ask that you join with me and lend me your power.*
>
> (Forcefully) *Shining Ones, be with me tonight and accept my sacrifice!*

Calling of the Primary Deities, Angus Mac Óg and Bláithíne

An offering of olive oil is poured on the fire or into the offering bowl, as each calling is spoken:

> *Now I call upon Angus Mac Óg, son of the Dagda, you who resided at Brug na Bóinne, the modern Newgrange. Angus the young, I ask you to come and join with me. I ask you to bring your fertility of youth to join with me here in this ritual. And to bring that fertility of youth to my fields to make my crops grow strong through the summer. Angus, to you I give this offering of fine oil and ask you to join with me tonight.*
>
> (Forcefully) *Angus Mac Óg, be with me tonight and accept my sacrifice!*

*Bláithíne, I have named you and so I call you forth. I call with the power within
me. I call with my own voice.*

*I use my hands and my being as the bridge across. Bláithíne, I call you. I have
named you blossom. I have named you flower face. You, whose wisdom comes
with the fertility of the land. Whose power is in that which shapes the soil.
Whose power is in that which causes trees to grow, flowers to bloom. Bláithíne, I
call you. I call you forth with the word and with the power within me.*

(Forcefully) *Bláithíne, I call you.*[91]

Praise Offering

This can be done through offers of song/ poetry, story, dance, artwork,
etc. You should prepare what you will be offering in advance of the
ritual and make sure that it is a worthy offering.

Prayer of Sacrifice and Key Offering

A large offering is given to the fire while the following is spoken:

*Bláithíne and Angus Mac Óg, I have called you tonight, made offerings to you
and shown you my love. I ask that you take this final sacrifice and know that I
will always love you!*

(Forcefully)*Bláithíne and Angus Mac Óg, accept my sacrifice!*

Omen

The omen is usually done with either runes or ogham cards or sticks
and the meaning to you can be incorporated into the return flow.

Return Flow

Having given offerings to the Kindred, you hope that blessings will flow
back to you magnified many times. The Return Flow is started by
holding up a cup of water, juice, beer, or ale. Energize the beverage by
visualizing while speaking:

*Once again, I turn my vision inward. I look to the area around me, to the trees.
I look at the faces of the beings gathered here around this ritual. I listen to the
noise they make as they move through the trees. Now I turn my vision upwards,
up to where the gate shines above me like a ring of gas jets, a circle of flame.
Looking up through that circle, I can see a host gathered there, look-ing down on
me with love. And looking downward through the gate below, I can see the host*

[91]Written by Phoenix, member of Muin Mound Grove, ADF. Used with permission.

gathered there as well, looking up at me with love. Now I call upon all those gathered around and above and below me to take the offerings I've made and to return your love to me. To give me the bounty of your blessings. A return, a bounty that has been magnified by your wondrous powers.

I can see how the flow of energy and love streams down from above and surrounds me! I can see how the energy fills the cup and spills over. I can see how the cup sparkles and shimmers. Gods and Goddesses, Spirits of Nature and Ancestors, I thank you for this gift in return.

(Forcefully) *Behold, the waters of life!"*

The waters are now drunk while contemplating everything that has gone on so far.

Thanking the Deities, Bláithíne and Angus Mac Óg

A gift of olive oil is poured on the fire or into the offering bowl, as the parting is spoken:

Bláithíne, I thank you for joining with me and for bringing your fertility to my fields. As this rite is ending, I give you this gift in parting, given out of love, with nothing asked in return.

(Forcefully) *Bláithíne, I thank you!*

Angus Mac Óg, I thank you for joining with me and for bringing your fertility to my fields. As this rite is ending, I give you this gift in parting, given out of love, with nothing asked in return.

(Forcefully) *Angus Mac Óg, I thank you!*

Thanking the Kindred

Another gift to the Gods and Goddesses of olive oil is poured on the fire or into the offering bowl, as the parting is spoken:

I call once again to the Shining Ones. I thank you for joining with me tonight. As this rite is ending, I give you this gift in parting, given out of love, with nothing asked in return.

(Forcefully) *Gods and Goddesses, I thank you!*

Another gift to the Sprits of Nature of olive oil is poured on the fire or into the offering bowl, as the parting is spoken:

I call once again to the Spirits of this Place. I thank you for joining with me tonight. As this rite is ending, I give you this gift in parting, given out of love, with nothing asked in return.

(Forcefully) *Spirits of Nature, I thank you!*

One more gift to the Ancestors of olive oil is poured on the fire or into the offering bowl, as the parting is spoken:

I call once again to the Ancestors. I thank you for joining with me tonight. As this rite is ending, I give you this gift in parting, given out of love, with nothing asked in return.

(Forcefully) *Ancestors, I thank you!*

Thanking the Gatekeeper and Closing the Gates

The gate is closed while saying something like:

As this ritual is ending, I ask now, let the Tree be once again a tree [pointing at the Tree and visualizing it shrinking back down to normal size].

And let the Fire be once again fire [pointing at the Fire and visualizing it simply as a candle or small fire].

And let the Well be once again a well [pointing at the Well and visualizing it as simply a bowl of water].

(Forcefully) *O Manannán mac Lir, let the gates be closed!*

One last time, a gift of olive oil is poured on the fire or into the offering bowl, as the parting is spoken:

Manannán mac Lir, I thank you for coming to me tonight as my magician, as my Druid, and as my Gatekeeper. Now that this rite is ending, I give you this gift in parting, given out of love, with nothing asked in return.

Thanking the Bards and the Earth Mother

Next, the Bards and the Earth Mother you called upon should be thanked. This can be done by pouring a offering of olive oil on the fire while saying something like:

Brigit, I thank you for being with me and aiding in my work. As this ritual comes to a close, I give you this gift of oil, given out of love with nothing asked in return.

(Forcefully) *Brigit, I thank you!*

Earth Mother, I thank you for upholding my work and give you this offering in parting. It is given out of love, with nothing asked in return.

(Forcefully) *Earth Mother, I thank you!*

Reversing the Two-Power Meditation

This meditation is reversed at the end of the ritual by allowing the energies to move back to their source. Again, you can record the following on tape and play it back during this part of the ritual:

Once again, look about using your inner vision. The gate has closed down, but the Spirits of Nature are still all around you. They never really leave. You can still see and feel the different types of energies swirling around your sacred space. Take those energies from the Sky into your being and start to move them upwards, back to where they came from. And as they pass through you, keep what you need to remain energized and at peace.

And once those energies from the Sky have left you, look around at the energies of the Earth that still flow around your sacred space. Allow those energies to flow into your being and start to move them downward, back to where they came from. As they pass through you, keep what you need and let the rest go.

Conclusion

Some type of formal closing must be spoken aloud, even if it is as simple as:

As I have given honor tonight, so will I do in the future! The rite has ended!

And then the bell or drum is sounded once again in the same way it was done to start the ritual.

Lúghnasadh

This Fire Festival marks the end of summer and the beginning of fall in the Northern Hemisphere. Traditionally up to a month long, held between July 15 and August 15, Lúghnasadh was the time of many gatherings for the Celtic tribes. Nowadays, it is usually celebrated on or near August 1.

The Holiday

Lúghnasadh is another of the festivals known by many names. Variant spellings include *Lughnasa* (Modern Irish), *Lugnasad* (Old Irish), *Lúnasa* (Reformed Modern Irish), *Lúnasdain, Lunasdal, Lunasduinn* (Scots Gaelic) and *Laa Luanisdyn* or *Laa Luanys* (both Manx). It is also called *Lammas* Day, Garland Day, *Domnash Chrom Dubh, Crom Dubh* Sunday, *Fraugham* Sunday, Billberry Sunday (also known as *Domthnach na bhFraochóga* in Ireland), *Cornucopia* (Strega), and *Thingtide* (Teutonic).[92]

British witches often refer to the astrological date of August 6 as Old Lammas, and folklorists call it Lammas O.S. ("Old Style"). This date has long been considered a "power point" of the Zodiac, and is symbolized by the Lion, one of the "tetramorphs," or "four elements" figures—the Lion, the Bull, the Eagle, and the Spirit—familiar to many from tarot cards called the World and the Wheel of Fortune. Astrologers know these four figures as the symbols of the four "fixed" signs of the Zodiac: Scorpio, Aquarius, Taurus, and Leo. The signs also align naturally with the four greater sabbaths of modern-day witchcraft, which are equivalent to the four Celtic Fire Festivals, Samhain, Imbolc, Beltane, and Lúghnasadh. Christians have adopted the same iconography to represent the writers of the four Gospels, Matthew, Mark, Luke, and John.

For the Irish, this was a feast to commemorate the funeral games, games held in honor of Tailtiu, the foster mother of the Celtic sun god Lúgh, the many-skilled god of the *Tuatha Dé Danann*, who had taken Lúgh in when he was young. An alternative interpretation of the holiday has been suggested by English scholar Miranda Green, who believes that this festival may have been held to celebrate Lúgh's marriage.[93]

For the ancient Irish, Lúghnasadh was celebrated in Telltown (in what is now County Meath) and in three other locations, Emain Macha in Ulster, Carman in Leinster, and at Tara for the whole of Ireland. Some folk tales tell us that Lúghnasadh was an occasion for the settling of legal and political matters, such as treaties, while games and feasting were held.[94] However, from a poem preserved in a medieval

---

[92]MacKillop, *Dictionary of Celtic Mythology*, 274.

[93]Miranda Aldhouse-Green, *Dictionary of Celtic Myth and Legend* (New York: Thames and Hudson, 1992), 136.

[94]Ibid.

manuscript, we learn that at Carman, there were prohibitions against: deeds of violence, abductions, the repudiation of husband or wife, and the levying of debts. The penalties ascribed by this poem for violating those prohibitions are severe—"Whoever transgresses the law of the King Berén prescribed firmly for ever that he should not thrive in his tribe, but should die for his mortal sin."[95]

One common feature of the games were the "Tailltean Marriages," a rather informal marriage that lasted for only "a year and a day" or until the next Lúghnasadh, at which time the couple would return to the place of the ceremony and decide whether to continue the arrangement if it pleased them. If it did not, they stood back to back, facing north and south, and walked away from each other, bringing the Tailltean marriage to a formal end (or divorce). These trial marriages are why the Lammas celebrations in Ireland are often called the "Tailltean Games." Such trial marriages (similar to a Wiccan handfasting, which also usually lasts a year and a day) were quite common into the 1500s, although the Church did not recognize them. It is said that at Kirkland in the Orkney Islands, there was a custom by which young men and women would choose "Lammas" brothers or sisters for themselves and spend the night with them on an improvised bed of sheaves,[96] a practice that appears to be the equivalent of the modern "one-night stand," and demonstrates the Celts' easygoing attitude toward expressing their sexuality.

The medieval Christian name for the holiday was Lammas which comes from the Anglo-Saxon "*hlaf-maes*," meaning "loaf feast" or "loaf mass." The term refers to the loaves that were baked from the first grains harvested, blessed by the Anglo-Saxon heathen clergy (and later by a Christian priest), and then distributed to the members of the tribe or congregation. The day called attention to first fruits and early harvest, and, in fact, Lammas usually falls between the hay harvest and the wheat harvest. In the ancient world, grain was thought of as a manifestation of the divine force. This force was personified as the "green man," a resilient God figure, growing sturdy and solid through spring and summer, cut down by the harvest's scythe, sleeping through the cold winter in the bosom of the Earth Mother, and returning once again, as an infant reborn, clothed in green with spring.[97] Later on, the green man became

---

[95]Rees, Alwin and Rees, Brinley, *Celtic Heritage: Ancient Tradition in Ireland and Wales*, 168.
[96]Rutherford, Ward, *Celtic Lore*, 95.
[97]Kia Marie Wolfe, *The Wheel of the Year*.

the basis for little John Barleycorn, an allegorical figure representing whiskey, who grew up to be a man and was cut down, ground between two stones, and remade into the strongest man of all. Bread and brew—products of the grain harvest—express the mystery of transformation, the metamorphosis of the grain by fire and fermentation.

It is said that at this time of the gathering of all the tribes, the complete mythological and chronological past of the tribes was conjured into the present by the skill of the *Seanchaí* (storyteller). Lammastide was also the traditional time of year for craft festivals. The medieval guilds would create elaborate displays of their wares, decorate their shops and themselves in bright colors and ribbons, march in parades, and perform ceremonial plays and dances for the entranced onlookers. This was the time of the year when apprentices would be promoted to journeyman status and were expected to demonstrate their skills. It was also the time when new apprentices would be hired. The atmosphere must have been quite similar to modern-day Renaissance Festivals or Native American Green Corn Dance festivals.

Lúghnasadh games would include horseracing and contests of strength and martial skills, one of which involved throwing a weight for distance. A chariot wheel attached to the end of an axle was the weight thrown! This was known as the "wheel feat" and was one at which Cú Chulainn, the great Irish hero, was said to excel.[98]

Lúghnasadh is also known as a new-wine festival and a kick-off for the hard work of the harvest season to come, which included such other chores as making candles, replacing curtains, tablecloths, and rugs, and preserving food for the winter months. It was also the time for weaning the calves and lambs.

A Personal Ritual for Lúghnasadh

Start the ritual in the same format as for the other holidays, with offerings and other items at hand. The primary deity honored is Lúgh, the many skilled sun God of the Irish pantheon. He was called *Lámfhada* or "of the long arm" in Irish because of his great prowess with the spear and sling. On his first visit into Tara, the seat of power and home of the high-king in Ireland, he was stopped at the gate because someone in Tara claimed to possess the skill Lúgh had, and only one person who

---

[98] Rutherford, Ward, *Celtic Lore*, 94.

excelled with a particular skill was allowed entry. Lúgh asked the gatekeeper if there was any one person in Tara who possessed all of the skills. The answer was no. Lúgh replied that he did possess them all, and so he was allowed to pass.

Musical Signal

A bell or drum is struck nine times in three groups of three rings.

Opening Prayer

A short declaration is made about the reason for the ritual:

> *Ancient Ones, I am here to honor you and to preserve the old ways. I have come tonight to celebrate the harvest and to consecrate its first fruits. I am here to renew my connection to you and to the sacred land.*
>
> (Forcefully) *I am here to honor the Gods!*

Two-Power Meditation—Earth and Sky

Again, the instructions that follow can be recorded on tape and played back during the ritual:

> *Close your eyes and find that quiet, still place within. Breathe deeply. Feel the warmth of the night around you. Listen to the sounds of the woods around you. Let your mind move, out of your body and then downward. Down through the soil, down through the rocks. As it moves down, feel the earth around you. Feel it with all your senses. Smell the rocks and the soil. Listen to the water flowing. Let your senses move down to where you can feel the movement of the energies of the Earth. This is the warming energy that continually flows around and through the Earth. Let these energies move into your being and then bring it back up with you. Back along the corridor of your being that you created when you sent your mind out. As this energy flows up with you, allow it to move out of your being and into the sacred space. Watch as it swirls and flows and moves around it.*
>
> *With that warming energy of the Earth, moving and flowing within the sacred space, allow your mind to again move out. This time let it move upward, up through the clouds and toward the stars. As it passes through the clouds, allow your senses to feel the clouds and the Sky. Smell the moisture as you pass the clouds. Hear the sound of the air moving past. Taste the water on your lips. As your mind moves even farther up, past the air, the stars become bright and strong to your feelings. You can feel the flow of cooling energy among and*

between the stars. Let that energy from the stars move into your being. Let that energy flow down along your being till it fills your body and then overflows into the sacred space. See the swirls of the energies as they mix the warming energies from the Earth and the cooling energies from the Sky and the mingled energies from you. Be at peace and filled with these energies as this ritual continues."

Purifying the Space

As you sprinkle yourself with the water, you can say something like:

I stand here prepared to begin this work. As this water touches me, may it wash away all earthly cares.

Then as you wave the incense around yourself, you can say something like:

May the Spirit rise within me.

After you are purified, you can carry the water and incense around the space you will be working in and repeat the same lines to purify it.

Honoring an Earth Mother

Make an offering to an Earth Mother and recite the chant "As One," as detailed under the ritual for Beltaine.

It is a usual custom among those following the Path of Druidry to bestow a kiss upon the Earth at this time.

Honoring the Bardic Deities

Another prayer to honor the bardic deities, again to Brigit, Goddess of the poets, is spoken:

Lady Brigit, first mother. Lady Brigit, I call to you. With the silence in my heart, from your call within my mind, with your kiss upon my lips. I call you, I call you, I call you. Lady Brigit I call to you. Bring me your inspiration. Lend me your honey tongue. O, Lady Brigit, O Lady Brigit, I call you home. I call you here.[99]

Establishing the Horizontal Axis

Walk around the boundary of your space sprinkling cornmeal while saying:

I ask that the Earth not open up and swallow me.

---

[99]Written by Phoenix, a bard within Muin Mound Grove, ADF. Used with permission.

Next walk around the space sprinkling water while saying:

I ask that the Seas not rise up and drown me.

And walk around the area one more time waving a stick on incense while saying:

I ask that the Sky not fall down upon me.

Establishing the Vertical Axis

At this time, offerings are given to each of the three in the sacred center as the words are sung about each. Usual offerings include silver to the well, oil to the fire, and incense or water to the tree.

Chant—"Portal Song" (words and music by Ian Corrigan)
Chorus:

By fire and by water, between the earth and sky
We stand like the world tree, rooted deep, crowned high
By fire and by water, between the earth and sky
We stand like the world tree, rooted deep, crowned high

Come we now to the well, the eye and the mouth of earth
Come we now to the well, and silver we bring
Come we now to the well, the waters of rebirth
Come we now to the well, together we sing

[Chorus]

We will kindle a fire, bless all and with harm to none
We will kindle a fire, and offerings pour
We will kindle a fire, a light 'neath the moon and sun
We will kindle a fire, our spirits will soar

[Chorus]

Gather we at the tree, the root and the crown of all
Gather we at the tree, below and above
Gather we at the tree, together we make our call
Gather we at the tree, in wisdom and love

[Chorus]

Calling Upon the Gatekeeper

This calling is usually done while placing an offering of olive oil to the fire or into the offering bowl.

Manannán mac Lir, once again I call upon you. I ask you to be my Gatekeeper. I ask you to come across the waves and open the ways for me. Manannán, I ask you to lend your magic with mine and I ask you to hold the ways open for me this day. Manannán, I give you this offering of fine oil in return for your aid and in love of you.

Manannán, once again I ask, let the well open as a gate [pointing to the Well and visualizing a gate, or ring of fire, opening over it]

Let the fire open as a gate [pointing to the Fire and visualizing a gate, or ring of fire, opening over it]

And let the tree open as the connection between all the planes [pointing to the Tree and visualizing it growing through the gates over the Fire and Well, both up and down, to all the planes of existence].

(Forcefully) *Manannán mac Lir, let the gates be opened!*

Kindred Callings

The offering to the Ancestors, such as cornmeal, is sprinkled around the inside of the sacred space or placed in the offering bowl. A calling is spoken while the offering is sprinkled:

Ancestors, I give you this offering of cornmeal and my love tonight. Ancestors of my blood, this place and my people, I ask you now to join with me in this ritual, to lend your strength to mine.

(Forcefully) *Ancestors, be with me tonight and accept my sacrifice!*

The offering to the Nature Spirits of a sweet-smelling herbal mix is sprinkled around the inside of the sacred space. If you are working indoors, walking around with a lit stick incense will work. A calling is spoken at this time as the offering is sprinkled or carried.

Spirits of this place and of Nature, I give you offerings of these sweet smelling herbs and my love tonight. I see and hear you each day and wonder at your beauty. I ask you now to join me in this ritual, and to lend your strength to mine.

(Forcefully) *Spirits of the Earth, be with me tonight and accept my sacrifice!*

The offering of olive oil to the Gods and Goddesses is sprinkled on the fire or into the offering bowl. A calling is spoken while the offering is sprinkled:

Shining Ones, Gods and Goddesses that I and my people have honored, I give you offerings of oil and my love tonight. I pledge to continue learning more about you and I ask you now to join with me in this ritual, and to lend your strength to mine.

(Forcefully) *Shining Ones, be with me tonight and accept my sacrifice!*

Calling of the Primary Deity, Lúgh

An offering of olive oil and part of a loaf of fresh bread, to symbolize the bounty of the harvest, is given to the fire or into the offering bowl, as the invocation is spoken:

> *I call to Lúgh, Lúgh of the long arm, master of all arts. I ask that you bring your skill to me once again as I ask you here to partake in the first fruits of the harvest. You've shown me how to take care of the grains and how to reap the harvest. Join with me now, Lúgh, to eat the breads baked with the harvest! My grain has grown heavy and ripe as I've brought back the wheat of our Ancestors. Join with me, Lúgh, and accept my offerings!*
>
> (Forcefully) *Lúgh, be with me tonight and accept my sacrifice!*

Praise Offering

The praise offerings are prepared in the usual way, making sure that they are worthy. Fresh grains and produce from the harvest are especially good at this time of year.

Prayer of Sacrifice and Key Offering

A large offering is given to the fire while the following is spoken:

> *Lúgh, I have called you tonight and shown you my love. I ask that you take this final sacrifice and know that I will always love you!*
>
> (Forcefully) *Lúgh, be with me tonight and accept my sacrifices!*

Omen

The omen is done as usual with either runes or ogham cards or sticks and the meaning to you can be incorporated into the return flow.

Return Flow

The Return Flow is started by holding up the customary cup of water, juice, beer, or ale, along with a loaf of bread. The bread is included at Lúghnasadh because of the importance of the grain harvest. Energize the beverage by visualizing while saying:

> *At this harvest season, I call now upon all those of the Mighty Kindred that have received my offerings. Using my inner vision, I can you all of you who have been called here watching me through the gates. I ask that you allow your blessings to*

flow into this cup of water, and into this loaf of bread. I ask that you allow your blessings to fill and sustain me.

(Forcefully) Behold, the waters of life!

The waters are now drunk while contemplating everything that has gone on so far.

Thanking the Deity, Lúgh

A gift of olive oil is poured on the fire or into the offering bowl, as the parting is spoken:

Lúgh, I thank you for the skill you have taught me. As this rite is ending, I give you this gift in parting, given out of love, with nothing asked in return.

(Forcefully) Lúgh, I thank you!

Thanking the Kindred

A gift to the Gods and Goddesses of olive oil is poured on the fire or into the offering bowl, as the parting is spoken:

To all the Shining Ones, I thank you for joining with me tonight. You know that you are always held close to my heart. As this rite is ending, I give you this gift in parting, given out of love, with nothing asked in return.

(Forcefully) Gods and Goddesses, I thank you!

Another gift to the Spirits of Nature of olive oil is poured on the fire or into the offering bowl, as the parting is spoken:

To all the Spirits of the Earth, I thank you for joining with me tonight. You never really leave me, but are around me every day. As this rite is ending, I give you this gift in parting, given out of love, with nothing asked in return.

(Forcefully) Spirits of Nature, I thank you!

One more gift to the Ancestors of olive oil is poured on the fire or into the offering bowl, as the parting is spoken:

To all of the Ancestors, I thank you for joining with me tonight. I will give honor to you and try to learn more about you each day. As this rite is ending, I give you this gift in parting, given out of love, with nothing asked in return.

(Forcefully) Ancestors, I thank you!

Thanking the Gatekeeper and Closing the Gates

The parting is spoken as the Gates are being closed:

> *I thank Manannán mac Lir for being in my rite as I celebrate this harvest. As this ritual is ending, I ask that the tree be once again a tree* [pointing at the Tree and visualizing it shrinking back down to normal size].
>
> *And let the fire be once again fire* [pointing to the Fire and visualizing it simply as a candle or small fire].
>
> *And let the well be once again a well* [pointing to the Well and visualizing it as simply a bowl of water].
>
> (Forcefully) *O Manannán mac Lir let the gates be closed!*

One last time, a gift of olive oil is poured as the following is said:

> *Manannán mac Lir, I thank you for working with me tonight, and give you this gift of oil, given out of love with nothing asked in return.*
>
> (Forcefully) *Manannán, I thank you!*

Thanking the Bards and Earth Mother

Parting gifts of olive oil are poured to both the Earth Mother and the Bards that were called upon while saying something like:

> *Lady Brigit, I thank you for hearing my call and coming in answer. As this rite is ending, I give you this gift in parting, given out of love, with nothing asked in return.*
>
> *Earth Mother, even though I called to you in song, I close this work with just the simple words, I thank you! I give you this gift in parting, given out of love, with nothing asked in return.*

Reversing the Two-Power Meditation

This meditation is reversed at the end of the ritual by allowing the energies to move back to their source. Again, record the following instructions on tape and play it back during this part of the ritual:

> *Close your eyes. This ritual is now coming to a close. Now it is time to take that cool energy from the Sky, which you brought down to this sacred place, and let it flow back through you, back to where it came from. Using your inner vision you can see the energies flowing around this sacred space. Let those energies from the Sky move into your being and let it move back up, up toward the stars. Keep what you need to remain filled and at peace, but let the rest go.*

And as you look around you, still using your inner vision, you can see the warm energies of the Earth flowing around this sacred space. Let these energies move into your being and, from there, go back to where they came from. And as they pass through you, keep what you need and let the rest go. Open your eyes and look around you at the sacred space itself. Be at peace with yourself.

Conclusion

Some type of formal closing must be spoken aloud, even if it is as simple as: *Our work tonight is done. The rite has ended!* The musical signal that started the ritual is repeated to close the ritual.

This concludes the chapter on the Fire Festivals. In our next chapter, I will be talking about the Quarter Days and give you examples of other types of rituals that can be done.

Chapter 7

Rituals for the Quarter Days and More

T he quarter days are the high days that fall on the actual solstices and equinoxes. While the dates for these vary from year to year, they are around December 21 for the Winter Solstice, March 21 for the Spring Equinox, June 21 for the Summer Solstice, and September 21 for the Fall Equinox.

You will see much similarity between the High Day rituals. As I said in the previous chapter, I believe that repetition is valuable; it allows you to become sufficiently familiar with the ritual that your mind is allowed to concentrate on the underlying "magic," the special feelings the ritual evokes, rather than on procedure.

Winter Solstice

The first of the Quarter Days is the Winter Solstice. Although there is no hard evidence that this holiday was celebrated by the Celts, it was celebrated by their close neighbors, the Germanic tribes (the Norse), and introduced to the British Isles by the Saxons and the Vikings. Much of our information comes from them.

The Holiday

Winter Solstice is called *Mean Geimredh,* meaning "mid-winter" in Modern Irish; *Alban Artha,* the point of roughness, in Welsh; *Modranicht,* mother night, to the Anglo-Saxons, *Saturnia* to the Romans, *Deuorius Riur,* great divine winter feast, in the Coligny calendar; and Yule to many modern NeoPagans. "Yule," according to Bede, an early Saxon historian, is derived from the archaic Norse word *Jol,* meaning "wheel."[100] The Norse visualized the year turning like a wheel (i.e., the

100IKia Marie Wolfe, *The Wheel of the Year.*

wheel of the zodiac), its spokes marking the equinoxes and solstices, and the holidays associated with them.

In the Clog Almanacs, a runic type of calendar system in use in the Scandinavian countries from the 12th to the 17th centuries, the symbol of a horn was used.

> *For Christmas there was a born* [horn], *'the ancient vessel in which the Danes used to wassail or drink healths* [sic], *signifying to us that this is the time we ought to make merry, cornua, exhaurienda notans, as Wormius will have it.'*[101]

Early books of English folklore tell us of the English custom of "wassailing the trees," which is still popular today and is an activity that many groves of Druids make a part of their Solstice celebrations. This custom can easily be done by a solitary Druid. The first thing necessary is the bowl or pitcher of the wassail. Wassail comes from the Old English *Waes hael*, meaning be well. This is a combination of fruit juices, mixed with whiskey or other distilled spirits. If you would rather not use spirits, then just the fruit juices will work. There are many recipes on the Internet today, but mainly if you combine apple cider, orange juice, a little lemon juice, then cinnamon, nutmeg and cloves, it will taste great! The next step is to take the drink to any fruit trees in your area, drink some for yourself, then give the tree a drink while wishing it "wassail!" If you have many fruit trees on your land, as I do, this can turn into a fun part of the night.

The Winter Solstice represents the rebirth of the sun, a particularly important turning point. The night of Winter Solstice is the longest night of the year. Darkness triumphs, and yet it gives way and changes into light. The breath of nature is suspended: everything waits while within the cauldron of rebirth, the dark king is transformed into the infant light. With the coming of dawn, the Earth Mother gives birth to the divine child sun, which is a bringer of hope and the promise of summer.

The divine child has been known by many names. To the Christians, he is Jesus; to the Welsh, he was Mabon; to the British in Roman-occupied Britain, he was Maponus; to the Romans, he was Mithras; and to the Irish, he was Lúgh. No matter what name he is known by, there are similarities in his story. For example, both Mabon and Lúgh were born

---

[101]"The Calendar - Primitive Almanacs," accessed December 11, 2012, *http:// www.thebookofdays.com/ misc/ primitive_almanacs.htm.*

to important mothers—Mabon to Queen Modron, and Lúgh to Eithne, daughter of Balor, the king of the Fomorians. Both children were taken into hiding right after their birth, Mabon to a prison on an island and Lúgh to be fostered with Tailtiu, queen of Leinster. Both played important roles in various folk tales, Mabon helping to get the razor, one of the magical tools needed in a quest, from the head of the boar Twrch Trwyth and Lúgh for leading the *Tuatha Dé Danann* in the *Second Battle of Mag Tuired* against the *Fomorians*.

One tale of this yearly rebirth comes from the *Mabinogion*. While out hunting, Pwyll, Lord of *Dyved* (an area in modern Wales) encounters Arawn, ruler of *Annwvyn* (the Otherworld). Pwyll sets his dogs on Arawn's stag, chasing a stag that Arawn was already chasing, and is caught. In pay-ment for his discourtesy, Pwyll must trade places with Arawn and, in a yearly fight kill Havgan, Arawn's enemy. Arawn tells Pwyll:

> *You will be there in my place; strike him one blow, which he will not survive, and if he asks you to finish him off hold your hand, no matter how much he begs you. For however often I struck him, the next day he would be fighting as well as before.*

I believe that this is a metaphor for the light returning each year as Havgan does. All turns out well for Pwyll and in the end; he becomes a fast friend with Arawn.[102]

In the books of early folklore, we find many examples of the rebirth that take place at this time of equilibrium. The Goddess of Sovereignty, the personification of the land itself, now shows her life-in-death aspect. Although at this season she is the "leprous-white lady" or "the *Cailleach Bhéirre*," the Queen of the cold darkness or Old Hag, this is her moment for giving birth to the Child of Promise, the Son/lover who will re-fertilize her and bring back light and warmth.

At York, there used to be a custom, which William Stukeley, an eighteenth-century writer on Druidism, describes:

> *On the Eve of Christmas Day they carry Mistletoe to the high altar of the Cathedral and proclaim a public and universal liberty, pardon, and freedom to*

---

[102]Jeffrey Gantz, *The Mabinogion* (New York: Dorset Press, 1985), 46–50.

all sorts of inferior and even wicked people at the gates of the city, towards the four quarters of Heaven.[103]

This custom was surely a relic of Druidry, as this was a time of the year that the chief Druid would cut the sacred mistletoe from the oak, as I quoted Pliny describing at the start of the book. This is a custom that survives in today's use of mistletoe as a Christmas decoration.

The Saxons brought the feast of Yule with them from Scandinavia and Germany and celebrated it with plenty of ale and with blazing fires, of which our Yule log and the Christmas tree are familiar elements. There is no evidence that the Celts adopted this custom directly from the Saxons, but it has come down to current NeoPagan practices through the English. The ritual importance of the Yule log is reflected in the custom of saving an unburned piece of the Yule log for luck, and using it to kindle the next year's log.

The evergreens for yuletide decorations were holly, ivy, mistletoe, sweet-smelling bay and rosemary, and green branches of the box tree, a small evergreen shrub better known as boxwood. Wood for the Yule log usually was, and still is, oak or ash, and was saved someplace other than in one's house. By Candlemas, February 2nd, all of this material having to do with the Yule holiday had to be gathered up and burnt or stored elsewhere, or hobgoblins would haunt the house.

A Personal Ritual For The Winter Solstice

The purpose of this ritual is to give honor to Gwion Bach (pronounced Gwee-**on** Bock) and Ceridwen (pronounced Ker-**id**-wen). Their story is found in the *Mabinogion*, one of the tales of the early Welsh.

In the lore, Ceridwen was a woman of great power, who some called a witch. Her second child was a boy called Morfran, who was so ugly that it hurt to look at him. He was also known by the name *Afagddu*, meaning "utter darkness." He was so ugly, that in battle no one would strike him because they thought he was a devil and the incarnation of evil. Ceridwen knew that she must do something to help him, and through her magical skills, she wanted to give him the gift of all knowledge and poetry.

---

[103]From "The Medallic History of Marcus Avrelivs Valerius Carausius, Emperor in Britian," by William Stukeley, as quoted in "The Golden Bough," by Sir James George Frazer. Sir James George Frazer, "The Golden Bough, a Study in Magic and Religion - Google Play," 291, accessed December 11, 2012, *https://play.google.com/books/reader? id=z3sIAQAAIAAJ&printsec=frontcover&output=reader&authuser=0&hl=en&pg=GBS.PA291.*

To prepare a spell to accomplish this took a long time. Numerous plants and tree barks and secret ingredients had to be gathered, many of them at special times of the year, and when they were assembled, they would have to be cooked in a special potion. The cooking would take a whole year, and the potion had to be stirred constantly at the right speed and temperature. This work was more than she wanted to do, so she hired an old man and a boy, Gwion Bach, from one of the villages on the shore of the lake where she lived.

Near the last day of the year, while Gwion Bach was stirring the brew, three drops splashed out of the cauldron and landed on his thumb. This gave him, instead of Morfran, the gift of all knowledge and poetry.

Ceridwen was furious and chased Gwion Bach., Both of them underwent transformations—with him as a hare and her as a greyhound, him as a fish and her as an otter, him as a bird and her as a hawk. Finally, he transformed himself into a grain of wheat in a chicken pen. Ceridwen transformed herself into a hen and ate him! Nine months later, she gave birth, and although the son she bore was beautiful, she vowed to kill him for what Gwion Bach had done. Nevertheless, she wanted to give him a chance to live, so she placed him in a basket and set it adrift on a river where it was found by a prince. The baby grew up to become the famous Welsh bard and poet, Taliesin.

This ritual works very well if it is performed before sunrise and timed so that the Praise Offering section occurs just as the sun rises. As was stated in the last chapter, the tunes for the chants used here are available on my Web site, located at *www.skipellison.us/chants.html*.

Musical Signal
A drum or bell is sounded nine times to start the ritual.

Opening Prayer
A short declaration is made about the reason for this ritual:

> *I come to this place to venerate the Gods and the Kindred. Bless me, O Shining Ones of the otherworld, Ancestors and Spirits of Nature. I give praise and offering in your honor on this shortest day.*

(Forcefully) *I am here to honor the Kindred!*

Two-Power Meditation—Earth and Sky

The purpose of this meditation is to incorporate the subtle energy difference between the Earth and the Sky. Start by slowing down your breathing, taking deep, full breaths, and clearing your mind. Start using your "inner vision," that found in your mind's eye. In this chapter, the words for this meditation are in the first person and meant to be spoken during the ritual instead of listening to them on tape. If this seems to be too much to learn in one chunk, you can break it down into smaller parts and read them, then do the visualization. Over time it becomes much easier, and when you have the "ideas behind it," internalized, you can just speak the words that come to you while you are doing it.

I begin this meditation by closing my eyes. I take slow, full breaths and let my mind settle and focus on the work to be done. I open myself to my inner vision by turning my vision inward. I can see my being moving slowly down through my body and into the ground. As it passes through the layers of earth, I can feel and smell the changes around me. As I move further down, I find the waters flowing and moving. I follow one of those streams down until I can sense the flow of warm energies flowing around me. These are the energies of the earth, the source of power that is as powerful as the Earth itself. I allow this energy to flow into my being and then I move my being back toward my physical body. Now that I am back in my physical body, I allow the energy of the Earth to move out of my being and around this sacred space. Still using my inner vision, I can watch as the energy I have brought back mixes with the energies already pres-ent in this sacred space. The air in this sacred space shimmers and glows with the warm energies of the Earth.

Now I let my inner vision move upward. As my being moves up through the layers of clouds and sky, I can feel the changes in the air, and smell the moisture in the clouds. As my being moves even higher, I can see one star above me shining more brightly than the others. This is my special star. My being moves up to where I can feel the energies flowing down from the star into myself. These energies are cooler than the energies of the Earth and they feel different. I let this energy move into my being and then slowly I bring my being back toward my physical body. When my being is back inside my body, I let the energy I've brought back flow out of my being to join and mix with the other energies present here. Using my inner vision to look around me, I can see the swirls of many different forms of energy moving around this sacred space. I now let my physical eyes open as I continue with this working.

Purifying the Space

For this part, have a shell full of water and a lit incense stick or three. Take a shell or cup of water and sprinkle yourself while saying:

I stand here prepared to begin this work. As this water touches me, may it wash away all earthly cares.

Then as you wave the incense around yourself, you can say something like:

May the Spirit rise within me.

After you are purified, you can carry the water and incense around the space you will be working in and repeat the same lines to purify it.

Honoring an Earth Mother

Honoring an Earth Mother can be done as described previously in Chapter 6, while singing a chant. One appropriate chant is as follows:

Chant—"Earth Mother" (author unknown)
Earth Mother, we honor your body
Earth Mother, we honor your bones
Earth Mother, we sing to your spirit
Earth Mother, we sing to your stones.
(Forcefully) *Earth Mother, I honor you!*

It is customary among people following the "Path of Druidry" to bestow a kiss upon the Earth at this time.

Honoring the Bardic Deities

One of the best ways to honor the bardic deities is through song. The following honors the Irish deity Birgita, another aspect of Brigit, goddess of the poets:

Chant – "Birgita" (words by Lisa Theil)
Birgita, Birgita, Goddess of the flame
Birgita, Birgita, Goddess of the flame
Awaken the flame within my being
Awaken the sacred fire within my being

Historical Precedent

For this section, you can tell why the ritual is held at this time, saying something like:

This is the night of the Solstice, the longest night of the year. Now darkness triumphs and yet, gives way and changes into Light. The breath of nature is suspended. All waits while within the Cauldron of Rebirth, the Dark King is transformed into the Infant Light. Watch for the coming of dawn, when the Great Mothers again give birth to the Divine Children of the Sun, who are the bringers of hope and the promise of summer. This is the hope within darkness, stillness behind motion, when time itself stops. The center which is also the circumference of all. I am awake in the night. I turn the Wheel of the year to bring the light. I call the sun from the womb of night.

Establishing the Horizontal Axis

Walk around the boundary of your space sprinkling cornmeal while saying:

I ask that the Earth not open up and swallow me.

Next walk around the space sprinkling water while saying:

I ask that the Seas not rise up and drown me.

And walk around the area one more time waving a stick of incense while saying:

I ask that the Sky not fall down upon me.

Establishing the Vertical Axis

At this time offerings can be given to each of the three in the sacred center as the words are sung about each. Usual offerings include silver to the well, oil to the fire, and incense or water to the tree. A suitable chant is as follows:

Chant—"Fire, Bright Fire" (Words and music by Pandora)
Fire, bright Fire, gate to the Shining Ones;
Fire, bright Fire, our passage to the Sky;
Fire, bright Fire, warmth of our community;
Spark of life, we honor you now.
Well, deep Well, gate to the underworld;
Well, deep Well, our passage to the sea;

Well, deep Well, wisdom of the Ancestors;
Waters of life, we honor you now.

Tree, great Tree, gate that reaches everywhere;
Tree, great Tree, with you we share the land;
Tree, great Tree, passage to the otherworld;
Source of life, we honor you now."

Calling Upon the Gatekeeper

This calling is usually done while making an offering of olive oil to the fire or into the offering bowl.

Manannán mac Lir, once again I call upon you and ask you to come across the waves to me. I ask that you act as my guide and magician. I ask you to lend your might to mine to work the magic of opening the gates! [During this calling, visualize the gates opening above the Well and Fire and see the Tree growing through them.]

(Forcefully) *Manannán mac Lir, let the gates be opened!*

Kindred Callings

The offering to the Ancestors of cornmeal or another type of food is sprinkled around the inside of the sacred space or into the offering bowl, while a calling is sung:

Chant—"Be with Us" (words by Phoenix)
Be with us,
Here tonight,
In the light,
Of the fires' life,
Ancestors
(Forcefully) *Ancestors, be with me tonight and accept my sacrifice!*

An offering to the Spirits of Nature of a sweet-smelling herbal mix is sprinkled around the inside of the sacred space or into the offering bowl, while a calling is sung:

Chant—"Earth Child" (words by Phoenix)
Earth child, wild one, born of the Earth;

Call to us, and sing to us, creatures of the Earth;
Ay ya, Ay ya Oh Ay ya, Ay ya Oh
(Forcefully) *Spirits of the Earth, be with me tonight and accept my sacrifice!*

An offering to the Gods and Goddesses of olive oil is sprinkled on the fire or into the offering bowl, while a chant is sung:

Chant—"Hail All the Gods" (words traditional)

Hail all the Gods,
Hail all the Goddesses,
Hail all the Holy Ones,
We dwell together.
(Forcefully) *Shining Ones, be with me tonight and accept my sacrifice!*

Calling of the Primary Deities, Gwion Bach and Ceridwen

An offering of oil is poured on the fire, as each calling is spoken:

I call to you now, Gwion Bach. As you were set to watch the cauldron of knowledge for Ceridwen, you worked diligently for almost the entire year. Then three drops of the scalding hot brew splashed onto your finger. As you sucked upon it to cool it off, you knew all that had been and would be. I ask that you bring that knowledge to me tonight. Aid me in my work to look with the cauldron.

(Forcefully) *Gwion Bach, accept my sacrifice!*

I call to you now, Ceridwen, keeper of the cauldron of knowledge. As you were preparing a potion to give your son, Morfran, the ugliest person in the world all knowledge, it was taken by Gwion Bach. You chased Gwion through many forms until at last you caught him while you were a chicken and he was a grain of wheat. After you ate him, you gave birth to him transformed into Taliesin. I call upon you to join with me tonight as I look into your cauldron.

(Forcefully) *Ceridwen, accept my sacrifice!*

Praise Offering

This can be done through offers of song, poetry, story; dance, artwork, or anything else you feel would honor the deities. You should prepare what you will be offering in advance of the ritual and make sure that it is a worthy offering.

Prayer of Sacrifice and Key Offering

A special large offering is given to the fire while the following is spoken:

Ceridwen and Gwion Bach, I have called you tonight and given you honor. I ask that you take this final sacrifice and know that I will continue to give you the honor that is due, and to tell others about you! (Forcefully) Ceridwen and Gwion Bach, accept my sacrifice!

Omen

The omen is usually done with either runes or ogham cards or sticks. After the omen is drawn and interpreted, take time to reflect upon how the omen is relevant to your personal life, and if you feel it needed, it can be worked into the return flow.

Return Flow

As before, hold up a cup of water, juice, beer, or ale, and energize the beverage by visualizing while saying:

I close my eyes and my inner vision looks upward. As I have given my sacrifices and praise to the Kindred, now I ask for them to return their blessings to me. I know that the blessings will be returned magnified many times by their greatness. Above, below, and through the gates, I can see the crowd of watchers looking at me with love. As I watch, I can see the streams of energy flowing into this cup.

(Forcefully) *Behold, the waters of life!*

The waters are now drunk while contemplating everything that has gone on so far.

Magical Working—Cauldron of Ceridwen

Most High Day rituals do not include magical workings because their main purpose is to honor the Mighty Kindred. But as this time of year is an occasion for introspection, the following magical working is detailed to allow you to reflect upon recent events in your life and to prepare for the next part of the cycle of the year. You will need the following:

- Cauldron or black bowl, filled with water, symbolizing the cauldron of knowledge
- 2 pillar candles
- 1 or more smaller candles
- Bowl of sand to hold the small candles
- A few drops of olive oil

A cauldron or black bowl is filled with water and positioned at a level where it can be easily gazed into. Two candles light the cauldron, so that their image is reflected in the water. A drop or two of olive oil added to the water gives the appearance of many different colors and aids in the working.

Before looking into the cauldron, take one or more small candles, lit from one of the two pillar candles, and place them into the bowl of sand nearby. While you gaze into the cauldron, say the following:

> *I now turn the wheel of the year to the longest night, the somber time of introspection and learning. Now is the time I face the cauldron of Ceridwen. This cauldron contained a potion for knowledge and inspiration. Ceridwen had made this potion for her son, Morfran, who was the ugliest person in the world. Ceridwen knew that if her son were the smartest person in the world, it wouldn't matter how ugly he was.*

> *Within this cauldron is all that I need to know, all that I need to learn. It is there waiting for me to look within and see it. I will take this knowledge with me as I gaze into it.*

After you feel that you have looked in the cauldron long enough to have seen any visions that may have appeared in it, focus upon the bowl of sand and the candle(s) while speaking the following:

> *I turn my attention now to the candle. I can see how bright the light shines! This light will be returning to me from this day forth. I call the light back to me now! I know in my heart that after today, I will be able to see the days becoming visibly longer as more and more light comes back to me.*

Thanking the Deities - Ceridwen and Gwion Bach

A gift of olive oil is poured on the fire or the offering bowl, as the parting is spoken:

> *Ceridwen, keeper of knowledge and magic, I thank you for joining with me. As this rite is ending, I give you this gift in parting, given out of love, with nothing asked in return.*

(Forcefully) *Ceridwen, I thank you!*

Another gift of olive oil is poured on the fire or the offering bowl, as the parting is spoken:

Gwion Bach, receiver of knowledge and magic, I thank you for joining with me. As this rite is ending, I give you this gift in parting, given out of love, with nothing asked in return.

(Forcefully) *Gwion Bach, I thank you!*

Thanking the Kindred

Similarly, a gift of olive oil is poured into the fire or into the offering bowl, as the parting is spoken:

To all of the Gods and Goddesses who were here but not named, I thank you for joining with me and giving me your blessings. As this rite is ending, I give you this gift in parting, given out of love with nothing asked in return.

(Forcefully) *Gods and Goddesses, I thank you!*

The gift of olive oil is repeated as the next parting is spoken:

To all of the Spirits of Nature, I know you are around me every day and are always in my life. I thank you for joining with me and giving me your blessings. As this rite is ending, I give you this gift in parting, given out of love, with nothing asked in return.

(Forcefully) *Spirits of Nature, I thank you!*

A gift of olive oil is repeated as the parting is spoken:

Ancestors without you I wouldn't be here. I thank you for joining with me and giving me your blessings. As this rite is ending, I give you this gift in parting, given out of love, with nothing asked in return.

(Forcefully) *Ancestors, I thank you!*

Thanking the Gatekeeper and Closing the Gates

The gates are now closed by saying something like:

Manannán mac Lir, I ask you once again to join your magic with mine, and let the Tree be again a tree [pointing at the Tree and visualizing it shrinking back down to normal size]

And let the Fire be again a fire [pointing at the Fire and visualizing it simply as a candle or small fire]

And let the Well be once again a well [pointing at the Well and visualizing it as simply a bowl of water].

(Forcefully) *Manannán mac Lir, let the gates be closed!*

A gift of olive oil is poured as this parting is spoken:

Manannán mac Lir, rider of the waves, you have been my guide to the Land of Eternal Youth tonight. As this rite is ending, I give you this gift in parting, given out of love, with nothing asked in return.

Thanking the Bards and Earth Mother

Parting gifts of olive oil are poured to both the Earth Mother and the Bards that were called upon while saying something like:

Birgita, I thank you for giving me a honeyed tongue, and as this rite is ending, I give you this gift in parting, given out of love, with nothing asked in return.

Mother of us All, I think you for upholding this work and as this rite comes to a close, I give you this gift in parting, given out of love, with nothing asked in return.

Reversing the Two-Power Meditation

This meditation is reversed at the end of the ritual by allowing the energies to move back to their source.

Once again I close my eyes. Using my inner vision, I look at the sacred space filled with bright swirls of energies— energies that have come from above and below and from within myself. I take those energies from the Sky above and bring them back within myself. Now, my being is expanding upward, back toward my special star. I'm bringing those energies with me and guiding them on their way back to the star. As the energies leave my being, I keep what I need for myself, and let the rest go. Now I let my being return to my body as I continue.

Now as I look around, I see that the energies of the Earth are still swirling around me. I take those energies into myself and start transferring them back into the Earth. I let my being flow with them, down into the Earth. When I've gone far enough, I allow the ener-gies to flow back to where they came from, keeping as much as I need. Then I let my being return to my body. As this phase of the work draws to a close, I allow my body to be energized by the forces that have gone through it. I open my eyes and look around at the sacred space. I am at peace.

Conclusion

Some type of formal closing must be spoken aloud, even if it is as simple as: *This rite has ended!* And then the bell or drum is sounded once again in the same way it was done to start the ritual.

Spring Equinox

As with the other Quarter Days, we have no evidence that the ancient Celts celebrated the Spring Equinox, but as they are a vital part of the modern NeoPagan tradition, we turn our attention to other parts of the world for sources of information and traditions. We do know that in present-day Wales the holiday is called *Alban Eilir* or Mid-Spring. For the Anglo Saxons, the holiday was a celebration of the Goddess Eostre and was called Eostre or Ostara.[104]

The Holiday

At this time of year, many cultures acknowledge the length-ening of the day and the greening of the Earth, and call attention to hares, eggs, and special flowers. Eostre, or Ostara, is the Anglo-Saxon Goddess of spring whose name was used for that of the spring festival we call Easter. The feast of Eostre was originally celebrated at the Spring Equinox. The Goddess' sacred month was the third lunar month, called the Moon of Eostre by the Saxons, which corresponds to the period from mid-February to mid-March; another modem name for it is the Month of the Greening of the Earth.[105]

The animal associated with Eostre in Old English literature was the hare, which has come down to us in folklore as the Easter Bunny. The icon of the Easter Bunny is much older than Christianity. It is the lunar hare, sacred to the moon Goddess in both the Orient and in western countries, such as Gaul. In China, people gazing at the full moon see in its shadows the image of the lovely young Goddess Chang-O, holding her pet hare in her arms. In Japan, it is said that the lunar hare constantly cuts the grass on the moon's surface, cleaning it so that the moon shines white and not green. In Europe, the hare, like the cat, was a common witch's familiar; and witches were said to have the power to turn themselves into hares. To this day, Irish peasants observe the taboo on hare meat, saying that to eat a hare is to eat one's grandmother. On the banners of the warrior-queen Boadicea of early Britain was the image of the lunar hare. In Germany, children were told that, if they were good, the hare, not the chickens, would lay eggs for them on Easter Eve. This hare was called the *Österhase*, or Easter hare.[106]

---

[104]"Eostre," accessed April 8, 2013, *http://www.englatheod.org/eostre.htm*.

[105]Nilah Foxglove, "The Goddess Eostre and Spring Equinox," *Circle Network News*, 1992 1991.

[106]Kondratiev, *The Apple Branch: a Path to Celtic Ritual*, 150.

Like all the Church's "movable feasts," Easter shows its Pagan roots in a dating system based on the old lunar calendar. Easter is fixed as the first Sunday after the first full moon after the Spring Equinox, formerly the "pregnant" or "growing" phase of Eostre as the earth passed into the fertile season. This was also the time when the vegetation God, the green God of the fields and forests, awoke for a new season, as did the Sleeping Lord, a figure usually associated with Fionn mac Cumhaill in the British Isles, who will awake when the time is ripe to return to the old Pagan ways.

In countries where Christian and Pagan religions coexisted, such as Iceland, Easter Sunday (sun-day) was devoted to honoring Christ and the Christian mysteries, while Easter Monday (moon-day) was dedicated to the older Pagan deities. We see a remnant of this in the fact that March 25 is now known as "Lady Day." In Bohemia, village girls, like ancient priestesses, symbolically sacrificed a dummy symbolizing the Lord of Death and threw him into a river while singing:

Death swims in the water, spring comes to visit us with eggs that are red, with yellow pancakes; we carried death out of the village, we are carrying summer into the village.[107]

A Personal Ritual For The Spring Equinox

We start our ritual in the usual way. The primary deities for this rite, Tiwaz (pronounced Tea-waz) and Eostre (pro-nounced E-o-stra), come from the Anglo-Saxon pantheon. Tiwaz, known as Tyr to the Germanic people, was the original Sky Father, the God of the Sky. In surviving Anglo-Saxon spells, he is paired with an Earth Goddess to restore fertility to unfertile fields.[108] It is to this end that we call upon him to help promote the new growth within the Earth.

Musical Signal

A bell is struck nine times in three groups of three rings.

Opening Prayer

Once again I establish this sacred place. I come here to give honor and love to the Shining Ones, Spirits of Nature, and the Ancestors.

---

[107]Sir James George Frazer, "Chapter 28. The Killing of the Tree-Spirit. § 4. Bringing in Summer. Frazer, Sir James George. 1922. The Golden Bough," accessed December 12, 2012, *http://www.bartleby.com/196/70.html*.

[108]"Odinswifeaecerbot.pdf," accessed April 8, 2013, http://www.germanicmythology.com/original/earthmother/odinswifeaecerbot.pdf.

(Forcefully) *I am here to honor the Gods!*

Two-Power Meditation – Earth and Sky

I close my eyes and take some slow, full breaths and allow my mind to settle and focus on the work to be done. I can feel the wind on my face as I listen to the sounds of the trees and smell the smell of the fire. I will allow all of these sensations to fill my mind.

Using my inner vision, that which lies behind my eyes, I can see my being, my spirit, start to move down my body and into the Earth. I let my being move down through the layers of the earth, feeling the dirt and stone and water around me. The smell of the earth and rock fill my being. I let my being move down farther until I can feel the warm flow of energy moving around me. This energy is one of the building blocks of the planet. I allow some of the energy to move into my being and slowly start to move it back toward my physical body.

As this energy moves into my body, I can sense the warmth filling me. As my body fills to overflowing, I let the warmth expand out from my body to interact with the energy of this Sacred Space.

Now filled with these energies of the Earth, I allow my inner vision to move upwards. Move up through the trees around me, feeling the leaves brush against my being as I pass through them. I allow myself to move up through the clouds into the open sky. I can smell the moisture in the clouds. As I look farther up, I notice one special star. This star is the source of the cooling energies of the Sky. I move to where I can feel that cooling energy mix with my being.

As the energy fills me, I slowly start to move back down toward my physical body, bringing the energy with me. When I am are back in this space, I allow the energies of the Sky to flow through me until it too spills out and mixes with the energies of the Sacred Space. With my inner vision, I can see the energies moving and mixing around this space. Energies that fill this special place and that I will use in my ritual tonight. I am at peace with myself. Now, I open my eyes and let my vision return to my mortal eyes as the work continues.

Purifying the Space

Purify yourself and the space by using water and incense together while saying:

By the Might of the Waters and the Light of the Fires, this Grove is made whole and holy.

Honoring an Earth Mother

Honoring an Earth Mother can be done by making an offering of flowers, cornmeal, or some other natural object, while speaking to her:

Chant—"Evening Breeze" (words by Phoenix)

Evening breeze, spirit song
Sings to me, when the day is done
Earth Mother, awaken me
With the power of the Spring
(Forcefully) *Earth Mother, I honor you!*

It is the usual custom to bestow a kiss upon the Earth at this time.

Honoring the Bardic Deities

Another piece spoken to honor the bardic deities, in this case for the Anglo-Saxon God of Poetry, along with many other titles, Wōden. He will also be called upon as the Gatekeeper for this rite. The Bardic calling is as follows:

Wōden, I call to you tonight as God of the poets. I ask for you to come to me tonight and to help bring the power of inspiration to my words. Grant me the power to speak with a silvered tongue and aid my words to be carried quickly and correctly to the High Ones.

Historical Precedent

Something like the following can be said to remind yourself why the ritual is being held now:

This is the night of the Spring Equinox, the festival of the greening of the Earth, when the hours of night and day stand in equilibrium. I look within myself to discover the balance that lies within me. As life on Earth peeps out after a long winter hibernation and plant life flourishes, so too may I thrive and prosper in all that I do.

Establishing the Horizontal Axis

Walk around the boundary of your space sprinkling cornmeal while saying:

I ask that the Earth not open up and swallow me.

Next walk around the space sprinkling water while saying:

I ask that the Seas not rise up and drown me.

And walk around the area one more time waving a stick of incense while saying:

I ask that the Sky not fall down upon me.

Establishing the Vertical Axis

At this time, offerings can be given to Fire, Well, and Tree. Usual offerings include silver jewelry to the well, olive oil to the fire, and incense or water to the tree.

Chant—"Fire, Bright Fire" (Words and music by Pandora)
Fire, bright Fire, gate to the Shining Ones;
Fire, bright Fire, our passage to the Sky;
Fire, bright Fire, warmth of our community;
Spark of life, we honor you now.

Well, deep Well, gate to the underworld;
Well, deep Well, our passage to the sea;
Well, deep Well, wisdom of the Ancestors;
Waters of life, we honor you now.

Tree, great Tree, gate that reaches everywhere;
Tree, great Tree, with you we share the land;
Tree, great Tree, passage to the otherworld;
Source of life, we honor you now."

Calling Upon the Gatekeeper

This calling is usually done while making an offering of olive oil to the fire or into the offering bowl.

As nature slowly reawakens from a long winter sleep, and the snow fades, giving nourishment to all that rests in the Earth's fertile soil, the seeds of rebirth begin to sprout up from the darkness. Let me awaken from the darkness of my sleep in praise of the life within and around me. Let the light shine forth from within my essence to illuminate the greening earth.

[During this calling, you can visualize the gates opening above the Well and Fire and see the Tree growing through them.]

I call now upon the keeper of the ways. You who will open the way for me so that I may tread the secret paths. Wōden, I call upon you now. Open the gates that I may commune with the Shining Ones.

(Forcefully) *Wōden, let the gates be opened!*

Kindred Callings

The offering to the Ancestors of cornmeal is sprinkled around the inside of the sacred space or into the offering bowl, while a calling is spoken:

I call now to my Ancestors. Without you I wouldn't be here. Ancestors of my people and Ancestors of this land, this offering is for you. I ask that you give me your aid and your blessings in this work tonight.

(Forcefully) *Ancestors, be with me tonight and accept my sacrifice!*

An offering to the Spirits of Nature of a sweet-smelling herbal mix is sprinkled around the inside of the sacred space or into the offering bowl, while a calling is spoken:

I call now to the spirits of this place. You who walk or crawl upon the Earth, you who swim in the waters, and you who fly in the skies. I also call to those of the Fair Folk that dwell upon this land. This offering is for you. I ask that you join with me tonight for this rite.

(Forcefully) *Spirits of Nature, be with me tonight and accept my sacrifice!*

An offering to the Gods and Goddesses of olive oil is sprinkled on the fire or into the offering bowl while a calling is spoken:

I call now to all the other Shining Ones. You who are honored but not named already. I give to you honor and this offering. I ask that you lend your might to mine for this rite.

(Forcefully) *Shining Ones, be with me tonight and accept my sacrifice!*

Calling of the Primary Deities, Tiwaz and Eostre

An offering of olive oil is poured on the fire or into the offering bowl for each, as the calling is spoken:

I call to you Tiwaz, god of fertility and the sky. I ask that you bring to me tonight the spirit of the bountiful Sky. Sky Father, come and celebrate with me the greening of the Earth! I ask that you bring to me the Sun's warming rays to help the growth of the new life in the Earth.

(Forcefully) *Tiwaz, I ask that you be with me tonight and accept my sacrfice!*

And I call to you, Eostre, Goddess of the dawn. I ask that you come to me tonight to celebrate the return of spring. I ask you to bring with you your hare, the symbol of the fertility, to give my fields and life the fertility needed for growth.

(Forcefully) *Eostre, I ask that you be with me tonight and accept my sacrifice!*

Praise Offering

This can be done through offers of song, poetry, story; dance, artwork, etc. You should prepare what you will be offering in advance of the ritual and make sure that it is a worthy offering.

Prayer of Sacrifice and Key Offering

A large offering is given to the fire while the following is spoken:

> *Eostre and Tiwaz, I have called you tonight and shown you my love. I ask that you take this final sacrifice and know that I will always honor and praise!*
>
> (Forcefully) *Eostre and Tiwaz, accept my sacrifice!*

Omen

The omen is usually done with either runes or ogham cards or sticks. Runes, and specifically the Anglo-Saxon Futhark would be appropriate for this rite. After the omen is drawn and interpreted, take time to reflect upon how the omen is relevant to your personal life, and if you feel it needed, it can be worked into the return flow.

Return Flow

Hold up a cup of water, juice, beer, or ale, and energize the beverage by visualizing what the words are describing while saying:

> *Looking through the gate, I can see the crowd of people, all of the deities and Ancestors and Spirits looking down upon me. The Kindred look down to me with love in their eyes! I ask you now, Kindred, let your blessings flow down to me. With my inner vision, I can see the blessings flowing down to fill the cup of liquid. I can see the sparkling moonbeams of light, the flickering of starlight flowing down through the gate and into this cup.*
>
> (Forcefully) *Behold, the waters of life!*

The waters are now drunk while contemplating everything that has gone on so far.

Thanking the Deities, Eostre and Tiwaz

A gift of olive oil is poured on the fire or into the offering bowl, as the parting is spoken:

Eostre, wondrous lady, I thank you for joining with me in this ritual. As this rite is ending, I give you this gift in parting, given out of love, with nothing asked in return.

(Forcefully) *Eostre, I thank you!*

Another gift of olive oil is poured on the fire or into the offering bowl, as the parting is spoken:

Tiwaz, Sky Father, I thank you for joining me in this ritual. As this rite is ending, I give you this gift in parting, given out of love, with nothing asked in return.

(Forcefully) *Tiwaz, I thank you!*

Thanking the Kindred

As the parting is spoken, a gift of oil is poured into the fire.

Shining Ones, I thank you for joining me in this ritual tonight. As this rite is ending, I give you this gift in parting, given out of love, with nothing asked in return.

(Forcefully) *Gods and Goddesses, I thank you!*

As the parting is spoken, a gift of oil is poured into the fire.

Spirits of this Place, I thank you for joining me in this ritual tonight. As this rite is ending, I give you this gift in parting, given out of love, with nothing asked in return.

(Forcefully) *Spirits of Nature, I thank you!*

As the parting is spoken, a gift of oil is poured into the fire.

Ancestors I thank you for joining me in this ritual tonight. As this rite is ending, I give you this gift in parting, given out of love, with nothing asked in return.

(Forcefully) *Ancestors, I thank you!*

Thanking the Gatekeeper and Closing the Gates

The parting is spoken as the Gates are being closed:

As the Earth greens and life flourishes below, upon, and above the Earth, I will remain firmly rooted with my knowledge—a light that shines from within and offers warmth, solace, and protection to all who wish to drink from its cup. Even though the gate is now being closed, I will remember that each time it is opened on this plane, it will be easier to open it again. The key to the gate exists within.

I thank Wōden for being in my rite as I celebrate this new life. As this ritual is ending, I ask that the Tree be once again a tree [pointing at the Tree and visualizing it shrinking back down to normal size].

And the Fire be once again fire [pointing to the Fire and visualizing it simply as a candle or small fire].

And let the well be once again a well [pointing to the Well and visualizing it as simply a bowl of water].

(Forcefully) *Wōden let the gates be closed!"*

One last time, a gift of olive oil is poured as the following is said:

Wōden, I thank you for working with me tonight, and give you this gift of oil, given out of love with nothing asked in return. (Forcefully) Wōden, I thank you!

Thanking the Bards and Earth Mother

Parting gifts of olive oil are poured to both the Bard and the Earth Mother that was called upon while saying something like:

Wōden, I thank you for hearing my words and joining with me. As this rite is ending, I give you this gift in parting, given out of love, with nothing asked in return.

Earth Mother, I close this work with just the simple words, I thank you! I give you this gift in parting, given out of love, with nothing asked in return.

Reversing the Two Power Meditation

Once again I close my eyes and I can feel the energies that were brought down from the sky around me. I let those energies flow back into my being. I let the energies that I no longer need flow out of my being, and back to where they came from. I keep all that I need to feel energized, relaxed and at peace.

I can feel the energies of the Earth moving through my Sacred Space. I let those energies flow back into my being. And I let the energies that I no longer need flow back down into the Earth where they came from. I open my eyes and look around me to the Sacred Space itself. I am at peace with myself.

Conclusion

Some type of formal closing must be spoken aloud, even if it is as simple as: For *tonight this work is over. The rite has ended!* And then the bell is rung once again in the same way it was done to start the ritual.

Summer Solstice

In the Northern Hemisphere, summer is the time when we are outdoors the most and become more in tune with the natural world around us: we work in gardens, camp at festivals, and swim in lakes and rivers. The Summer Solstice is the midpoint of summer, when the sun is above the horizon for the longest period, has its northernmost rising and setting, and its highest elevation at noon. It is the apex of the sun's splendor, the longest day and the shortest night, and marks the turning of the year from waxing to waning. Astrologers know this as the date on which the sun enters the sign of Cancer. Modern calendars are quite misguided in suggesting that summer "begins" on the solstice. According to the old Irish folk calendar, summer begins on May Day and ends on Lammas (August 1); the solstice, occurring midway between the two, marks midsummer. This is more logical than suggesting that summer begins on the day when the sun's power begins to wane and the days grow shorter.[109]

The Holiday

No specific evidence exists that proves that this holiday was observed by the ancient Celts, even though it is a part of the modern NeoPagan calendar. Old Celtic, however, did have a word for "midsummer," *medrosaminos*,[110] and we know from the writings of Romans, such as Pomponius Mela, that the Druids "knew the ways of the stars and moon."[111] It is also highly likely that even though the Druids did not build the great stone monuments, such as Stonehenge, they noticed celestial alignments at certain times of the year. With all this circumstantial evidence, I feel that it is just a question of not having found the hard evidence yet, rather than that the Celts did not celebrate it.

Midsummer is also known as Litha to many modern NeoPagans and *Alban Hefin* (from the Welsh, meaning "point of summer"). "Litha" means "stone" and is associated with calendars. Among the Norse, midsummer is sacred to the Norse God Balder the Beautiful, and to Thor, God of thunder and protector from giants, and his consort Sif, she of the "golden hair." Modern-day Christians celebrate St. John's day on June 24 to honor St. John the Baptist.[112]

---

[109]Kia Marie Wolfe, *The Wheel of the Year*.

[110]Kondratiev, *The Apple Branch: a Path to Celtic Ritual*, 68.

[111]As quoted in Bonwick, *Irish Druids and Old Irish Religions*, 39 Original from De Situ Orbis, page 109.

[112]Ronald Hutton, *The Stations of the Sun: a History of the Ritual Year in Britain.* (Oxford: Oxford University Press, 1997), 311.

Symbols of the Sun are found throughout the folk customs that have come down to us from the Indo-European peoples. One interesting tradition from the 1820s, performed in Glamorgan, Wales, was to roll wheels stuffed with straw down the sides of the hills and set them ablaze. It was said that if the wheel stayed lit until it reached the bottom of the hill, the harvest would be abundant. This custom survived in the hills around Dartmoor in Devon, England, until the mid 1900s.[113]

The Summer Solstice is the one Quarter Day festival strongly associated with bonfires. Records going back to the sixteenth century refer to the number of bonfires seen on hills throughout the British Isles. These fires would be lit around sunset and as they died down, people would jump through them, believing that such fire would "burn away" bad luck while brushing against them. The embers would be taken home to be scattered across the fields the next day to ensure a bountiful harvest.[114]

This was also an important herb-gathering time. The folk custom of making and blessing the *Brat Aitmeithe*, the "Airmid's mantle" that is similar to the *Brat Bride* made on Imbolc for Brigit, is still celebrated today. Usually this starts with a recitation of the story of Dian Cécht and his killing of his son, Míach. Dian Cécht, the healer of the *Tuatha Dé Danann*, could not reattach the arm of Nuada, king of the *Tuatha Dé Danann*, after it was cut off in battle. Míach, however, accomplished the feat, which made Dian Cécht so jealous of his son that he killed him. After Míach's death, 365 healing herbs, one for each human ailment, grew from his grave. His sister, Airmid, gathered the herbs and laid them out on an outline shaped like a human body to show how they were to be used, so that the knowledge could be passed down to later generations. But Dian Cécht scattered the herbs so that the knowledge of how to cure all ailments was lost to us. The *Brat Aitmeithe* is usually a large piece of cloth with the outline of a human body stitched on it. On this outline are placed pictures of the herbs that are beneficial for each part of the body. This custom has preserved much of the old lore of herbalism in the Celtic countries.[115]

---

[113]Sir James George Frazer, "Chapter 62. The Fire-Festivals of Europe. § 5. The Midsummer Fires. Frazer, Sir James George. 1922. The Golden Bough," accessed December 12, 2012, *http://www.bartleby.com/196/156.html*.

[114]Kondratiev, *The Apple Branch: a Path to Celtic Ritual*, 173–174.

[115]Ibid., 171.

On the Isle of Man, it is said that people marked the Summer Solstice by gathering green meadow grass and carrying it to the top of the cliffs above the sea. They would then throw it into the sea for Manannán mac Lir as payment of rent for the year. After this, the people would continue with revels "too shocking to be told," very likely festivities that expressed the open sexuality of the Celts, as talked about in Chapter 2.[116]

In Wales, summer was the time for dancing and raising the *y fedwen haf,* the summer pole. Similar to the maypole, it appears to also celebrate fertility, but at a different time of the year.

In many Pagan cultures, the Sun God is split between two rival personalities: a God of light and his twin, a God of darkness. In Arthurian tales they are Sir Gawain of the Round Table and the Green Knight. For the Welsh in the *Mabinogion* they are represented by Lleu, the God of light, and Gronw Pebyr, his wife Blodeuwedd's lover and the person who tried to kill him with her help. For the Irish they are Lúgh, of the *Tuatha Dé Danann,* and Balor, of the *Fomorians.* For modern NeoPagans, they are the Holly King, who wins the seasonal battle between them at the Summer Solstice and the Oak King, who wins the battle at the Winter Solstice. Often these figures are depicted as fighting seasonal battles for the favor of their goddess/lovers, such as Blodeuwedd, the lover of Gronw, who represents Nature. The God of Light is always born at the Winter Solstice and his strength waxes with the lengthening days, until the moment of his greatest powers, the Summer Solstice, the longest day. And, like a look in a mirror, his "shadow self," the Lord of Darkness, is born at the Summer Solstice, and his strength waxes with the lengthening nights until the moment of his greatest power, the Winter Solstice, the longest night.[117]

A Personal Ritual For The Summer Solstice

Although for liturgical reasons I tend not to mix deities from different pantheons in the same ritual, this is an exception. We will honor and call upon as the primary deities Taranis (pronounced **Tair**-an-us), from the Gaulish pantheon and Boann (pronounced **Bow**-an), from the Irish pantheon.

---

[116]Rutherford, Ward, *Celtic Lore,* 98.

[117]Kia Marie Wolfe, *The Wheel of the Year.*

Taranis and Boann are both associated with storms and water and are very good deities to call upon if there is a need for rain. Taranis is the Gaulish god of storms and thunder. Boann's association with water is recounted in a story in which she approached a Sacred Well, *Sídh Nectán*, and walked around it in the wrong direction, counter-clockwise. (All sacred objects should be approached by walking sun-wise, or clockwise, around them.) The well rebelled and overflowed, with the water chasing her. As she ran to the edge of the island and the sea, the river Boyne was created. In 1999, while in the midst of a month-long drought, my grove, a local congregation of ADF, called upon Taranis and Boann during our Summer Solstice ritual. We had rain the next morning!

We start our ritual in the usual way.

Musical Signal

A bell is struck nine times in three groups of three rings.

Opening Prayer

A short declaration is spoken:

> *I am in this sacred space to give honor to the Kindred! Gods and Goddesses, Spirits of this Place and Ancestors I am here to remember, love and worship you.*
>
> *(Forcefully) I am here to honor the Gods!*

Two-Power Meditation—Earth and Sky

This meditation places your mind in a receptive state for the messages returned from the Mighty Kindred and to bring energies from the Earth and Sky to the sacred space.

> *I close my eyes and take nice deep breaths. In and out, in and out. My body relaxes as my breathing slows. In and out, in and out. I move my consciousness to that place behind my eyes where I can travel to all worlds, all places. That place inside me that allows me to move freely, wherever I choose to go. And with my consciousness in that place behind my eyes, I allow my consciousness to move out of my body. Out through my feet and down into the Earth. I allow my mind and my consciousness to sink further down. Down so I can feel the currents of the Earth. The flow of energy through the Earth. The flow of warmth, the flow of dark power that moves and flows through the Earth. And when my mind has moved down to the point where I can feel the Earth's energies, the Earth's powers, moving and flowing freely, I allow that energy to flow back up the*

channel I've created. Back up into my body. I bring that Earth-energy, that warm flow of energy, in to fill my body. To fill my body and then overflow. And as it leaves my body it moves to fill this sacred space. I can feel as the energy flows up through the Earth and out and around through this sacred space. I can feel it, as it grows stronger, as it moves around the area. Around and around, around and around.

From my hands, to my heart, to my mouth, to my eyes it flows. Up to where my visions dance, to my mind, opened and enlightened, and then out. Out to the path that stretches between the Earth and the moon and the stars and planets. That which is the universe. That which breathes back and forth, back and forth. The rhythm that echoes across time and space, the dance of life itself. And I let my mind and heart grow tree form. And stretch and grow tall, out to where the stars dance. I can see the heavens ahead and around, behind and in front of me. That which surrounds me and holds me. That which explodes and rains down upon the Earth, as light. Glistening through me, softly, softly. That which nurtures and strengthens. I let that light flow down upon the Earth, upon this sacred space, and let that energy flow out from my being. Out and around this sacred space. A dance that never ends. Never ends. Never ends. I am at peace with myself. Now, I open my eyes and let my vision return to my mortal eyes as this work continues.

Purifying the Space

For this part, have a shell full of water and a lit incense stick or three. Take a shell or cup of water and sprinkle yourself while saying:

I stand here prepared to begin this work. As this water touches me, may it wash away all earthly cares.

Then as you wave the incense around yourself, you can say something like:

May the Spirit rise within me.

After you are purified, you can carry the water and incense around the space you will be working in and repeat the same lines to purify it.

Honoring an Earth Mother

Honoring an Earth Mother can be done by making an offering of flowers, cornmeal, or some other natural object, while speaking to her:

Earth Mother, you support me in all that I do and I thank you for that. I give this offering to you in love and ask you to join with me in this ritual. I pray that you bring your strength and grounding to this rite.

(Forcefully) *Earth Mother, I honor you!*

It is usual to bestow a kiss upon the Earth at this time.

Honoring the Bardic Deities

An offering of sweet-smelling herbs can be sprinkled on the earth or into the offering bowl while speaking the following to honor Ogma, an Irish deity of poets:

Ogma, honey-mouthed, I call upon you tonight to ask for your aid. I call upon you, patron of the poets and the eloquent speakers. I ask that you aid me in finding the best words, the sweetest-sounding chants, and the most wonderful offerings to give to the Kindred!

(Forcefully) *Ogma, accept this offering and grant me this boon!"*

Historical Precedent

This section is included to allow yourself to be reminded a little of the history of the holiday.

All flows in cycles. The cycle of history has evolved for us a religious symbolism to acknowledge the seasonal cycle of the sun's apparent path through the sky. The midsummer solstice is the time when, because of the earth's tilt, the sun is at its peak of power and the day is the longest. While it is natural and good to celebrate the sun's blessings at this apex of summer, I also recognize that from this moment forward the light and warmth will begin to wane in a never ending cycle which guarantees its eventual return.

Establishing the Horizontal Axis

Walk around the boundary of your space sprinkling cornmeal while saying:

I ask that the Earth not open up and swallow me.

Next walk around the space sprinkling water while saying:

I ask that the Seas not rise up and drown me.

And walk around the area one more time waving a stick of incense while saying:

I ask that the Sky not fall down upon me.

Establishing the Vertical Axis

Again, establish the vertical axis by reconnecting the Well, Fire, and Tree with their roots in all the other sacred fires, wells, and trees in the cosmos. Offerings (such as silver jewelry to the well, olive oil to the fire, and incense or water to the tree) can be made as the following is said:

> [While pointing to the Well with one hand and giving the offering with the other.] *Sacred Well, I give this offering of silver to you. At this time, I ask that you allow your waters to move down into the Earth and reconnect with all the Sacred Wells that have flowed upon the earth.*

> [Point to the Fire with one hand and give the offering with the other.] *Sacred Fire, I give this offering of fine olive oil to you. At this time, I ask that you allow your flame to reconnect with all of the Sacred Fires that have burned throughout time.*

> [Point to the Tree with one hand and give the offering with the other.] *Sacred Tree, I give this offering of water to you. At this time I ask that your roots extend deep into the earth and reconnect with all of the Sacred Trees that have grown upon the earth.*

Calling Upon the Gatekeeper

This calling is usually done while giving an offering of olive oil to the fire.

> *And now I call to Manannán mac Lir. Manannán mac Lir, I ask you to come to me tonight to be my guide between the worlds. I ask you to hold open the ways for me and to lend your strength to mine as the gates are being opened. Manannán mac Lir, once again I ask, let the fire open as a gate. And let the well open as a gate. And let the tree open as the conduit between all the worlds.*
>
> (Forcefully) *Manannán mac Lir let the gates be opened!*

Kindred Callings

An offering to the Ancestors of cornmeal is sprinkled around the inside of the sacred space or into the offering bowl. A calling is spoken while the offering is sprinkled:

> *Ancestors I ask that you be with me tonight. Mothers and Fathers of all, not just of me, but of the earlier inhabitants of this land as well. I call to you tonight and ask you to join with me and lend me your wisdom.*

(Forcefully) *Ancestors, be with me tonight and accept my sacrifice!*

An offering to the Spirits of Nature of a sweet-smelling herbal mix is sprinkled around the inside of the sacred space or into the offering bowl. A calling is spoken while the offering is sprinkled:

Spirits of Nature, I ask that you accept this sacrifice of sweet-smelling herbs and join in this ritual. Spirits of this land and all the lands around it, Spirits of the waters and of the air and skies above it, I call to you now. I ask that you join with me and lend me your strength.

(Forcefully) *Spirits of Nature, be with me tonight and accept my sacrifice!*

An offering of olive oil to the Gods and Goddesses is sprinkled on the fire or into the offering bowl. A calling is spoken while the offering is sprinkled:

I call now to all the Gods and Goddesses that have not been named. I give you this offering of fine oil and ask that you join with me for this ritual tonight. I ask that you join with me and lend me your power.

(Forcefully) *Shining Ones, be with me tonight and accept my sacrifice!*

Calling of the Primary Deities, Taranis and Boann

The wording that follows is based on the version used in 1999, when our grove prayed for rain. If you are not in a time of drought, I would suggest changing the wording. As each calling is spoken, an offering of olive oil is poured on the fire.

I call upon you tonight, great thunderer Taranis. I ask that you bring the rains to make my crops grow. I have been in a time of drought and my crops are calling for water! Taranis, I call to you to come in your great wheeled chariot that goes across the skies. I ask that you bring your great hammer that makes the thunder. And most of all, I ask that you bring the rains that we all need.

(Forcefully) *Taranis, I call you and ask that you accept my sacrifice!*

I call you, white cow woman. You are the mother, the beginning, and the start of the river Boyne. The river that flows across the land. Let that water, that river cascade, descend, and gently move down upon me. Upon my body, within my mind, and upon my land. You who stepped across the boundaries, and who looked into the well at Sídh Nectán [pronounced She Ne-tain], You who called forth that river with your actions, who let it follow you and to run its course.

You who gave yourself to that river, I call you, Boann, the beginning of the Boyne. I ask that you let your river move, cascade, and gently descend upon me.

(Forcefully) Boann, I call you and ask that you accept my sacrifice!"

Praise Offering

This can be done through offers of song, poetry, story, dance, artwork, etc. You should plan what you will be offering in advance of the ritual and make sure that it is a worthy offering.

Prayer of sacrifice and key offering

A large special offering of your choice is given to the fire while the following is spoken:

Boann and Taranis, I have called you tonight, made offerings to you and shown you my love. I ask that you take this final sacrifice and know that I will always honor you and give you praise!

(Forcefully) Boann and Taranis, accept my sacrifice!

Omen

The omen is usually done with either runes or ogham cards/sticks. After the omen is drawn and interpreted, take time to reflect upon how the omen is relevant to your personal life, and if you feel it needed, it can be worked into the return flow.

Return Flow

The return flow section is started by holding up a cup of water, juice, or ale. Energize the beverage by visualizing while saying something like:

As I have given sacrifices of song, poems and praise to the Kindred, now I ask for them to return the blessings to me. I know that the blessings will be returned magnified many times by their greatness. Above, I can see the crowd of watchers looking down with love. I can see their love and blessings stream down like moonbeams to fill this cup.

(Forcefully) Behold, the Waters of Life!"

The waters are now drunk while contemplating everything that has gone on so far.

Thanking the Deities, Boann and Taranis

A gift of olive oil is poured on the fire or into the offering bowl, as the parting is spoken:

> *Boann, white cow woman, mother of rivers, I thank you for joining with me. As this rite is ending, I give you this gift in parting, given out of love, with nothing asked in return,*
>
> (Forcefully) *Boann, I thank you!*

Another gift of olive oil is poured on the fire or into the offering bowl, as the parting is spoken:

> *Taranis, great thunderer, bringer of the rains, I thank you for joining with me. As this rite is ending, I give you this gift in parting, given out of love, with nothing asked in return.*
>
> (Forcefully) *Taranis, I thank you!*

Thanking the Kindred

As the parting is spoken, a gift of oil is poured into the fire.

> *I turn now to all the other Gods and Goddesses. I thank you for joining with me tonight in this work. As this rite is ending, I give you this gift in parting, given out of love, with nothing asked in return.*
>
> (Forcefully) *Gods and Goddesses, I thank you!*

As the parting is spoken, a gift of oil is poured into the fire.

> *I call now to all the Spirits of this place. I see and feel you around me every day. I know you are never far from me. As this rite is ending, I give you this gift in parting, given out of love, with nothing asked in return.*
>
> (Forcefully) *Spirits of Nature, I thank you!*

As the parting is spoken, a gift of oil is poured into the fire.

> *I call now to the ancestors of my people. I acknowledge you in my life and vow that you will be remembered. As this rite is ending, I give you this gift in parting, given out of love, with nothing asked in return.*
>
> (Forcefully) *Ancestors, I thank you!*

Thanking the Gatekeeper and Closing the Gates

The parting is spoken as the Gates are being closed:

Gatekeeper, great Manannán mac Lir, I call upon you one last time during this ritual. As this ritual comes to an end, I thank you for working with me, for holding open the ways between. I thank Manannán mac Lir for being in my rite as I call for rain. As this ritual is ending, I ask, let the Tree be once again a tree [pointing at the Tree and visualizing it shrinking back down to normal size].

And let the Fire be once again fire [pointing at the Fire and visualizing it simply as a candle or small fire].

And let the Well be once again a well [pointing at the Well and visualizing it as simply a bowl of water].

(Forcefully) *Manannán mac Lir, let the gates be closed!"*

One last time, a gift of olive oil is poured as the following is said:

Manannán mac Lir, I thank you for working with me tonight, and give you this gift of oil, given out of love with nothing asked in return.

(Forcefully) *Manannán, I thank you!*

Thanking the Bards and Earth Mother

Parting gifts of olive oil are poured to both the Bard and the Earth Mother that was called upon while saying something like:

Ogma, I thank you for hearing my words and joining with me. As this rite is ending, I give you this gift in parting, given out of love, with nothing asked in return.

Earth Mother, I close this work with just the simple words, I thank you! I give you this gift in parting, given out of love, with nothing asked in return.

Reversing the Two-Power Meditation

This meditation allows the energies to move back to their source.

I close my eyes and look around me with the vision that sits behind my eyes. This sacred place is now filled with flows of energy, with love, and with the host of otherworldly beings gathered here. All are visible when I use my inner vision. As this ritual comes to a close, it is time to let those energies that I have brought in at the start, go back to where they came from. I let those energies that came into me from above, from the dance of the universe, go back to the Sky. As that energy moves through me, I keep what I need, but let the rest go.

And as those energies from the Sky go through me and have gone, I look around again to the energies from the Earth. I let those energies move into and through

me as they too go back to where they came from. I keep all that I need to feel
energized, relaxed, and at peace. I open my eyes and look around at the sacred
space. I am at peace with myself and with the land.

Conclusion

A formal closing should be spoken, such as: *For tonight this work is over. The*
rite has ended! The bell is then rung the same as it was to start the ritual.

Autumnal Equinox

The Autumnal Equinox, also known to modern NeoPagans as Mabon,
Harvesttide, or *Alban Elfed* (Welsh for "the point of reaping"), is usually
celebrated on the evening of the actual date of the Equinox, September
21. This is a time when day and night are of equal length. As Druids
strive for balance—harmony between the male and female, the positive
and negative, the light and dark forces of life—it is especially important
at this time to look within yourself to see how well you balance these
complementary elements.

The Holiday

Although Mabon is not considered one of the original Celtic festivals,
the solstices and the equinoxes have been adopted as Quarter Days
into the NeoPagan wheel of the year. Just as Lúghnasadh marks the
gathering of the first fruits of the harvest, Mabon marks the
completion of the harvest—a time of thanksgiving which emphasizes
future returns of abundance.

The Autumnal Equinox is a time of transition, and though festive, it is
connected with the relationship between the Sun and the Earth. The
modern Wiccan author Doreen Valiente has written that "in the months
of March and September, the months of equinoxes [are] periods well
known to occultists as being times of psychic stress."[118] The equinoxes,
being times of balance and of suspended activity, when the veil between
the seen and the unseen is at a thin point, are also times when human
beings "change gear" to a different phase. Therefore, they can signal
periods of psychological and psychic disturbances. Realizing the
significance of these natural phases enables us to be exhilarated by them,
instead of being distressed, and to work with them to achieve the balance.

---

[118]Doreen Valiente, *An ABC of Witchcraft: Past and Present*, [1986 ed.]. (Blaine Wash.: Phoenix
Pub., 1986), 166.

The Autumnal Equinox is also known as Harvest Home to modern agrarian NeoPagans and occurs during the height of the harvest season. As summer ends, the agricultural work for the year has been completed and food is being stored for the winter. The time is marked by leaves turning; bird migrations; winemaking; harvesting corn, grains, fruits, and nuts; and spending time with friends around the fire, as the chill of winter is anticipated.

Most of the customs that have been passed down to us from the ancient Celts concern harvest practices. When the last sheaf of grain was to be cut, the reapers would stand with their backs to it and throw their scythes until one of them cut it off. This sheaf was then formed into a "dolly," similar to the modern corn dollies but usually in the shape of an animal. In Scotland, if the harvest had been good and reflected the fertility of the land, the dolly was called a young woman, the "Harvest Queen." If the harvest had been bad, it was called an old woman, the "Sterile Hag." Most communities held on to this dolly for a full year, and burned it at the end of the next harvest. The reaper of the dolly was usually its keeper and received special favors from the Otherworld and the spirits of the land during the year.[119]

During this season we thank the Shining Ones and the Spirits of Nature for the harvest and ask their blessings on that which has been set aside for future nourishment. The seeds of desire that were planted during the Spring Equinox are realized and made manifest to those who sowed and nurtured them. And the annual cycle continues as autumn's grain is spring's seed.

Significant colors for this holiday are gold, brown, warm reds, soft greens, orange, and other harvest colors. Decorate your sacred space and your personal altar with wheat, corn, nuts, and other harvest items to bring the feeling of the season to the forefront, to please the senses, and to stimu-late the inner mind in your daily work.

A Personal Ritual For The Autumnal Equinox

We start our ritual in what should now be the familiar manner, but bear in mind that a ritual meal follows this Quarter Day ritual. It should include pork, apples, carrots, and other seasonal vegetables, along with

---

[119]Kondratiev, *The Apple Branch: a Path to Celtic Ritual*, 192–193.

corn and breads baked from whole grains. You should prepare as many of the dishes as possible by yourself, rather than buying them. Traditionally, this feast was presided over by the dolly cut from the last sheaf; if you can create one from corn husks for your altar and table, it would be appropriate.

The purpose of this ritual is to honor the Welsh deity for whom this holiday is named—that is, Mabon and his mother Modron. The tale talking about Mabon and his mother is found in the *Mabinogion*, the great tales of Wales. The tale takes place during the time of Arthur and is called "How Culhwch (pronounced Cul-**thok**) won Olwen."

The tale itself is long but to summarize it, Culhwch fell in love with Olwen who was the daughter of a giant, Ysbaddaden (pronounced Uss-path-**ad**-an). Ysbaddaden didn't want her to marry for it had been foretold that on the day she was wed, he would die. To prevent Culhwch from marrying her, Ysbaddaden gave Culhwch a long list of deeds to be done before the wedding could take place. One of the deeds was to get the comb and shears that lay between the ears of the giant boar, Twrch Trwyth (pronounced Turkh **Troo**-ith). Many conditions had to be met and one of them was that the only hound that could bring down the boar could only be controlled by Mabon. This led to the successful hunt for Mabon who had been stolen from his mother on a Beltane eve and was hidden away in a secluded prison.

Musical Signal

A bell is struck nine times in three groups of three rings.

Opening Prayer

A short declaration of the purpose of the ritual is spoken:

> *I come to this sacred space to give honor, worship, and my love to all of the Mighty Kindred. Shining Ones, Spirits of Nature and Mighty Ancestors, I vow to hold to the Old Ways.*
>
> (Forcefully) *I am here to honor the Kindred!*

Two-Power Meditation—Earth and Sky

This meditation places your mind in a receptive state for the messages returned from the Mighty Kindred and to bring energies from the Earth and Sky to the sacred space.

I close my eyes and let my breathing slow as I take deep full breaths, in and out, in and out. And as my breathing slows, I let my mind turn inward. I look within with my inner vision. The vision that exists behind my eyes. Using this vision I let my mind move downward. Out of my body through my feet, then down farther still. I let it move down into the Earth itself. Down still, through the layers of rock and the waters that flows beneath the surface. Down to where I can feel the flow and play of the fields of energy that moves below the Earth. I take theses energies within myself and then move back up toward my physical body. I bring them with me and when my being is back in my body, I allow them to flow out from me. And as those energies flow, I can see them filling this Sacred Space with light.

And as those energies of the Earth fill this Sacred Space, I let my inner vision travel upwards. Up and out of my body again to move up towards the Sky. I let my vision move up past the clouds, out through the atmosphere, out to where the stars are. And here above the clouds and the air, I can feel the flow of the energies of the stars. A cooler, different feeling energy. I let this energy flow into me and then move back down, down toward my physical body. And as my being moves back into my body, I allow these energies from the stars to move out of my body to mix with the energies of the Earth. And as I can see this Sacred Space filled with glowing, swirling energies, I open my eyes and am at peace.

Purifying the Space

Purify the space by saying the following while sprinkling water and carrying around a lit incense stick.

By the might of the Waters and the Light of the Fires, this Grove is made whole and holy.

Honoring an Earth Mother

Honoring an Earth Mother can be done by making an offering of flowers, cornmeal, or some other natural object, while speaking to her:

Earth Mother, you are my foundation, my place of safety, and the source of my strength. I give honor to you with this offering and ask that you join with me this night to honor the Mighty Kindred.

(Forcefully) *Earth Mother, I honor you!*

It is usual to bestow a kiss upon the Earth at this time.

Honoring the Bardic Deities

An offering of olive oil can be given to the fire, as the following is spoken:

I stand here tonight as the bard. Mine is the face of all the bards that have come before and all that will follow. My voice rings down the corridors of time and will resound in the future. My memory reaches beyond the mist of years, centuries, and eons. My song is the melody that sings through eternity. My voice the remembrance of the Ancestors and the cries of our children. But for this time and in this place, I am the bard. And I call now to Ogma, the silver-tongued, leader of people with his words. Help me to find that spark of inspiration that burns within and let it burn bright this night.[120]

Historical Precedent

This section is included to allow yourself to be reminded a little of the history of the holiday.

Now is the time of Balance, with Day and Night facing each other as equals. I pledge to try to find that same balance within myself. The Yin and the Yang. The Active and the Passive. Without one the other cannot exist. The end is just a reawakening of the beginning - life is reincarnated. Energy is never destroyed - it simply changes form. Nothing ever remains without change, in the tides of Earth and Sky. Autumn's grain is spring's seed. Know and remember that whatsoever rises must also set and whatsoever sets must also rise.

Establishing the Horizontal Axis

Walk around the boundary of your space sprinkling cornmeal while saying:

I ask that the Earth not open up and swallow me.

Next walk around the space sprinkling water while saying:

I ask that the Seas not rise up and drown me.

And walk around the area one more time waving a stick of incense while saying:

I ask that the Sky not fall down upon me.

Establishing the Vertical Axis

Offerings are made in the usual manner—silver jewelry to the Well, olive oil to the Fire, and incense or water to the Tree.

Chant—"Fire, Bright Fire" (Words and music by Pandora)
"Fire, bright Fire, gate to the Shining Ones;
Fire, bright Fire, our passage to the Sky;

---

[120]Created by Willow, a member of Muin Mound Grove, ADF. Used with permission.

Fire, bright Fire, warmth of our community;
Spark of life, we honor you now.

Well, deep Well, gate to the underworld;
Well, deep Well, our passage to the sea;
Well, deep Well, wisdom of the Ancestors;
Waters of life, we honor you now.

Tree, great Tree, gate that reaches everywhere;
Tree, great Tree, with you we share the land;
Tree, great Tree, passage to the otherworld;
Source of life, we honor you now."

Calling upon the Gatekeeper

This calling is usually done while giving an offering of oil to the fire.

I call out to the gatekeepers, openers of the ways between, guardians of the
portals. I call now to Manannán mac Lir. I wish to walk between the worlds,
to follow the secret trails. I ask you to open the gates so that I may give praise to
the Great Ones, to the honored dead and to the Spirits around me. I ask this
Manannán mac Lir! Manannán, once again I ask, let the fire open as a gate.
And let the well open as a gate. And let the tree open as the conduit between all
the worlds.

(Forcefully) *O Manannán let the gates be opened!*

Kindred Callings

The offering of cornmeal is sprinkled around the inside of the Sacred
Space. A calling is spoken at this time as the offering is sprinkled.

This offering is to you Ancestors. Without you I wouldn't be here. I owe you
my very live. Ancestors, I ask you to aid me in this ritual tonight.

(Forcefully) *Ancestors, be with me tonight and accept my sacrifice!*

The offering of a sweet smelling herbal mix is sprinkled around the
inside of the Sacred Space. A calling is spoken at this time as the
offering is sprinkled.

This offering is for you Spirits of this Place, of the Earth. You are around and
near me all the time. Nature Spirits, I ask you to aid me in this ritual tonight.

(Forcefully) *Spirits of Nature, be with me tonight and accept my sacrifice!*

The offering of oil is sprinkled on the fire. A calling is spoken at this time as the offering is sprinkled.

This offering is for you Shining Ones. Even though you are not named in this ritual, you are always in my heart. Shining ones, I ask you to aid me in this ritual tonight.

(Forcefully) *Shining Ones, be with me tonight and accept my sacrifice!*

Calling of the Primary Deities, Mabon and Modron

An offering of oil is poured on the fire, as each calling is spoken:

I call now upon Mabon. You were stolen from your mother as she slept. And you were one of the three exalted prisoners of Britain. Put in a prison near Gloucester, you were kept there till you were grown. After being rescued on Kei's back while Arthur and his men were attacking the prison, you helped them to recover the razor from behind the ear of the boar, Twrch Trwyth.

(Forcefully) *Mabon, I call to you to join me in this ritual tonight, and accept my sacrifice!*

I call now upon Modron. Mother of Mabon, you had your son stolen when he was only three days old. Long though you searched for him, he wasn't to be found. Then years later he was returned to you by Arthur and his men.

(Forcefully) *Modron, I call to you to join me in this ritual tonight and accept my sacrifice!*

Praise Offering

This can be done through offers of song, poetry, story; dance, artwork, etc. You should prepare what you will be offering in advance of the ritual and make sure that it is a worthy offering.

Prayer of Sacrifice and Key Offering

A large offering is given to the fire while the following is spoken:

Modron and Mabon, I have called you tonight and shown you my honor. I ask that you take this final sacrifice and know that I will always honor and praise you!

(Forcefully) *Modron and Mabon, accept my sacrifice!*

Omen

The omen is done as usual with either runes or ogham cards or sticks and the meaning to you can be incorporated into the return flow.

Return Flow

Hold up a cup of water, juice, beer, or ale and energize the beverage by visualizing what the words are saying while saying:

> *I close my eyes and let my body go still. Using my inner vision, my mind roams to look around and above me. I can see the crowd of spirits gathered on this plane and on the other planes. The Spirits of this Place, the Ancestors and the Shining Ones, all of them looking at me with love in their hearts! I ask you now, gathered host, return to me your blessings! Give them to me into this cup of water. Gathered host, I ask this of you!*
>
> (Forcefully) *Behold, the Waters of Life!*

The waters are now drunk while contemplating everything that has gone on so far.

Thanking the Deities, Modron and Mabon

A gift of olive oil is poured on the fire or into the offering bowl, as the parting is spoken:

> *Modron, I thank you for joining with me. As this rite is ending, I give you this gift in parting, given out of love, with nothing asked in return.*
>
> (Forcefully) *Modron, I thank you!*

Another gift of olive oil is poured on the fire or into the offering bowl, as the parting is spoken:

> *Mabon, I thank you for joining with me. As this rite is ending, I give you this gift in parting, given out of love, with nothing asked in return.*
>
> (Forcefully) *Mabon, I thank you!*

Thanking the Kindred

As the parting is spoken, a gift of olive oil is poured into the fire.

> *Shining Ones, I thank you for joining me in this ritual tonight. As this rite is ending, I give you this gift in parting, given out of love, with nothing asked in return.*
>
> (Forcefully) *Gods and Goddesses, I thank you!*

As the parting is spoken, a gift of olive oil is poured into the fire.

Spirits of this Place, I thank you for joining me in this ritual tonight. As this rite is ending, I give you this gift in parting, given out of love, with nothing asked in return.

(Forcefully) *Spirits of Nature, I thank you!*

As the parting is spoken, a gift of olive oil is poured into the fire.

Ancestors, I thank you for joining me in this ritual tonight. As this rite is ending, I give you this gift in parting, given out of love, with nothing asked in return.

(Forcefully) *Ancestors, I thank you!*

Thanking the Gatekeeper and Closing the Gates

The parting is spoken as the Gates are being closed:

I call out to the gatekeepers, openers of the ways between, guardians of the portals. I call now to Manannán mac Lir, and I thank you for allowing me to walk between the worlds, and to follow the secret trails. This ritual is coming to a close, so it is time once again to close the gates, knowing that every time I open them, the ways between become clearer! As this ritual is ending, I ask, let the Tree be once again a tree, and let the Fire be once again fire. And let the Well be once again a well.

(Forcefully) *Manannán let the gates be closed!*

One last time, a gift of olive oil is poured as the following is said:

Manannán mac Lir, I thank you for working with me tonight, and give you this gift of oil, given out of love with nothing asked in return.

(Forcefully) *Manannán, I thank you!*

Thanking the Bards and the Earth Mother

Parting gifts of olive oil are poured to both the Earth Mother and the Spirits of the Bards that were called upon while saying something like:

Ogma, I thank you for hearing my call and coming in answer. As this rite is ending, I give you this gift in parting, given out of love, with nothing asked in return.

Earth Mother, I close this work with just the simple words, I thank you! I give you this gift in parting, given out of love, with nothing asked in return.

Reversing the Two-Power Meditation

I close my eyes. For one last time tonight, I let my vision move back to the place behind my eyes where the inner vision lies. I look about me at the energy still flowing around this Sacred Space, and then I let that energy from the Skies, from the stars, flow into my being. And with that energy in my being, I let it move upwards, back to where it came. As it moves out of my physical body, I keep enough so that I will be filled with energy, refreshed and at peace.

And as those energies from the Skies pass through my being and leave my body, I let my inner vision move out, out to this Sacred Space. I can see the energies from the Earth still moving about and around this Sacred Space. I let those energies move into my being, then allow them to move down, back to where they came from. As they move out, I keep all that I need to feel energized, relaxed and at peace. I open my eyes and look around at the Sacred Space itself. I am at peace with myself and with the land.

Conclusion

Some type of formal closing must be spoken aloud, even if it is as simple as: *My work tonight is done. The rite has ended!* The musical signal that started the ritual is repeated to close the ritual.

Other Rituals

For this next section, having finished both the Fire Festivals Rituals and the Quarter Day Rituals, we move on to other types of rituals you can do. Since these rituals are not "High Day" rituals, I am not going to be strictly following the ADF Core Order of Ritual. Since they serve a different purpose than giving honor to the Kindred, they will be tailored specifically to the purpose of the rite.

Protecting a Space or House

To protect a space or a house, it is important to begin at the foundations, both figuratively and literally. The space to be protected needs to be cleaned thoroughly before it can be protected by magic. The physically cleaner it is to start, the better the magic protection will be. With these preparations completed, go to the center of the cellar, or crawl space if there is no cellar, and give an offering to the Earth for supporting the structure. Because the Earth grows many of the usual offerings, in this case "made" offerings, either hand-made or bought are appropriate. Then move one by one to each of the four corners of the house and leave offerings there for the Spirits of Nature that surround the area. This can be done either inside or outside of the house.

When this has been done, you can begin to work on protecting the center. Move to the central point of the house or grounds and perform the Two-Power Meditation, and when you have reached a very relaxed and meditative state, call upon the Kindred as follows:

> *Mighty Kindred, I call upon you this day to ask your aid in protecting this house. I ask that you join with me here to make this a safe place, a loving environment. I ask that you help me make this a place where all will feel comfortable and welcomed. I ask that you work with me to keep out all influences that will harm this space or the people within it. I give you these offerings, Mighty Kindred, out of my love and respect for you. I pledge that those in this space will honor you and love you.*

Offerings of herbs, artwork, flowers, and whiskey can be given to the Kindred at this time. Those that need to, can be placed in an offering bowl that will eventually go outside. To further enhance the protection, artwork depicting the Kindred can be placed on the walls of the home.

After these steps are completed, you can use one of the techniques described previously in the section "Land Taking." This is done by taking a lit candle, in a glass holder to protect it from the wind, and carrying it around the out-side perimeter of your house and property while saying the following:

> *Spirits of this Land and Place; I claim and hallow this property in the old ways. Ancestors of this land, I ask your blessings on my stay here. Gods and Goddesses who have been worshipped on this land, I pray your friendship to the Gods and Goddesses I hold sacred.* [Repeat this continuously while walking around the property.]

This completes the work that initially needs to be done to protect a house or space. Subsequent rituals to the Kindred, either as High Day rituals or as daily devotionals, will further protect it.

Creating a *Nemeton* (Sacred Space)

If there is sufficient space where you live, it is wonderful to have a private outdoor sanctuary where you can worship in nature. The Irish word for such a sacred space is *Nemeton*, and it has been adopted by many people following the Path of Druidry. A *Nemeton* can range in size from a small area in a backyard for individual use, to large enclosures for eighty people or more for group work. Some can accommodate 500 or more people for gatherings and festivals.

When setting up your own *Nemeton*, the location on your property is important. Try to find a shaded area that feels good and has "good vibrations" as you walk through it. If you have the option of using a grove of trees for your *Nemeton*, you will find that a special feeling very quickly develops from working there.

When you have chosen the area you want, perform the following ritual in that location to show the Kindred that they will again be given honor. Leave offerings there and go there to meditate. Try to think of ways that the area can be enhanced.

These may include more plantings, a water fountain to attract birds and small animals, or bird feeders and bird houses. Plan well, but before making any changes, make sure to meditate several times to ask the Kindred if they will be happy with the changes. If you get the message in your meditations that they will be unhappy with your changes, try something else until you get the message that they will be happy. Unhappy Spirits of the Land or discontent Kindred can easily defeat the purpose of the space.

Another way to enhance your space is by building altars to each of the individual Kindred. Around the altars, you can add statues or pictures of the Shining Ones, the Ancestors, and the Spirits of Nature. One nice touch for a Nature Spirits altar is to include a bird feeder and a birdbath in its design, which will attract many Nature Spirits to it.

As you meditate and conduct rituals in the space, the Kindred will let you know of other "improvements" that can be made. These do not have to be physical improvements; they can take the form of other types of rituals, offerings, or different meditation techniques that will occur to you whenever you are in a receptive state. The more the space is used, the better the connections with the Kindred will be and you will find it easier to interact with them.

A Ritual For Dedicating A *Nemeton*

The work of digging a place for the fire, and one for the container for a well, and sinking a pole if there are no living trees, are actions that need to be part of the ritual. Do not do them beforehand, but have the necessary tools present so they can be carried out easily.

The ritual is started by carrying a candle around the sacred space while saying the following:

(Forcefully) *Mighty Kindred, hear my words!*

I ask your blessings on making this space once again reserved for the continuation of the old ways. I pledge to give honor to all of the Mighty Kindred here. Furthermore, I pledge that this space will grow as you desire.

Spirits of this land, guide my hand, heart, and mind in this work.

Ancestors guide my hand, heart, and mind in this work.

Gods and Goddesses, guide my hand, heart, and mind in this work.

Move to the center of the area and give an offering to the Earth while saying:

Mother Earth, once again this place is being held sacred. You are always honored and revered, not only here but in my life as well. This I pledge to you.

(Forcefully) *Mother Earth, aid me in my work and accept my offering!*

In the center of the space, slowly dig a place for a fire to be built. This will become permanent over time and can be enhanced by the use of cement or the addition of a fire ring. Kindle a fire while saying:

Sacred Fire, once again you burn in this land. I ask that you now reconnect with all the Sacred Fires that have ever burned. I pledge to you that my practice will con-tinue and that offerings will be given to you. I pray that you carry my words and offerings to the Shining Ones.

(Forcefully) *Sacred Fire, hear my words and accept my offering!*

Then pour an offering of olive oil on the fire after it is burning well.

Near the fire in another depression, place a bowl of water, cauldron, or other container, to be your Sacred Well. You will want this receptacle to be pleasing to look at, so take care in choosing it. After you have filled it with water, say the following while giving the well an offering of silver:

Sacred Well, once again you flow in this land. I ask that you now reconnect with all of the Sacred Wells through the Earth. I pledge to you that my practice will continue and that offerings will be given to you. I pray that you carry my words and offerings to the Ancestors.

(Forcefully) *Sacred Well, hear my words and accept my offering!"*

If there is a suitable tree growing in your *Nemeton*, then it can become your *Bilé* (Old Irish), your sacred tree. If not, dig a hole and insert a pole, steadying it with the earth to keep it in place. Over time, a permanent pole can be placed in a pipe in a cement holder. When one pole becomes unstable, it can be replaced with a new one.

With the *Bilé* established, say the following while pouring an offering of water on the tree:

Sacred Tree, once again you grow in this land. I ask that you now reconnect with all of the Bilé, the sacred trees, on the Earth. I pledge to you that my practice will continue and that offerings will be given to you. I pray that you act as the conduit through all the planes so my words and offerings will reach the Mighty Kindred.

(Forcefully)*Sacred Tree, hear my words and accept my offering!*

If you use a real tree for your *Bilé*, then an offering of fertilizer, in what ever form you feel is most appropriate, works very well. The *Nemeton* is now established and it is appropriate to sit and meditate there on how the Mighty Kindred wish it to grow. Every time a ritual is held in the sacred place, the connections created grow stronger. I am confident that as more rituals are performed in the *Nemeton*, you will notice many creatures, seen and unseen, around it.

A Funeral Ritual for an Animal Companion

Many of us have animal companions that have been with us for a long time. There comes a time when that loved one passes from this world. For many of us, it is as sad a time as when a member of our human family dies. A funeral ritual helps us remember the times spent with our companion, both good and bad. It is an occasion to say goodbye.

A memorial ritual can be a memorial service without the burial, or one followed by a service at the burial site. You may not be able to bury your companion, as vets often want to dispose of the body by cremation rather than allow you to take care of it. When this is the case, a memorial service without the burial can be used.

To begin, gather together friends that remember your com-panion and objects the animal used. Pick a spot that was loved by your companion—a park, a yard, or someplace where your companion felt free. A bowl of water and a candle can be used for the Well and Fire. You can start by saying:

> *We are gathered here today to remember our friend* [insert the companion's name here]. *Even though he/she has passed from this plane, he/she will always be remembered. I give first an offering to the mother of us all, the mother of this place.* [An offering is given to the Earth.]

Continue by calling upon the Kindred to join you in your remembering:

> *I call now to the Mighty Kindred.*
>
> *First to the Ancestors, I give you this offering* [an offering is given to the Well or Earth], *and ask that you aid* [insert the companion's name here] *in his/her journey to the Summer Lands. He/she was a true companion. He/she was loyal and true and gave me unconditional love.*
>
> *Next, I call to the Spirits of Nature, those beings of the land, sea, and sky who reside in this place. I give you this offering* [an offering is given to the Earth] *and ask that you aid* [insert the companion's name here] *in his/her journey to the Summer Lands.*
>
> *Now I call upon the Shining Ones. Mighty deities that are honored by me, I give you this offering* [an offering is given to the Fire or Earth], *and ask that you aid* [insert the companion's name here] *in his/her journey to the Summer Lands.*

After the offerings are given and the Kindred called, it is proper for the people gathered to share stories of their time spent with the departed companion. Allow enough time so that everyone can say what needs to be said. Have on hand the objects that the animal companion played with and loved so that people can pick them up and hold them while they reminisce.

After people are finished with the remembering, it is fitting to give thanks to the Mighty Kindred. This can be done by saying:

I give thanks to the Mighty Kindred that have joined us to remember [insert the companion's name here].

Shining Ones, thank you for joining with us and for helping [insert the companion's name here] *make his/her journey to the Summer Lands.*

Spirits of Nature, thank you for joining with us and for helping [insert the companion's name here] *make his/her journey to the Summer Lands.*

Ancestors, thank you for joining with us and for helping [insert the companion's name here] *make his/her journey to the Summer Lands.*

To all of you who have come together to remember [insert the companion's name here], *I thank you for helping me and the others gathered here in this time of sorrow. This rite has ended.*

One thing that I've found personally helpful to work through this period of grief is a poem called *The Rainbow Bridge*. It can be found here - *http://www.rainbowbridge.com/Poem.htm* and I highly recommend everyone reading it![121]

---

[121]"The Rainbow Bridge Poem - A Pet Loss Poem," accessed December 13, 2012, *http://www.rainbowbridge.com/Poem.htm.*

Chapter 8
What We Know About the Ancient Druids

With your walk along the "Path of Druidry" well along the way, it is now time to think about what more you can do. One branch of the Path involves learning more about the ancient Druids and Celts. The information in this chapter is meant to be a **starting point** for your study. Such studies may not be for everyone, but even the introduction to such a course of study in this chapter is worthwhile. As Julius Caesar observed about the Druids, they "learn by heart a great number of verses; accordingly some remain in the course of training twenty years."[122] For most of us, twenty years of training requires immense dedication.

In my opinion, the best place to start is to read contemporary accounts of the ancient Druids. This information is found in the work of Greek, Roman, Irish, and Welsh authors. Another way to learn about them is from the archaeological record. This source is a little less reliable because it has to be interpreted though modern eyes, rather than from the written words of the people themselves.

In this chapter, I will mention some of the more important writings about the Druids and the Celts. The material on the Celts is included to give the background necessary to understand the Druids. Reading these books will increase your understanding considerably. For all of the authors, I have included either in print or internet links for where you can find the writing. I cannot guarantee that these links will still be active after the book has gone to the publisher, but a simple search on

---

[122]Caesar, Julius, "The Gallic Wars," trans. McDevitte, William Alexander and Bohn, W.S., Book 1, section 6.14, accessed January 31, 2012, *http://www.brainfly.net/html/books/brn0004.htm.*

the author's name combined with the name of the work, should bring up an internet link.

Greek Literary Sources

Greek writings on the Celts and the Druids first appear around 500 BCE, when the historian Herodotus wrote about the Celts, and continue to the end of the third Century CE. Many of the authors discussed here can be found in *The Celtic Heroic Age: Literary Sources for Ancient Celtic Europe and Early Ireland and Wales*, edited by John T. Koch and John Carey published by Celtic Studies Publications in 1994, ISBN 0964244616; or in Celts and the Classical World by David Rankin, published by Rutledge in 1987, ISBN 0415150906. These books are an invaluable historical aid to understanding the Celts and the Druids and ones that I personally recommend highly. An invaluable online source is *www.brainfly.net*, a cyber-library that has many of the works of the Greek and Roman authors available in electronic format.[123]

Many of the works that have come down to us are in fragmentary manuscripts, sections in one and other sections in different manuscripts. To make it easier to reference individual parts of the works, they are usually listed by work and then section in the work. These section numbers can be used, especially in online editions where you can do a text search on the page for the number, to find the information you are looking for.

We start our journey into the works of the Greek authors, listed alphabetically, by looking at what an **anonymous** poet wrote in the second Century BCE. In the *Greek Anthology*, in section 9.125, we read that in what is now Germany, as soon as a Celtic child was born, the father would carry him or her to the Rhine River and place them in it to be judged. If they were strong enough to survive, they would live, if they were not strong enough, the river would carry them away.[124]

Next we turn to a very prolific author, **Aristotle**, who lived from 384 to 322 BCE. Aristotle was a great philosopher and statesman who had studied under Plato. His interests were varied and he wrote on many subjects including logic, metaphysics, nature, ethics, politics, art and life in general. In his work *Politics*, which deals with the political structures of many of the lands around Greece, in book 2, section 9, he discusses

---

[123]Brainfly, Inc., "Brainfly.Net," accessed January 31, 2012, *http://www.brainfly.net/*.
[124]As quoted in - Koch, *The Celtic Heroic Age*.

the Celts and homosexuality, telling how the Celts openly approve of sexual relationships between men.[125] In the *Nicomachean Ethics*, one of his many works of ethics, in sections 3.7.6 and 3.7.7, he talks about the Celts being foolishly brave, stating:

> *Of those who go to excess he who exceeds in fearlessness has no name (we have said previously that many states of character have no names), but he would be a sort of madman or insensible person if he feared nothing, neither earthquakes nor the waves, as they say the Celts do not...*[126]

In his work *Eudemian Ethics*, in section 3.1.25, he also talks about the Celts taking up arms against the sea.[127]

We move next to **Athenaeus**, who lived in the early second Century CE. Writing in the book *Deipnosophistae (The Learned Banquet)*, which describes the conversations of learned men at a banquet extending over several days, he discusses sections from Posidonius' work, *Histories*, written originally in the first century BCE. In Book IV, page 244-245, section 36, he talks about the Celtic eating and drinking habits, how they eat sitting on the ground and consume small quantities of bread but large amounts of meat. In Book IV, page 246, section 37, he talks about the wealth and hospitality of Louernius, a Gaulish chieftain who put on a feast for thousands of people in which is says:

> *...that he enclosed a fenced space of twelve furlongs in length every way, square, in which he erected wine-presses, and filled them with expensive liquors; and that he prepared so vast a quantity of eatables that for very many days any one who chose was at liberty to go and enjoy what was there prepared, being waited on without interruption or cessation.*[128]

In Book IV, page 248, section 40, he talks about the "hero's portion," which was the best cut of meat that was given to the greatest hero, usually considered to be the person who had killed the most warriors, at the feast. In Book VI, page 387, section 49, he gives us a brief description of the Bards, who are described as poets who recite in song.[129]

---

[125]Aristotle, "POLITICS," trans. Jowett, Benjamin, book 2, section 9, accessed January 31, 2012, *http://www.brainfly.net/html/books/brn0061.htm.*

[126]Aristotle, "Nicomachean Ethics," trans. Ross, W.D., Book 3, accessed January 31, 2012, *http://www.brainfly.net/html/books/brn0042.htm.*

[127]As quoted in - Koch, *The Celtic Heroic Age*, 6.

[128]"Athenaeus: Deipnosophistæ - Book 13 (d)", n.d., Book IV, page 246, section 37, *http://www.attalus.org/old/athenaeus13d.html.*

[129]"Athenaeus: Deipnosophistæ - Book 13 (d)."

Our next author is **Callimachus of Cyrene**, who lived from about 285 to about 246 BCE. He was a very prolific author and is credited with over eight hundred books, although few still survive. Writing around the time of the Celtic invasion of Delphi, 278 BCE, in the work *Hymn to Delos*, one of three books he had written in the style of the *Homeric Hymns*, he tells about the Celtic invasion, where they came as far south as the Greek Isles, and about a prophecy by Apollo at his birth about the Celts invading Greece.[130]

Next we hear from **Clement of Alexandria**, who lived from about 150 CE to 210 CE. Writing in the work *Stromata*, in book 15-70.1, he talks about Pythagoras and how the mathematician had studied with the Gauls and Brahmins. In book 15-70.3 of the same work, he tells us that the philosophers of the Celts, the Druids, were among the most important in the world.[131]

Dio Chrysostom (a.k.a. Dio Cocceianus), was a Greek orator and philosopher who lived from the forties of the first Century CE to sometime after 110. He wrote in the work *Orations*, section 49, that the Druids were the primary advisors to the chiefs and that the chiefs would make no decision without them, so in fact, the Druids were the real leaders of the tribes.[132]

Lucius Cassius Dio was a Greek senator and historian who lived from 164 to sometime after 229 CE. In the work *Roman History*, section 62, he tells the story of Boadicea (Boudica), a Queen who took over the rule of her people, the British tribe called the Iceni, after her husband was killed and her daughters were raped by the Romans. He further tells of a method of augury used by her, based on the direction a rabbit dedicated to Andraste, a local goddess, ran as it was released.[133]

We now turn to another prolific author, **Diodorus Siculus**, who wrote between 60 and 30 BCE. Due to the similarity in descriptions, it is very likely that in his book, *The Historical Library*, he is getting his information from an earlier work by Posidonius. In book 5, section 24 he wrote on

[130]Callimachus, "Classical E-Text: CALLIMACHUS, HYMNS 4 - 6," trans. Mair, A.W., n. 52, accessed January 31, 2012, *http://www.theoi.com/Text/CallimachusHymns2.html.*

[131]Clement of Alexandria, "Logos Virtual Library: Clement of Alexandria: The Stromata," trans. Wilson, Wiliam, bk. 15, accessed January 31, 2012, *http://www.logoslibrary.org/clement/stromata/index.html.*

[132]Koch, *The Celtic Heroic Age*, 24.

[133]Unknown, "Cath Maige Tuired."

the origin of the name Galatia, stating that it was named after a son of Hercules. In book 5, section 27 he talks about the Celts, the availability of gold in their lands and how, when they placed gold offerings in their temples and sanctuaries, no one touched it because it had been given to the gods. In book 5, section 28 he describes the Celts physical appearance as being very tall with white skin and blond hair, and long mustaches among the nobles. He also tells that for their feasts they sit on the ground and eat large amounts of meat. He continues on to tell what they believe about reincarnation, saying:

> *They do not fear death, but subscribe to the doctrine of Pythagoras that the human spirit is immortal and will enter a new body after a fixed number of years. For this reason some will cast letters to their relatives on funeral pyres, believing that the dead will be able to read them.*[134]

In book 5, section 29 he talks about dealing with war customs, where they fight from two-horse chariots and favor single combat between a champion from each side to settle conflicts, and heads, where they take the heads of slain enemies and keep them as trophies. In book 5, section 30 he tells about clothes and adornments. He describes the clothes as being multi-colored with pants and that cloaks with checkered patterns are worn fastened with a clasp. In book 5, section 31 he discusses bards, who sing both praise and satire, Druids, the philosophers and theologians who can step between two warring armies and stop them with a word; seers, who are highly respected; and augury, a method of foretelling the future by birds. In book 5, section 32 he tells about how there are many tribes but when they are considered together, they are called the Galatae by the Romans, about burning sacrifices (both prisoners and animals), and about the Celts and homosexuality. In book 5, section 33 he compared the Celts with the Celtiberians saying that the Celtiberians were hairier and darker skinned. Finally, in book 5, section 34 he talks about Celts drinking wine flavored with honey.[135]

Diogenes Laërtius is our next author, writing in the first half of the third Century CE. In *Vitae*, Introduction, part 1, he writes on the Druids, philosophy, and the names of some of the other philosophers, such as the Magi of Persia and the Gymnosophists of India. In the

---

[134]Diodorus Siculus, "LacusCurtius • Diodorus Siculus — Book V Chapters 19-40," sec. 28, accessed January 31, 2012, *http://penelope.uchicago.edu/Thayer/E/Roman/Texts/Diodorus_Siculus/5B*.html.*

[135]Diodorus Siculus, "LacusCurtius • Diodorus Siculus — Book V Chapters 19-40."

Introduction, part 6, he wrote on what the Druids taught, worshiping the Gods, abstinence from evil and practicing "manly virtue" (bravery).[136]

The historian **Ephorus'** work was lost, so all we have is what is quoted by Strabo (described below) in *Geography*, book 4, section 4.6. Written originally by Ephorus, who lived from 405 to 330 BCE, it talks about the physical nature of the Celts and their aversion to obesity, enough so that if a persons belly stuck over their belt, they were punished.[137]

Herodotus, who lived sometime in the fifth Century BCE, in his book *Histories*, book 1, section 33, writes on the Celts, simply saying that they lived beyond the Pillars of Hercules, the modern Straits of Gibraltar.[138]

Nicander of Colophon, who lived in the second Century BCE, is another author whose major works are lost. One section is quoted by Tertullian, a Greek jurist and author who lived from 160 to 240 CE, in *De Anima*, chapter 57, section 10, about the Celts receiving visions by spending the night on the tombs of famous men.[139]

Pausanias, writing in the second Century CE, in the essay *Description of Greece*, about the Celtic invasion of Greece in 278 BCE, compliments the information given us by Callimachus of Cyrene, described above.

Phylarchus, who lived in the third Century BCE, is another author whose material is lost. It was quoted by Athenaeus, see above, in *Deipnosophistae (The Learned Banquet)*, book 4, page 187, section 150:d-f, on the wealth of the Galatians, especially of Ariamnes, a chieftain who held a yearlong feast for all the people of Gaul.[140]

Plato, who lived from 427 to 348 BCE, writing in the book Laws, sections 1.637d-e, talks about the Celts and how they are prone to

---

[136]Diogenes Laërtius, "Lives of the Eminent Philosophers/Book I - Wikisource," trans. Hicks, Robert Drew, accessed January 31, 2012, *http://en.wikisource.org/wiki/Lives_of_the_Eminent_Philosophers/Book_I#Prologue.*

[137]Strabo, "LacusCurtius • Strabo's Geography — Book IV Chapter 4," trans. Jones, H.L., accessed January 31, 2012, *http://penelope.uchicago.edu/Thayer/E/Roman/Texts/Strabo/4D*.html.*

[138]Herodotus, "The History of Herodotus Vol. 1," trans. Macaula, G.C., sec. 33, accessed January 31, 2012, *http://www.brainfly.net/html/books/brn0098a.htm.*

[139]Tertullian, "A Treatise on the Soul/De Anima," trans. Holmes, Peter, accessed January 31, 2012, *http://www.brainfly.net/html/books/brn0169.htm.*

[140]Athenaeus of Naucratis, "The Literature Collection: The Deipnosophistæ, or, Banquet of the Learned of Athenæus (volume I): Book IV", n.d., *http://digicoll.library.wisc.edu/cgi-bin/Literature/Literature-idx?type=turn&id=Literature.AthV1&entity=Literature.AthV1.p0252&q1=celts&pview=hide.*

drunkenness, along with the Scythians, Persians, Carthaginians, Iberians, and Thracians.[141]

Plutarch, who lived from 50 to 125 CE, talks about the women of Gaul and how brave they are in On the Bravery of Women, section 6, page 495. In the work Camillus, section 22.4 (page 151), he talks about the Gauls invading Rome in 348 BCE and how the Centurion Lucius Camillus came to the city's rescue.[142]

Polyaenus writes in the book *History*, section 8.39, on the bravery of the Gaulish women and how one of them publicly poisoned a man that had raped her.[143]

Polybius, writing in the second Century BCE, in the work *History*, sections 2.28.3-10, 29.5-9, 31.1-2 and 21.38.1-6, talks about the Battle of Telamon in northern Italy where a large group, about forty thousand Celts, were trapped between two Roman armies and killed.[144]

Posidonius, who was writing in the first Century BCE, talks about the hero's portion, as has been previously described under Athenaeus, and the Celtic love of fighting at feasts. It appears that many later authors were referring to his original accounts in their writings.

Pseudo-Scymnus, writing in the first Century BCE, in the work *Periplus*, lines 183-187, talks about how nice the Celtic hospitality is and how they have music at their feasts.[145]

Ptolemy I, who lived from 367 or 366 to 282 BCE, is another author whose work is lost other than in quotes. As quoted by Strabo [see below] in *Geography*, section 7.3.8, he tells about the life of Alexander the Great and on what the Celts feared most—that the sky would fall. This fear is given by several authors but in none of the cases do they

[141]Plato, "The Internet Classics Archive | Laws by Plato," trans. Benjamin Jowett, accessed February 7, 2012, *http://classics.mit.edu/Plato/laws.1.i.html*.

[142]Plutarch, "Plutarch • On the Bravery of Women — Sections I-XV," trans. Frank Cole Babbitt, 495, accessed February 7, 2012, *http://penelope.uchicago.edu/Thayer/E/Roman/Texts/Plutarch/Moralia/Bravery_of_Women*/A.html#VI*; Plutarch, "Plutarch • Life of Camillus," trans. Bernadotte Perrin, 151, accessed February 7, 2012, *http://penelope.uchicago.edu/Thayer/E/Roman/Texts/Plutarch/Lives/Camillus*.html*.

[143]Koch, The Celtic Heroic Age, 35–36.

[144]Polybius, "Polybius," trans. Evelyn S. Shuckburgh, accessed February 7, 2012, *http://www.brainfly.net/html/polybius.htm*.

[145]Pseudo-Scymnus, "Fjor.net - eTOME," l. 183–187, accessed February 7, 2012, *http://fjor.net/etome/grecoroman/pseudoscymnus.html*.

actually describe how this fear came about or what they feared would fall on them.

Another author whose work only survives in quotation is **Sopater**, who wrote in the third century BCE. As quoted by Athenaeus [see above] in *Deipnosophistae (The Learned Banquet)*, book IV, section 51, page 258, he talks about the Celts sacri-ficing the losers in battle to the Gods:

> *Among them is the custom, whenever they win a victory in battle, to sacrifice their prisoners to the gods. So I, imitating the Celts, have vowed to the divine powers to burn as an offering Three of those false dialecticians.*[146]

Another author who wrote extensively on the Celts is **Strabo**, who lived from 66 BCE to 24 CE. It is very likely that much of his work was taken from the earlier author Posidonius [see above]. In Strabo's book *Geography*, in section 3.4.16, he talks about the Celtiberians, who lived in modem Spain, worshipping an unnamed god on the full moon. In section 4.1.13, he talks about the large amounts of gold and silver that was sacrificed to the gods by throwing it into lakes and lists tribal names, such as the Tectosages. In section 4.4.1, he talks about ships and in section 4.4.2, on the Celts' physical appearance and strength in battle. In section 4.4.3, he talks about the Celts and Germans, clothes, weapons and diet and in section 4.4.4, about the Druids, bards, and Vates. In section 4.4.5, he talks about how heads were taken in battle and used as trophies, divinations where enemies were stabbed and the message was read from their death throes, and Druids and the wicker man—a large man-shaped wickerwork that was filled with sacrificial victims, including humans at times. In section 4.4.6, he talks about an island inhabited by women where each year they have to strip the roof off of their temple and put a new one on in one day and how in the harbor called Two Crows, the disputes are settled by sacred crows: Barley cakes are set out by the people involved in the dispute and whichever one is pecked first by the crow is declared the winner. In section 4.5.4, he talks about the Britons and how they sleep with each other's wives as well has their own mothers and sisters. He does say that this may be a myth and that he has no hard evidence. In section 7.2.3, he talks about human sacrifice by drowning. In section 7.3.8, he talks about the Celts fearing nothing but that the sky should fall; this may be a repeat of information from Ptolemy I.[147]

---

[146]Koch, *The Celtic Heroic Age*, 6.

[147]Strabo, "Geography," trans. H. C. Hamilton and W. Falconer, accessed February 7, 2012, *http://www.brainfly.net/html/strabo.htm*.

Theopompus, writing originally in the fourth Century BCE, is quoted by Athenaeus [see above], in *Deipnosophistae (The Learned Ban*quet), sections 10.443b-c, on the Celts military strategy, where in this case, they placed a powerful purgative in their enemies' food so that they could be easily killed.[148]

And last in this section on Greek authors, **Xenophon**, who lived from 431 to 354 BCE, writing in the book *Hellenica*, book 7, section 1, and verse 18, talks about the use of the Celts as mercenaries in 367 BCE by the Lacedeamonians [Spartans].[149]

Roman Literary Sources

In this section, I will list the Roman sources of information about the Druids and the Celts. Some of the authors, such as Julius Caesar, need to be read with a critical eye. With Caesar, we know that he was writing his books while at war with the Germans and Gauls and therefore was likely using them as propaganda to back his war effort. Even when he is fairly accurate, you still need to consider why he was writing as he did.

This list does not cover all Roman authors who talk about the Druids or the Celts, there just isn't enough room in the book, but it does cover a good portion of them. As you move along this branch of the "Path of Druidry" and research further on your own, I am sure that you will find many others.

Ammianus Marcellinus, who lived from about 330 to 391 CE, writing in the *Roman History*, in book 15, section 9.4, talks about what the Druids said of the people in Gaul and where they came from: beyond the Rhine river and from outlaying islands. Book 15, section 9.8 tells that the Druids believed, as Pythagoras did, that the soul was immortal.[150]

Arrian (a.k.a. Lucius Flavius Arrianus), who lived from 80 to 160 CE, in the work *Anabasis of Alexander*, Book 1, sections 1.4.6 to 1.5.2, tells about Alexander and the Celts he met on the Ionian gulf [the Adriatic]. He reported that what they feared the most was that the sky would fall. He also reported that they were large in stature and brave.[151]

---

[148]Koch, *The Celtic Heroic Age*, 6.

[149]Xenophon, "Hellenica," trans. H. G. Dakyns, accessed February 7, 2012, http://www.brainfly.net/html/books/brn0191.htm.

[150]Ammianus Marcellinus, "The Roman History," trans. J. C. Rolfe, accessed February 7, 2012, http://penelope.uchicago.edu/Thayer/E/Roman/Texts/Ammian/home.html.

[151]Arrian, "The Anabasis of Alexander; or, The History of T...," trans. Chinnock, Edward James, accessed February 7, 2012, http://www.archive.org/stream/cu31924026460752#page/n53/mode/2up.

Decimus Magnus Ausonius was an early teacher and writer from Gaul, in what is now the Bordeaux region of France. He died about 395 CE and wrote about the Gaulish Druids in the work *Commem Professorum*, first in sections 4.7 to 4.10. Here he talks about how the Gaulish Druids are descended from Belenus, an early Gaulish god. Then in sections 10.22 to 10.30 he relates that the Druids are similar to those in Amorica [Brittany].[152]

Marcus Tullius Cicero, better known simply as Cicero, lived from 106 to 43 BCE. Writing in the work *De Divinatione*, in section 1.41.90, he tells about the Druid method of divination, mainly augury: predicting from natural events, birds, the sky, and sun etc.[153]

Hippolytus lived from 170 to 236 CE. He wrote in the work *Philosophumena* (*Refutation of All Heresies*), in section 1.22, on the Druids as philosophers and their use of divination and magic, saying:

> *The Celts hold the Druids as prophets and foretellers of future events because they can predict certain events by Pythagorean science and mathematics. . . . The Druids also use magic.*[154]

Gaius Julius Caesar, who lived from 100 (or 102) to 44 BCE gave us much of our information about the Druids. Most of this comes from *De Bello Gallica* (*The Gallic Wars*), written from 58 to 50 BCE. In section 6.11, he talks about the politics and customs of the Celts and how they have numerous factions not only among the tribes but even among the same families. Then in section 6.12, on the tribes, he continues to list their names. In section 6.13, he talks about how people of the tribes who do not abide by the Druids' decisions are prohibited from ritual sacrifice—the strongest punishment, other than banishment, classes of men [Druids and knights are the main ones], the Archdruid, yearly meetings held in the central region of Gaul where all assemble to hear judgments, and the Druids from Britain. In section 6.14, he talks about the Druids and their training [quoted at the start of this chapter], their rights [an exemption from war and taxes], types of knowledge they possess [of the stars, nature, and the gods, among others], and warriors in general being unafraid of death because of the Druids' teachings. In section 6.16, he talks about the Gauls and how their religion was based

---

[152]Koch, *The Celtic Heroic Age*, 29.

[153]Marcus Cicero, *The Nature of the Gods and, On Divination* (Amherst N.Y.: Prometheus Books, 1997).

[154]Hipppolytus, "Philosophumena; or, The Refutation of All Heres...," trans. F. Legge, 61–62, accessed February 7, 2012, *http://www.archive.org/stream/philosophumenaor01hippuoft#page/62/mode/2up.*

on sacrifice to the Gods and Spirits, their use of wicker men. In section 6.17, he discusses their deities, substituting Roman names for the local ones. In section 6.18, he tells how the Gauls believe that the start of the day occurs at the sunset of the previous evening, not at the sunrise, and how fathers did not feel it was manly to be seen in public with their young sons until they were old enough to go to war, and mentions the Gaulish God Dis. In section 6.19, he tells that men hold the "power of life and death" over their women and children, describes methods of gathering information [torture and any other way necessary], and funerals, where when a man had died, all of his prized possessions, including living animals, slaves, and favorite wives were killed and burned with him. Finally, in section 6.20, he discusses the magistrate's power to deal with any rumors or accusations.[155]

Justin (a.k.a. Marcus Junian(i)us Justinus), who lived in the second Century CE, writing in the Philippic Histories, in section 43.3, tells about a wedding custom among the Gauls where the groom was chosen by the bride on the day of the wedding from among the suitors present at the wedding feast. In section 43.5 he talks about a battle between the Gauls arid the Greeks. During the battle, the Greek commander had a dream of a Goddess and asked for peace. As he entered one temple in the city, he found the image of the Goddess he had dreamed of and sacrificed a golden torc [neck ring] to her.

Aelius Lampridius, dates unknown, writing in the work Alexander Severus (about the emperor who reigned 222- 35 CE), section 60, tells that a woman Druid gave Alexander a bad omen:

> *Furthermore, as he went to war a Druid prophetess cried out in the Gallic tongue, 'Go, but do not hope for victory, and put no trust in your soldiers.'*[156]

Livy (a.k.a. Titus Livius), who lived from about 59 BCE to 17 CE, described the origins of the city of Rome in the work The Early History of Rome. In volume 3, book 23, paragraph 31, he talks about the Gauls' battle strategy, in this case cutting most of the way through trees on both sides of a major road and then pushing the trees down on the enemy soldiers, and how they made a drinking cup for the temple from the head of one of the conquered enemy.[157]

---

[155]Caesar, Julius, "The Gallic Wars."

[156]Aelius Lampridius, "Historia Augusta - The Life of Severus Alexander," trans. David Magie, accessed February 7, 2012, *http://www.severusalexander.com/historia.htm*.

[157]Livy, "The History of Rome, Vol. III," trans. Reverend Canon Roberts, accessed February 7, 2012, *http://www.brainfly.net/html/books/brn0131c.htm*.

Lucan (a.k.a. Marcus Annaeus Lucanus), wrote between 39 and 65 CE, in the work *The Civil War* or *Pharsalia*, sections 1.490-510, on the Gods Taranis and Tuetates, two Gaulish Gods and the strange rites the Druids do.[158] And in sections 3.399-425, he talks about the Sacred Groves and their destruction by Caesar.[159]

Pliny the Elder (a.k.a. Gaius Plinius Secundus), who lived from 23 or 24 to 79 CE, in the work *Natural History*, section 16.24, writes on mistletoe, how it must be gathered and its uses against poisons (quoted above). In sections 24.103-104, he talks about *selagos*, an unknown plant: how it is gathered by "stealing" it while passing the right arm through the left sleeve of one's tunic, as well as a long list of other prohibitions, and its uses as a charm against evil and for eye diseases. In section 29.52, he talks about the "Druid's egg" or *anguinum*—supposedly something made from a sexual grouping of serpents, but thought by many scholars today to be the egg cases of whelks, he also tells where it comes from—balls of snakes in the summertime, and how it is used—to ensure successful litigations. Finally, in section 30.4, he writes about the Druids and their knowledge of magic, which was famous throughout the ancient world.[160]

Pomponius Mela, a Roman geographer, wrote the work *De Situ Orbis* from about 37 to 50 CE. In it, he describes the Druids and where they teach—in caves or hidden groves—and what—reincarnation, that the spirit is eternal and people will be born again in new bodies. He also discusses what they know about the stars and planets.[161]

Avienus Postumius Rufus Festus, a Roman poet who lived late in the mid-fourth Century CE, writes in the work *Ora Maritime*, on the inhabitants of the Mediterranean and the British Isles, describing them as vigorous and energetic.[162]

[158]Lucan, "OMACL: Pharsalia: Book I: The Crossing of the Rubicon," trans. Sir Edward Ridley, accessed February 7, 2012, *http://omacl.org/Pharsalia/book1.html*.

[159]Lucan, "M. Annaeus Lucanus, Pharsalia, Book 3, Line 399," accessed December 20, 2012, *http://www.perseus.tufts.edu/hopper/text?doc=Perseus%3Atext%3A1999.02.0134%3Abook%3D3% 3Acard%3D399*.

[160]Pliny the Elder, "Works of Pliny the Elder - Gaius Plinius Secundus," trans. John Bostock and H. T. Riley, accessed February 7, 2012, *http://www.brainfly.net/html/pliny_e.htm*.

[161]Koch, *The Celtic Heroic Age*, 25.

[162]Avienus, "Avienus - Fjor.net - eTOME," trans. JP Murphy, accessed February 7, 2012, *http://fjor.net/etome/grecoroman/avienus-iberia.html*.

Suetonius (a.k.a. Gaius Suetonius Tranquillus), who lived from about 69 to 140 CE, writes in the work *The Lives of the Caesars: Claudius*, section 25, about the Roman emperor who had his troops wipe out the Druids, whom Claudius called cruel and inhuman.[163]

Tacitus (a.k.a. Publius Cornelius Tacitus), who lived from about 55 to 120 CE, writes in the work *Annals*, section 14.30, about the invasion of Mona, which is modem Anglesey in Wales, and the destruction of the Druids as ordered by Claudius. In section 14.35 of the *Annals*, he talks about Boadicea [Boudica] and her daughters, referred to above, in the section on Greek authors, under Lucius Cassius Dio. Then in section 14.32 he talks about an omen in Camulodunum, modern Colchester in England, where a statue of "Winged Victory" fell over on its back. Also in the same work, section 12.40, 2-7, he tells of the capture of Caratacus, the king of the Catuvellauni and an early Celtic hero, and the leadership of Cartimandua, the warrior queen of the Brigantes, the largest tribe in Britain at the time. Then, in the work *Histories*, section 5.54, he talks about the Druids' interpretation of omens, during the Gauls' invasion of Rome, showing that the Gauls would be victorious. In addition, in Histories, sections 4.61 and 4.62 he talks about the prophet Veleda of the Germans. Many scholars today think that "Veleda" is actually a title meaning "seeress" for both the Germanic and Celtic tribes. Finally, in the Histories, section 3.45, he tells more about Cartimandua, giving more of her history. In the work, *Agricola*, section 16, he tells more about Boudica, giving more of her history.[164]

Valerius Maximus, writing about 35 CE in a handbook of illustrative examples of memorable deeds and sayings, *Factorum ac dictorum memorabilium libre IX*, talks about the Gauls and their belief in the immortality of the spirit.[165]

Flavius Vopiscus, writing in the fourth Century CE, in the work *Numerianus*, section 14, talks about a woman Druid prophesying to the Diocletian about becoming the emperor, which came to be soon afterward, and in the work *Aurelianus*, section 63.4.5, on women Druids prophesying to the emperor Claudius.[166]

---

[163]Suetonius, "The Lives of the Caesars," trans. J. C. Rolfe, accessed February 7, 2012, *http://www.brainfly.net/html/books/brn0140.htm*.

[164]Tacitus, "Publius Cornelius Tacitus," accessed February 7, 2012, *http://www.brainfly.net/html/tacitus.htm*.

[165]Valerius Maximus, *Memorable Deeds and Sayings: A Thousand Tales from Ancient Rome*, trans. Henry John Walker (Hackett Pub Co Inc, 2004), 59.

[166]Koch, *The Celtic Heroic Age*, 28.

Irish Literary Sources

We also gain much of our information about the Druids from early Irish sources (i.e., prior to the 1500s), but one problem with using them is that they all have a Christian gloss over them. In other words, they were written by Christian monks and most of the overtly Pagan references were taken out or referred to with euphemisms. Druids were referred to in many of the tales, such as the *Book of Invasions*, written around 1150 CE, which told of the histories of the tribes that had come into Ireland, *The Cattle Raid of Cúailnge* which tells of the invasion of Ulster by the armies of Queen Medb and her king, Ailill, and several others. These texts, written down in Old or Medieval Irish between 700 and 1200 CE, were the written record of an older oral tradition very likely dating from before the fifth Century CE.

In this section, I will list the major tales and give a location where translations can be found online. As with any online references, URLs do change over time, so if the link does not work, please try doing a search for the name of the tale on one of the major search engines.

There are two very good online sources for the early Irish texts: One is *www.maryjones.us/ctexts/index.html*, which is good for Irish, Welsh, and the Lives of the Saints; the other is the Corpus of Electronic Texts (CELT), located at *www.ucc.ie/celt/captured.html*. The following tales are all available on one of the two Web sites.

Annála Connacht **(The Annals of Connaught)** - This tale tells about the major happenings in the province of Connaught for the years 1224 to 1562 CE. From this work, we can delve into the lives of the people of Ireland and find out how they interacted with the Druids and invaders.[167]

Aislinge Meic Con Glinne **(The Vision of Mac Conglinne)** – Supposedly written in the province of Munster by Anier MacConglinne, a bard of the Onaght Glenowra tribe, in the late 11th or early 12th century CE, this tale tells about his visions as he was trying to overcome his gluttony and has many interesting details of the food and lives of the people, both nobles and the common folk. The descriptions of the food alone are worthwhile if you are working on recreating the life of the early Irish Celts for the SCA or other reenactment groups.[168]

---

[167]Unknown, "Annála Connacht," accessed February 8, 2012, *http://www.ucc.ie/celt/published/G100011/index.html*.

[168]Unknown, "Aislinge Meic Con Glinne," accessed February 8, 2012, *http://www.ucc.ie/celt/online/T308002/*.

Annals of the Four Masters - This set of manuscripts is the most complete and extensive of all the many different annals of Ireland. It holds the records of the happenings in Ireland from 2242 BCE (?) to 1616 CE. The earliest parts are very sparse and were "reconstructed" to cover the period from the creation of the world to the time they were actually written, with the history being filled in from the Bible instead of using the oldest oral legends. As such, the earliest part has to be ignored, but the later sections have proven to be fairly accurate.[169]

Bethu Brigte (The Life of Brigit) - This anonymous tale covers the life of Saint Brigit, with many of the stories also attributed to the Goddess Brigit, from her birth in a cowshed to a bondmaid of the Druid Dubthach to her later life as a nun and saint.[170]

Buile Suibhne (The Frenzy of Suibhne): Being the Adventures of Suibhne Geilt—author unknown. Another anonymous tale, this of a king who goes mad and goes to live in the woods. There are many bits of lore about the trees of the Ogham, the alphabet used by the Druids, hidden in here![171]

Cath Maige Tuired (The Second Battle of Mag Tuired) - This tale deals with the second battle between the Fomoire, the main tribe in Ireland before the *Tuatha Dé Danann* arrived, and the *Tuatha Dé Danann*, the tribe of people that many NeoPagans worship as deities today. At the start of the battle, each of the members of the tribe list what they will do during the battle, such as taking on many opponents or creating wondrous weapons to be used, and what skills they will bring to the battle, such as magic and strength and weapon skill.[172]

Chronicon Scotorum (The Chronicles of the Scots) - This tale was translated by William M. Hennessy & Gearóid Mac Niocaill, and is by an unknown author. It is a chronicle of Irish affairs from the earliest times to 1135 CE, with a supplement containing the events from 1141 to 1150 CE. Much of this work is based on the people that left Ireland to found Scotland.[173]

---

[169]Unknown, "Annals of the Four Masters," accessed February 8, 2012, *http://www.ucc.ie/celt/online/T100005A/*.

[170]Unknown, "Bethu Brigte - The Life of Brigit," trans. D. Ó hAodha, accessed February 8, 2012, *http://www.ucc.ie/celt/published/T201002/index.html*.

[171]Unknown, "Buile Suibhne," trans. J. G. O'Keeffe, accessed February 8, 2012, *http://www.ucc.ie/celt/published/T302018/index.html*.

[172]Unknown, "Cath Maige Tuired."

[173]Unknown, "Chronicon Scotorum," trans. William M. Hennessy & Gearóid Mac Niocaill, accessed February 8, 2012, *http://www.ucc.ie/celt/published/T100016/index.html*.

Deirdre of the Sorrows - In this love story, we learn about Deirdre, the wife of King Conchobar. She falls in love with Naisi, one of King Conchobar's warriors. Deirdre and Naisi along with his two brothers travel through the land, spending time in any area where they can hide, to escape from Conchobar. This is another tale with many interesting details about the life of the people that can allow us to fill in the picture of what life was like at the time. By doing this, we can see why and how the Mighty Kindred were worshipped then, allowing us to bring that form of worship back.[174]

***Lebor Gabala Erren* (The Book of Invasions)** – This is from the *Book of Leinster*, written in 1150 CE. This tale tells of the successive waves of tribes coming into Ireland, as was described previously. It is one of the primary sources for our information about the *Tuatha Dé Danann*, the children of Danu, whom many NeoPagans worship.[175]

***Táin Bó Cúalnge* (The Cattle Raid of Cúalnge)** - Written down about 1100 CE, this story is one of the primary tales of the Ulster Cycle, those tales concerned with the province of Ulster. This one talks about a battle between two beings that took place through several transformations. They started out as humans and ended up in the shape of a brown bull and a white bull. In it, we hear of Queen Medb and her husband, Ailill, and the hero Cú Chulainn, with his skill at battle, and learn many fascinating details about the lives of the people.[176]

The Fate of the Children of Lir – This is another one of the primary tales, those tales that give us such a wealth of information about the Irish. Transformed by their stepmother Aoife, the four children spend the rest of their lives living as swans on three of the lakes of Ireland, three hundred years on Loch Derravaragh, three hundred years on Straits of Moyle, and three hundred years at the Isle of Inish Glora. Along with being a wonderful story, this tale also teaches us of the magic of the Druids.[177]

Along with the tales listed above, we can gain many useful bits of information on the Druids and the Celts from reading the works dealing with the lives of the saints. Even though the books on the saints' lives

[174]Unknown, "Deirdre," trans. Douglas Hyde, accessed February 8, 2012, *http://www.ucc.ie/celt/published/T301020/index.html*.

[175]Unknown, "Táin Bó Cúalnge from the Book of Leinster," trans. Cecile O'Rahilly, accessed February 8, 2012, *http://www.ucc.ie/celt/online/T301035/*.

[176]Ibid.

[177]Unknown, "The Children Of Lir."

are told from a Christian point of view, we can learn a lot by seeing what the saints railed against in their battles with the Pagan forces, what powers the Druids they faced possessed, and what rituals celebrating the Old Ways were held on special days.

Welsh Literary Sources

Another good source of material on the Druids comes from early Welsh manuscripts written down by Christian monks in Britain in the 1300s and 1400s. We run into the same problem with this material as with the Irish: the Christian recorders put their own glosses on the tales they copied and took out the overt Pagan references. The Welsh records do show that the oral tradition, which had kept the tales alive, persisted from an early date. Some of this material appears to have been composed in the early sixth and seventh centuries CE, and were still being told the same way when they were written down seven or eight hundred years later.

The main source of Welsh information about the Druids is the *Mabinogion*. This is a collection of eleven individual tales, divided into *The Four Main Branches, The Native Tales,* and *The Three Romances. The Four Main Branches* are: *Pwyll - Lord of Dyfed, Branwen, the Daughter of Llyr, Manawyddan, the Son of Llyr,* and *Math, the Son of Mathonwy. The Native Tales* are: *Lludd and Llefelys, The Dream of Macsen Wledig, Culhwch and Olwen,* and *The Dream of Rhonabwy.* And *The Three Romances* are: *Owain* or *The Lady of the Fountain, The History of Peredur,* and *Geraint and Enid.*

There are several translations of the *Mabinogion* available, with Lady Charlotte E. Guest, Jeffrey Gantz, Gwyn Jones, and Patrick K. Ford being the principal translators. In my opinion, the Patrick Ford version is the best and most accurate based on the references to it from noted Celtic scholars . The main problem is that none of the translations have all eleven tales in them, so to do a real study of them you need to have all four translations. You will also find many books dealing with the individual stories of the *Mabinogion.* Many of these are very interesting and worthwhile, and several have been popularized from dissertations for advanced degrees, such as *"Culhwch and Olwen": An Edition and Study of the Oldest Arthurian Tale* by Rachel Bromwich and D. Simon Evans, published by the University of Wales Press in 1993, ISBN 070831127X.[178]

---

[178]Rachel Bromwich, *Culhwch and Olwen: an Edition and Study of the Oldest Arthurian Tale* (Cardiff: Univ. of Wales Press, 1992).

As noted below, there are many other stories from Welsh literature that give us background material on the Druids and the people of the land. Along with the Web site located at *http://www.maryjones.us/ctexts/index.html*, mentioned in connection with Irish sources, another very good online resource is the Internet Medieval Sourcebook, located at the Fordham University Center for Medieval Studies. Their Web site is *http://www.fordham.edu/halsall/sbook.asp*.[179]

The Life of Gildas - Written between 1130 and 1150 CE by Caradoc of Llancarfan, a Welsh historian, this tale deals heavily with the life of Arthur and his struggles to be declared king by the people.[180]

De Excidio Britanniae (Concerning the Ruin of Britain) - Written by St. Gildas, one of the primary authors about early British life, in the sixth Century CE does not mention Arthur at all but does mention Ambrosius Aurelianus, the Roman given rule over all of Britain. In this tale, St. Gildas talks about the wickedness that is spreading over the land.[181]

Historia Brittonum - This was written by Nennius, an early British historian, about 835 CE. This work is one of the best sources for information on Arthur, but it has been said by some scholars that Nennius was "very inventive" in his retelling. Still he did have access to texts that are no longer available—we no longer even have the names for them, so his work should be read with "the BS meter fully on."[182]

Black Book of Carmarthen - This is the oldest manuscript written in Welsh, dating from the middle of the thirteenth Century CE. This manuscript has a lot of information on Arthur, Merlin, and other figures from the Arthurian tales.[183]

White Book of Rhydderch - Written about 1325 CE, the manuscript contains the oldest complete texts of ten of the eleven *Mabinogion* tales.

---

[179]Halsall, Paul, "Internet Medieval Sourcebooks," accessed February 8, 2012, *http://www.fordham.edu/halsall/sbook.asp*.

[180]Caradoc of Llancarfan, "The Life of Gildas," trans. Hugh Williams, accessed February 8, 2012, *http://www.fordham.edu/Halsall/basis/1150-Caradoc-LifeofGildas.asp*.

[181]Gildas Bandonicus, "Concerningthe Ruin of Britian," trans. J. A. Giles & Alan Lupack, accessed February 8, 2012, *http://www.fordham.edu/Halsall/source/gildas.asp*.

[182]Nennius, "Historia Brittonum," trans. J. A. Giles, accessed February 8, 2012, *http://www.fordham.edu/halsall/basis/nennius-full.asp*.

[183]Multiple, "The Black Book of Carmarthen," accessed February 8, 2012, *http://www.maryjones.us/ctexts/bbcindex.html*.

The *White Book* also provides the earliest texts for many other early Welsh tales.[184]

Red Book of Hergest - Written between 1375 and 1425 CE, this is a collection of early Welsh material, including many of the *Mabinogion* tales, a selection of early Welsh proverbs, an early herbal, and others. Much of it is starting to be online in translation.[185]

Archaeological Sources

Much of Celtic archaeological evidence comes from inscriptions on statues and references on metal plates. Two "curse tables" have been found in France, each of which describes a Druid (?—this is still being debated by scholars) ritual. The texts from both of these, the Tablet of Chamalieres, dated about 50 CE, and the Tablet of Larzac, dated about 90 CE, can be found in *The Celtic Heroic Age*, edited by John T. Koch. Written in an early Italic language, the Tablet of Chamalieres has been translated to read:

> *I. I beseech the very divine, the divine Maponos Avernatis by means of that magic tablet: quicken[?] us, i.e., those [named below] by the magic of the underworld Spirits[?]:*
>
> *II. C. Lucios, Floros Nigrinos the invoker, Aemilios Paterinos, Claudios Legitumos, Caelios Pelignos, Claudios Pelignos, Marcios Victorinos, Asiaticos son of A00edillos.*
>
> *III. And it is the destiny of the Victor to which they shall be destined [or and it is the oath of the Strong One that they shall swear]; the centre—when he sows it—[it] shall be whole; [and] I right the wrong [:] blindly[;] thus [?] by means of this tablet [of incantation?] I shall see what shall be. By Lugus I prepare them; by Lugus I prepare them; by Lugus I prepare them, by Lugus.[186]*

Other archaeological evidence can be found in the grave goods of the people that who were buried in the large burial mounds and from excavations of their villages and towns, such as around London and other early towns on the British Isles and in Europe. There are many popular books available dealing with this type of evidence, such as *The Druids* by Steward Piggott and *Pagan Celtic Britain* by Dr. Anne Ross, so I will not be dealing further with this material in this book.

---

[184]Jones, Mary, "White Book of Rhydderch," accessed February 8, 2012, *http://www.maryjones.us/jce/rhydderch.html.*

[185]Jones, Mary, "The Red Book of Hergest," accessed February 8, 2012, *http://www.maryjones.us/ctexts/hindex.html.*

[186]Koch, *The Celtic Heroic Age*, 3.

Chapter 9

When You No Longer Want to Be Solitary

Theremay come a time in your journey along the Path of Druidry when you feel the need to be with other like-minded people. There are several ways to do this. First, you can investigate the Druid groups listed in this chapter and decide whether any of them resonate with your personal beliefs or strike you as worthy of further exploration. Many of them have sites on the Internet and that is a good way to learn about their beliefs. We are lucky to live at a time when the ways of the Druids are widespread, and there are groves in many areas. If there are no groves near you, most organizations will gladly assist you in forming a local grove or help you work on your studies over the Internet.

Another approach is to form a group in your town to study the ways of the Celts, if you find others who share your interests. Along with group study, consider taking courses at a local college or university in the fields of History, Celtic Studies, or Comparative Religion. Among your classmates you may find others who feel as you do. However you find colleagues, the process of working with others, sharing knowledge of our Ancestors, and worshipping the Shining Ones together, increases our awareness of the Kindred.

Ár nDraíocht Féin (ADF)

Ár nDraíocht Féin is the Druid church that I led for nine years. Its name, pronounced "arn ree-ocht fane," is modern Irish for "our own Druidism" and is as well, a play on words for "our own magic." Most people call it ADF. As an organization, we allow our groves to worship pantheons of deities, from Irish to Norse to Roman to Vedic, as long as they are from the Indo-European peoples. We understand that the term

Druid is a Celtic term, but feel that all of the Indo-European peoples followed the "Path of Druidry" even though they had different names for their priests.

This organization is primarily a church that follows the "Path of Druidry", a way of lifelong learning and worship of the Kindred. The Archdruid leads ADF's Mother Grove, which acts as its board of directors. The function of the Mother Grove is comparable to most nonprofit organization's board of directors.

Other officers who are appointed include the Administrator, the Treasurer, the Chronicler, the Store Manager, and the Office Manager. The Archdruid, Administrator and Office Manager hold the only paid positions in ADF. The Office Manager enters information into our membership database and performs all the office work associated with the corporation at ADF's international office, located in Tucson, Arizona. Solitaires, traditionally almost half of our members, are ADF members who live in areas where there are no other ADF members, or individuals who choose not to participate in the local groves in their area. Much of the activity in ADF is conducted online, and solitaires with computer access enjoy a large online support network even if they do not participate in any grove's activities. This support network can help immensely in your growth on the "Path of Druidry."

A new subgroup has been formed within ADF called "The Solitary Druid Fellowship (SDF). This subgroup of ADF has liturgy written specifically for solitaries, and seeks to create the experience of "congregation in solitude" through the adoption of a shared liturgical practice. It was started by Teo Bishop and is now facilitated by Kristin McFarland, and can be found at *http://www.solitarydruid.org/*.[187]

An ADF member who finds two other people interested in joining ADF may form a protogrove. Members of the protogrove are encouraged to find others who are interested in our organization, and if they succeed, they are allowed to move to the next level, the provisionally chartered grove.

The Grove Organizing Committee can charter a provisionally chartered grove whenever three protogrove members are willing to sign a charter application and do the work necessary to keep the grove active.

---

[187]Teo Bishop, "Solitary Druid Fellowship," accessed December 19, 2012, *http://www.solitarydruid.org/*.

Provisionally chartered groves are required to hold open public rituals for each of the eight High Days and to meet at least twice monthly to study and practice our form of Druidism. They are also required to perform some type of community service in their area at least once each quarter.

When a provisionally chartered grove has been in existence for three years, has had at least nine voting ADF members for the past two years, one of whom is recognized by ADF as a Clergy person, it can apply to become a fully chartered grove. ADF is a nonprofit corporation registered in the state of Delaware and has 501(c) (3) tax-exempt status as a church in the United States. Work has also begun to gain official recognition as a church in Canada as well.

Other Druid Resources

Along with ADF, there are numerous Druid coalitions, organizations, and networking groups that meet only on the Internet. Many Web sites of interest to Druids offer resources for meeting others involved in the Path of Druidry. In addition to my own Web site, *www.skipellison.us*, there are many others that maintain listings of Druid groups or Druid-related sites including:

www.neopagan.net/CurrentDruidGroups.html, the site of Isaac Bonewits, the founder of ADF, who was a popular NeoPagan author and lecturer. He passed away on 8/12/2010, but his website is being maintained, but not updated.

The Druid Network, the largest Druid networking organization, located at *http://druidnetwork.org/en/community*. More information about their organization is included in the section on Networking Only Groups.

The Witches Voice, one of the best NeoPagan Web sites on the planet, is located at *www.witchvox.com/lx/lx_druidic.html*. For all of the organizations below, if no source is given, the material is from their website.

Druid Coalitions

Druid coalitions are of comparatively recent origin. They are associations of people following many different Paths of Druidry who join together for learning and companionship. Most of the groups have formed within the past five years in the U.S., but U.K. groups have been around much longer. Along with the groups listed below, there is an e-mail group for people interested in forming new coalitions: *groups.yahoo.com/group/druidCI*.

ArkOkla Druids

Web site: *arkokla_druids.tripod.com*

E-group: *groups.yahoo.com/group/arkokladruids*

A group of students of Druidism and Celtic Reconstructionism who live within driving distance of west-central Arkansas, drawn from various organizations and orders that meet casually and more formally for seasonal rites in person. The e-group, ArkOkla Druids, can be contacted for information.

California Druids

E-group: *http://groups.yahoo.com/group/CA-Druids/*

California Druids seeks to facilitate different Druid groups helping each other with local projects throughout the state. It also provides a contact point for individuals seeking involvement in a local Druid group, produces a calendar of Druidic and Celtic events in the state, and performs social work.

Canadian Druid Fellowship

E-group: *http://groups.yahoo.com/group/Canadian_Druid_Fellowship/*

This is a group for those who follow the Path of Druidry that live in Canada. It is a very active group.

Celtic Druids of Austin

E-group: *http://groups.yahoo.com/group/AustinCelticDruidism/*

This is an e-group located on Yahoo that was formed to help facilitate Celtic focus Groves in the Austin area.

Christian Druids

E-group: *http://groups.yahoo.com/group/christiandruids/*

This is an e-group for people who follow the path of Christianity as well as one of the philosophical orders of Druidry. It appears to be a very active group.

Druids of Texas

E-group: *http://groups.yahoo.com/group/DruidsOfTexas/*

Druids of Texas was begun by Judith Prueitt to provide a comfortable online meeting place for those interested in and devoted to Druidism in Texas. It remains one of the oldest Druid lists in the area, and its members include Texans and Druids from across the U.S. and internationally who are interested in and connected to the unique and independent spirit of the Texas Druidic community.

Iowa Druid Coalition (IDC)

E-group: *http://groups.yahoo.com/group/iowadruidry/*

This is a group for all Druids, of any organization, that live in Iowa.

Pacific Northwest Druid Coalition

E-group: *http://groups.yahoo.com/group/PNWDC/*

The e-groupon Yahoo is formed for people who follow the Path of Druidry and live in the Pacific Northwest. They define the Pacific Northwest as Northern California, Oregon, Washington state, and British Columbia.

South Central Druid Coalition

Web site: *http://scdruidcoalition.tripod.com/southcentraldruidcoalition/id2.html*

The Coalition serves Texas, Arkansas, Oklahoma, Mis-souri, Louisiana and friends. It works to provide greater visibility for Druidism in these regions, provide networking opportunities and con-tacts for those on or wishing to be on the Path of Druidry, provides support for the projects of various orders and organ-izations, and sponsors events.

South East Druid Coalition—USA

E-group: *http://groups.yahoo.com/group/SEDC-USA/*

The intention of the SEDC-USA (Southeast Druid Coalition-USA) is to facilitate, on a regional level, different Druidic groups helping each other with local projects, provide a contact point for individuals seeking involvement in local Druidic groups, produce a regional calendar of Druidic and Celtic events, as well as to make a difference in the region by doing social work and seeking a voice in ecological matters within the region. The SEDC-USA also hopes to help in the establishment of state Druidic coalitions in the region. Open to all people on a Druidic path in NC, SC, Virginia, Georgia, Florida, Alabama, and eastern Tennessee.

Druid Organizations

The following organizations accept new members. Most have an active presence on the Internet.

Ancient Order of Druids in America (AODA)

Web site: *http://www.aoda.org/*

Founded in 1912 and rooted in the Druid Revival of the eighteenth and nineteenth centuries, the Ancient Order of Druids in America provides an opportunity for modern people to experience the teachings and practices of Druidry in today's world. AODA understands Druidry as a path of nature spirituality and inner transformation founded on personal experience rather than dogmatic belief. It welcomes men and women of all national origins, cultural and linguistic backgrounds, and affiliations with other Druidic and spiritual traditions. Ecological awareness and commitment to an earth-honoring lifestyle, celebration of the cycles of nature through seasonal ritual, and personal development through meditation and other spiritual exercises form the core of its work, and involvement in the arts, sciences, and esoteric studies are among its applications and expressions.[188]

Anderida Gorsedd

Web site: *http://www.anderidagorsedd.org/Anderida_Gorsedd/Home.html*

This is an eclectic Druid group that holds regular open rituals and camps in Sussex, in southern England. Facilitated by Damh the Bard and Cerri Lee, the group is open to all who bring a warm heart and open mind.

Avalon Druid Order (ADO)

Web site: *http://www.avalondruidorder.org/index.html*

Over the ages, the Avalon Mystery Tradition has amassed a daunting body of wisdom and lore far beyond what can be learned in one lifetime by any one person or group. Thus, contemporary Avalonian groups

---

[188]John Michael Greer, "Fwd: Fwd: A Piece About Your Organization for My Book," December 22, 2012 Used with permission.

tend to found their spiritual practices on specific Avalonian archetypes and eras, forming Tradition branches not unlike the denominations of mainstream religions; our spiritual focus is the "Faery" (native) Druidry of the Age of the Mothers, in the time before the Celts. Avalon's is a re-emerging Tradition, whose isolated adherents were reunited only recently through the web-working of the Celtic Sisterhoods; a reunion which opened the way to the very roots of Avalon's wisdom. Avalon Druid Order (ADO) is a product of this reflowering of Avalonian Tradition and Avalon's root wisdoms form the basis for our spiritual teachings and practice.[189]

Berengaria Order of Druids

Web site: *http://www.berengariaorder.co.nr/*

The Order's name comes from the classic Star Trek episode "This Side of Paradise," in which Spock refers to the planet Berengaria, "where there be dragons." The Order is dedicated to the aims, ideals and whatever else of Star Trek, Babylon 5, and other sci-fi that takes its fancy.[190]

Black Mountain Druid Order

Web site: *http://www.bmdo.org/*

The Black Mountain Druid Order was founded in 1997. Their purpose from the website is:

> *There are two major schools of thought in modern Druidry. One believes that Druids should try to be as authentic as possible in reconstructing the original Druid path by painstakingly studying history and archaeology for clues. The other is more experiential and believes that Druidry is a more inner, individual path. This school teaches that whatever is true for you as you walk the path is the 'true' Druidry. Since the 'True Druidry' of our ancestors is lost to antiquity, neither of these schools of thought can lay claim to representing true historical Druidry. In this sense, we are all Reconstructionists. Black Mountain Druid Order strives to strike a balance between these two schools of thought by learning from the past while focusing on the future. Our philosophy is to try to remain as free of dogma as possible. By doing so we allow for new experience and insight. We use the tools and knowledge of the past to find our way to the future. It is*

---

[189]"Avalon Druid Order," accessed December 19, 2012, *http://www.avalondruidorder.org/index.html* Used with permission.

[190]"Berengaria Order Of Druids Website," accessed December 19, 2012, *http://www.berengariaorder.co.nr/*.

our belief that if the <u>Gods and Goddesses</u> are real, then they will guide us as we recreate Druidry; and if the Gods and Goddesses aren't real, and we're just making this up as we go along, then what was done in the past doesn't matter anyway as long as the rituals have meaning for us now.[191]

British Druid Order

Web site: *http://www.cobdo.org.uk/*

Contact: Liz Murray, Liaison Officer, BM Oakgrove, London WC1N 3XX, UK (An SAE would be much appreciated.) For an up-to-date list of CoBDO members, please click the 'Members' button on the website.

The Council developed out of discussions between four Druid Orders, some of whose members met at the Summer Solstice of 1988, at Stonehenge. That year saw unpleasant scenes following the imposition of a four mile exclusion zone around the Henge to prevent those who had previously attended an annual free festival there from gaining access to the site. These Orders decided to meet regularly to discuss problems surrounding Stonehenge and other issues of mutual interest. Quarterly meetings began in February 1989 and over the next few years several other groups joined us. By 1995/1996 the Heads of three Orders, in particular, had been vociferous in pursuing the issue of access to Stonehenge. Subsequently, especially due to LAW and GODS, meetings were set up with English Heritage to bring together interested parties at a 'Round Table'. These discussions resulted in free and open access to the Stones being restored for the Midsummer dawn in 2000 and yearly since then.[192]

Charnwood Grove

Web site: *http://www.charnwoodgrove.org/*

The Grove is a group of Pagans, based in the east Mid-lands of the U.K., from various traditions and backgrounds, who meet to celebrate the eight seasonal festivals. Their focus is celebratory, and their rites, while encompassing many different approaches to spiritual expression, are conducted within the Druidic tradition.

---

[191]"Home Page of the Black Mountain Druid Order," accessed December 19, 2012, *http://www.bmdo.org/* Used with permission.

[192]From personal correspondence from Liz Murry dated 4/2/04.

Comardia Druvidiacta (a.k.a. Fellowship of the Men of Greater Ireland/Nemeton Dearraich OBOD Grove)

Web sites: *www.Keltia.de or www.KultURgeister.de* (both in German)

The program's druidic teaching is based on traditional lore and includes theoretical as well as practical training. Its aim is to understand the inner self and nature and to give people the opportunity to develop their spiritual, emotional, physical, and intellectual potential.

Comhaltacht-Draiocht

Web site: *http://www.comhaltacht-draiocht.org/*

This is a religious fellowship that meets to practice Draiocht, or *Gnatha na Sinsear*. Draiocht means Druidry or Druid-way, *Gnatha na Sinsear* means ancestral traditions.

Druidic Association of North America (DANA)

Web site: *http://danagrove.wordpress.com/*

DANA is a New Hampshire non-profit corporation formed for the purpose of Celtic Reconstructionist Druidic Practice honoring the Kindred.

Druid Clan of Dana

Web site: *http://www.fellowshipofisis.com/druidclanofdana.htm*

The Druid Clan of Dana (DCD) is a Foundation-Center Society of the Fellowship of Isis. It was established by Olivia and Lawrence Durdin-Robertson in 1992. Groups within the DCD are organized into Groves, and each Grove is founded by an Archdruidess or Archdruid of the Clan. The Grove Goddess (or Goddess and God) may be of any race or tradition. Archdruid/esses are qualified to act as Grove preceptors for those who wish to attain DCD Initiations. There is an established Liturgy and Initiation structure for the Druid Clan of Dana, but there is no one curriculum. Archdruid/esses, through inspiration from their own dedicatory Deity (or Deities) produce their own unique training program.

Druid Order of the Sacred Grove

Web site: *http://groups.yahoo.com/group/Druid_Order_SG/?tab=s*

The Druid Order of the Sacred Grove was founded on Beltane, May 1st, 2003, by Jaron McLlyr in Las Vegas, Nevada along traditional

Druidic lines. According to the "Great Charter" of the Order, it exists "to revive and rediscover the Druidic mysteries, further the Druidic communities and provide a safe and nurturing environment for its members; based in the teachings and wisdom of the Celtic Reconstruction." As an "Order," it follows more structured lines than most other types of Pagan group. It is administered by the Founding Grove Council headed by the Keeper of the Sacred Oak Bard Ollaire Rose Wolfbane, the Keeper of the Sacred Well Bard Ollaire Airmid McLlyr and the Keeper of the Sacred Flame Arch Druid Jaron McLlyr. An Ordination Board oversees the training and ordination of the state recognized clergy. The Druidic College Board directs the educational program and sets criteria for advancement.[193]

Fellowship of Druidism for the Latter Age (FoDLA)

Web site: *http://www.fodla.org/index.html*

FoDLA is a church composed of American polytheistic Pagans following the path of *Draíocht Nua* or Neo-Druidism. It started as an offshoot of ADF, but its members follow only a Celtic Path.

Gaelic Druid Order of the Southern Cross

Web site: *http://gdosc.bravepages.com/druidorder.html*

An Australian-based order, with a growing worldwide membership, focused along traditional lines. This group promotes the belief that a connection to one's ancestry is important and that the study of the Gaelic language and culture forms an integral part of bardic studies. People of all racial back-grounds are welcome.

Genesis Order of Druids

Web site: *http://druidnetwork.org/affiliatedgroups/groves/genesis*

This is a group that was formed in 2008 in the UK to concentrate on learning the real meaning of Druidry. They also hold public rituals and meetings, and have a yearlong training program.

Glastonbury Order of Druids

Web site: *http://www.glastonburyorderofdruids.com/*

The Order acknowledges Glastonbury as the fountain-head of three major religions—Wicca, Druidry, and Christianity—and Stonehenge as

---

[193]Glenn Hall, "Druid Order of the Sacred Grove," June 4, 2006 Used with permission.

the omphalos of the natural ecology of Britain. This group encourages practice of the Druid arts appropriate to the spiritual development of those who work with the Order.

Gorsedd of Bards of *Caer Abiri*

Web site: *http://www.druidry.co.uk/getting-involved/the-gorsedd-of-bards-of-caer-abiri/*

Now meeting at Avebury, on the Spring and Autumn Equinoxes, the Gorsedd of Bards of *Caer Abiri* conducts rituals of gentle "folk" Druidry, its power coming from the dedication of each person attending, the acknowledgment of community, and the reverence for Spirits of Place and for the power of heritage.

Gorsedd of Bards of *Caer Pugetia* (a.k.a. Bards of Turtle Island)

Web site: *http://www.caerpugetia.com/*

A group of some 250 bards in the Seattle area who hold *Gorsedds* (bardic meetings) and *Eistedfodd* (offerings of poetry, song, and storytelling) eight times a year in local natural holy places with ancient trees and forests. Their Goddess is personified as Pugetia, and its God Pugetius, or Akrasentansit, representing the male and female powers of Puget Sound.

Gorsedd of Bards of *Cor Gawr*

Web site: *http://www.facebook.com/groups/56826550944/*

The Gorsedd of Bards of *Cor Gawr* was first inaugurated at Stonehenge in the late 1990s. Since then the Gorsedd has regularly gathered at the temple at the festivals of Midsummer and Midwinter. Because the Access Committee has now allowed for the temple to be completely open overnight and for the dawn of the Summer Solstice, the Gorsedd of *Cor Gawr*, meeting closer to the traditional date of Midsummer (usually 24 June), offers members of the Druid and Pagan community an opportunity for focused ritual, meditation and celebration with a smaller group. As it works on a Special Access pass, the *Cor Gawr* rituals are ticketed events, with a number limit of 100 people.

Green Mountain Druid Training (GMDO)

Web site: *http://greenmountaindruidorder.org/*

This order was created by Ivan McBeth and Fearn Lickfield and became active in the spring of 2006. It is a mystery based school located in Vermont. It works to align its students with the power of the Earth and to heal and teach.

Henge of Keltria

Web site: *www.keltria.org*

Keltrian Druidism was founded in 1985 by members of Ar nDraiocht Fein who were looking for a Celtic-specific Path. The Henge of Keltria is a US based group that honors the Ancestors, reveres the Spirits of Nature, and worships the Gods and Goddesses of Celtic heritage. The group oversees groves and study groups in several states. Individuals who practice Keltrian Druid Ritual in a solitary environment may meet with other individuals and study groups.

Hermetic Druidry

Contact: P.O. Box 2101, Byron Bay, New South Wales 2481 Australia.

This grove is widely known in the southern hemisphere, having been responsible for inaugurating and hosting the Druid Assembly in Australia, enabling initiates of Druidry to celebrate together for the first time across the expansive region of New South Wales. Druidry in Australia presents the opportunity to live the ancestral paths in new terrain. Hermetic Druidry maintains the core knowledge of its Druidic line, combined with ever-increasing knowledge of the Spirits of Time and Place there.

Insular Order of Druids (IOD)

Web site: *http://www.lugodoc.demon.co.uk/Druids/IOD.htm*

From their website, we learn that this group organized seasonal festivals for the Pagan community, as well as handfastings, naming and other Rites of Passage. While the original group disbanded in June of 2005, new groups are forming in the Portsmouth area of the UK.

Kengerzhouriezh Drouizel an Dreist-Hanternoz (KDAD)

Web site: *http://www.bretagne-celtic.com/rencontre_myrdhin.htm* (French)

Placing an emphasis on the philosophical as well as the esoteric aspects of Druidry, the group's references are the Irish mythological accounts and all the texts of the Celtic tradition. Members always meet outdoors and celebrate the eight traditional festivals. Admission is by proposal and presentation by present members, after several applications. Women are welcomed. Work is performed in the Breton and French languages. Teaching is by oral transmission.

Kredenn Geltiek Hollvedel/Goursez Tud Donn

Web site: *http://www.druidisme.org/* (French)

Kredenn Geltiek Hollvedel (Breton for "Wideworld Celtic Creed") or *Goursez Tud Donn* ("Gathering of Ana's Folk in Breton"), was founded in 1936 by Raffig Tullou (died in 1990). The *Comardiia Druuidiacta Aremorica Uecorectus* (an Old Celtic designation meaning: "Armorican Druidical Fellowship of Strict Obedience"), the assembly of its clergy of Brittany and sister fellowships (of Quebec, Canada, America, Germany, Ireland and Northern Italy, Padana). Goals: the modern world is on an inevitable crash course towards catastrophe—a shared feeling—due mainly by all the forms of pollution secreted: mentally, intellectually, ecologically, and so on! Druidism hopes to defend its adepts against the effects of such a situation, and assure their survival, both physically and mentally, through the integral pagan reappropriation of ancestral "means," patiently crafted by past generations, henceforth the imperative for cultural survival.[194]

Loyal Arthurian Warband

Web site: *http://www.warband.org.uk/*

Initiation is by the Sword in all instances. The sword in question being Excalibur, the Sword of Britain, held in trust by Arthur the sword bearer. There are, in fact, three separate orders within the Loyal Arthurian Warband; the differences are fairly self explanatory. King Arthur Pendragon is the Titular Head and Chosen Chief of what has

---

[194]From their website.

[195]"The Loyal Arthurian Warband - Druid Network," accessed December 20, 2012, *http://druidnetwork.org/node/1000816.*

become known as the LAW Band, cLAW Band and Warband. Or as is oft times called Wizard, Witches and Warriors; each order being sworn to the ancient virtues of Truth, of Honor and of Justice.[195]

Llygedyn Grove

Web site: *http://www.llygedyngrove.com/*

Established in 1999 by Rev. Warren and Carolyne Kleinman, this grove was formed to serve the needs of the Central Texas community. It offers public rituals, potlucks and other ways for the community to grow.

Order of Bards, Ovates, and Druids (OBOD)

Web site: *http://www.druidry.org/*

One of the largest Druid Orders in the world, its method of teaching is via an experiential home learning course. A worldwide fellowship with more than six thousand mem-bers and eighty groups, members stay in touch by the monthly journal Touchstone. Four camps are held each year in the Vale of the White Horse in Wiltshire, England, and two assemblies are held on the Solstices at Glastonbury, as well as gatherings in Australia, New Zealand, and the U.S.

Phoenix Order Of Druids (POD)

Web site: *http://www.p-o-d.org.uk/*

This is a family based order from Liverpool, England. It is an offshoot from both King Arthur's Loyal Warband and the Insular Order of Druids that was formed in 2005. it is a teaching and learning order that meets monthly.

Reformed Druids of Gaia

Web site: *http://reformed-druids.org/*

The mission of the Reformed Druids of Gaia is to invoke a web of knowledge, mythos and experience that provides a framework for reconnecting with the Earth Mother, and regathering her progeny through tribal collectives consecrated to responsible conservatorship and progressive cognizance within the ever evolving tradition of Neo-Pagan Druidism. Their teaching Order is called the order of the Mithral Star, and more information can be found here - *http://mithrilstar.org/*.

Reformed Druids of North America

Web site: *http://apps.carleton.edu/student/orgs/druids/*

In 2004, the group consists of about forty groves and proto-groves in a loose confederacy, without a central grove; their focus is primarily on Nature, but eclectically draws inspiration from a vast array of cultures around the world. The RDNA has produced many magazines, established a massive international archive of materials from other groups, published several thousand pages of free anthologies of their own non-dogmatic (and often humorous) material, of which A Reformed Druid Anthology is the largest.

Stonehenge & Amesbury Druids (Aes Dana Grove)

Web site: *http://www.stonehenge-druids.org/index.html*

This group is one of the British groups that take the lead in organizing rituals held at Stonehenge and Amesbury.

The Druid Order of the Yew

Web site: *http://druidnetwork.org/br/yew*

The Order is a gathering of people brought together by the power of a shared intention. Membership is open to members of The Druid Network. Each applicant is asked to submit a Statement of Dedication, an expression of the individual's commitment to Druidry in terms of action.

The Gaelic Druid Order

Web site: *http://www.gaelicdruidorder.org/*

This is a group formed in the Scottish highlands, with a daughter grove in Australia. They work with nature and work to develop the spiritual potential of their members, using the three levels of the Druids: Bards, Ovates and Druids.

The Invisible Druid Order

Web site: *http://invisibledruidorder.net/*

Contact: P.O. Box 1060, Anoka, MN USA 55303-1060

The Order calls us to honor our relationship with ourselves, with each other, with the natural world, and with the Spirits. Its purpose is to foster women and men who exercise spiritual discipline; develop a constructive relationship with the Otherworld, and who make themselves useful to the world in which they live. The three guiding principles of the IDO are training of the mind, a reverence for nature and its source, and social responsibility.

The International Grand Lodge of Druidism
Web site: *http://www.igld.org/*

IGLD`s general aim is to create and further promote contact, friendship, and peace among peoples, members of Druidic Orders and nations worldwide and to extend Druidism to new countries. The members and Officers at all levels are committed to finding and following ways to achieve these goals. IGLD is a forum for the exchange of views and news on mutual activities and objectives; however members and affiliated societies must retain their autonomy. IGLD shall endeavor to coordinate the rituals of affiliated Orders and aim to exchange news between them. IGLD shall also encourage coordination between Orders in a region.

The New Order of Druids (NOD)
Web site: *www.druidcircle.net*

Some believe that present-day Druids are people who live with their minds in the past, and that the Druidic wisdom had its place in time only, and thus cannot be applied any more today. But in our current society, it may well turn out that this very same ancient wisdom will be our future.

The concept of the New Order of Druids was created by David Dom (Belgium) in 2002, and was opened in January 2003. The fundamental ideas on which we based this organ-ization, is to offer a totally free-of-charge alternative for people through the means of internet, with three main goals: to learn, to grow, to exchange.

The New Order of Druids (N.O.D. in short) is, in truth, a free online community Circle for people of all ages young and old, for both men and women, no matter where in the world you live. To this day, the New Order of Druids has members both male and female of all ages, from Europe, America, Australia and even Turkey.

The Order of Druids in Ireland

Web site: *http://www.wightdruids.co.uk/ODI.html*

The ODI was founded in 1993 and led the return of the Irish Druids to Tara. The head of the order is Archdruid Michael McGrath, who claims to be the Hereditary Druid of Munster.

The Order of White Oak

Web site: *http://www.whiteoakdruids.org/*

This modern Druidic order bases its beliefs and practices on what is known of the original faith and practices of the pagan Celts, using historical research and poetic inspiration to build a viable tradition. Membership is by invitation only.

The Sisterhood of Avalon

Web site: *www.sisterhoodofavalon.org*

The sisterhood is an international Celtic women's mysteries organization that seeks to balance intuitive wisdom with scholastic achievement.

Tuatha de Brighid

Web site: *http://www.tuatha-de-brighid.org/*

This clan of modern Druids seeks to find common ground amid all non -harmful spiritual loyalties and believes in the interconnectedness of all faiths. Brighid, who is both Goddess of the Gaels and Saint Brigid of the Christians, is a fitting matron for this endeavor, and its members are her folk.

United Ancient Order of Druids

Web site: *http://www.aod-uk.org.uk/home.htm*

The UAOD may be the oldest of the surviving Meso-Pagan Druid organizations.

Internet-Only Druid Groups

As the name suggests, these groups do not have physical locations, but operate strictly on the Internet.

Druidic Dawn, CIC

Web site: *http://www.druidicdawn.org/*

Druidic Dawn is an online group interested in networking and celebrating Druid diversity.

DruidNews Blog

Web site: *http://druidry.blogspot.com/*

This is a blog written by a Druid that includes news of interest to other Druids everywhere. Many of the articles are drawn from the U.K. press and are about various environmental issues; others report on the establishment of new Druid Orders. Readers' comments are encouraged.

Oaklight

Web site: *http://www.oaklight.org/*

This site is mainly a networking and resource for people following the Path of Druidry online. It features the blog of well known Druid teacher and author, Duir.

OBOD Oaks Group

E-group: *http://dir.groups.yahoo.com/group/OBOD_Oaks_III/*

In this Internet discussion group, everyone is a teacher and everyone a learner, sharing commentary on particular avenues of study and practical pursuits from which all may benefit.

The Solitary Druid Fellowship (SDF)

Web site: *http://www.solitarydruid.org/*

This subgroup of ADF has liturgy written specifically for solitaries, and seeks to create the experience of "congregation in solitude" through the adoption of a shared liturgical practice. It was started by Teo Bishop and now facilitated by Kristin McFarland. Membership is not necessary in order to participate in SDF's shared worship. The Fellowship provides free liturgies for each of the Eight High Days of the Pagan Wheel of the Year, each based on ADF's Core Order of Ritual. SDF seeks to create opportunities for solitaries to experience ritual celebration through a shared form with other solitaries across the globe.

The Summerlands, Inc.

Web site: *http://www.summerlands.com/*

A Celtic Pagan community dedicated to rediscovering, preserving, disseminating, and when necessary, recreating that which has been lost—the magic, history, customs, and religions of our Ancestors. The group worships and celebrates the old Gods and Goddesses in ways both ancient and new. The Summerlands online community serves the Pagan, Celtic and Druidic communities through its Summerlands Press Publishing Company, the Rowan Leaf Bookstore, and the Summerlands Druid Seminary. It was created by Searles and Deborah O'Dubhain.

Networking-Only Groups

Networking groups act as a resource for the community by maintaining up-to-date lists of Druid organizations, and making it easy for solitary members to reach out to others.

Irish Druid Network

Web site: *http://www.irishdruidnetwork.org/*

This site began in 2006, and is set up to bring together people from all over Ireland who follow the Path of Druidry. It is not affiliated with any group, but is there for all to use.

The Druid Network

Web site: *http://druidnetwork.org/*

The Network is an international organization bringing together Orders, groves and individuals, offering a forum for sharing skills, teachings, inspiration, and experience, and encouraging the creative active expression of living Druidry. The Druid Network is not an Order. It is effectively a clearinghouse for information about Druidry, including in its online directory Druidic organizations from all around the globe and providing details of public rituals, courses, and other resources useful to anyone on a Druid Path or just interested in Paganism in general. The membership area of the site gives details on affiliated groves and a database enables members to contact each other. There are also forums on various matters pertaining to Druidry.

The Witches' Voice

Web site: *http://www.witchvox.com/lx/lx_druidic.html*

I consider the Witches' Voice to be one of the best all around sites today for news of the Pagan community. They are up-to-the-minute in reporting, and cover everything of interests to Pagans of all persuasions. They are also a great networking site, and have pages to allow you to find any type of organizations you desire. The page listed above is the link to their page of Druid resources.

Other Web Sites of Interest to Druids

The following Web sites contain many interesting pages for those following the Path of Druidry. The subjects covered range from stone circles to historical research.

Ancient Scotland Tour

Web site: *www.stonepages.com/tour*

CELT: Corpus of Electronic Texts

Web site: *www.ucc.ie/celt/captured.html*

Celtic League

Web site: *http://www.celticleague.net/*

Columcille Megalith Park

Web site: *www.columcille.org*

IMBAS

Web site: *www.imbas.org* Contact: *imbas@imbas.org*

Irish Myth Concordance

Web site: *http://www.sacred-texts.com/bos/bos106.htm*

Mary Jones's Celtic Encyclopedia

Web site: *http://www.maryjones.us/jce/jce_index.html*

Mary Jones's Celtic Literature Collective

Web site: *http://www.maryjones.us/ctexts/index.html*

The Preserving Shrine

Web site: *http://www.seanet.com/~inisglas/*

Stone Pages

Web site: *http://www.stonepages.com/*

A Welsh Myth Concordance

Web site: *http://esoteric.2hav.net/articleviewer.php?artid=307*

Bibliography

Aelius Lampridius. "Historia Augusta - The Life of Severus Alexander." Translated by David Magie. Accessed February 7, 2012. *http:// www.severusalexander.com/historia.htm*.

Aldhouse-Green, Miranda. *Dictionary of Celtic Myth and Legend*. New York: Thames and Hudson, 1992.

Ammianus Marcellinus. "LacusCurtius • Ammianus Marcellinus — Book XXXI." Translated by Bill Thayer. Accessed January 19, 2012. *http:// penelope.uchicago.edu/Thayer/E/Roman/Texts/Ammian/31*.html*.

———. "The Roman History." Translated by J. C. Rolfe. Accessed February 7, 2012. *http://penelope.uchicago.edu/Thayer/E/Roman/Texts/Ammian/ home.html*.

Aristotle. "Nicomachean Ethics." Translated by Ross, W.D. Accessed January 31, 2012. *http://www.brainfly.net/html/books/brn0042.htm*.

———. "POLITICS." Translated by Jowett, Benjamin. Accessed January 31, 2012. *http://www.brainfly.net/html/books/brn0061.htm*.

Arrian. "The Anabasis of Alexander; or, The History of T..." Translated by Chinnock, Edward James. Accessed February 7, 2012. *http://www.archive.org/ stream/cu31924026460752#page/n53/mode/2up*.

Athenaeus of Naucratis. "Athenaeus: Deipnosophists - Book 13 (d)." Translated by C.D.Yonge. Accessed January 19, 2012. *http://www.attalus.org/old/ athenaeus13d.html*.

———. "The Literature Collection: The Deipnosophists, or, Banquet of the Learned of Athenæus (volume I): Book IV." Accessed January 31, 2012. *http:// digicoll.library.wisc.edu/cgi-bin/Literature/Literature-idx? type=turn&id=Literature.AthV1&entity=Literature.AthV1.p0252&q1=celts&pview=hide*.

"Avalon Druid Order." Accessed December 19, 2012. *http://www.avalondruidorder.org/index.html.*

Avienus. "Avienus - Fjor.net - eTOME." Translated by JP Murphy. Accessed February 7, 2012. *http://fjor.net/etome/grecoroman/avienus-iberia.html.*

"Berengaria Order Of Druids Website." Accessed December 19, 2012. *http://www.berengariaorder.co.nr/.*

Bonewits, Isaac. *Rites of Worship: a Neopagan Approach.* Miami Florida: Earth Religions Press, 2003.

Bonewits, Isaac. "Neopagan Net: Table of Contents / Site Map." Accessed January 19, 2012. *http://www.neopagan.net/Contents.html#PartEleven.*

Bonwick, James. *Irish Druids and Old Irish Religions.* New York: Dorset Press, 1986.

Brainfly, Inc. "Brainfly.Net." Accessed January 31, 2012. *http://www.brainfly.net/.*

"Brídeóg." Accessed November 29, 2012. *http://www.djibnet.com/photo/brideog/brideog-5415130689.html.*

"Brigid's Cross - Wikipedia, the Free Encyclopedia." Accessed November 29, 2012. *http://en.wikipedia.org/wiki/Brigid%27s_cross.*

Bromwich, Rachel. *Culhwch and Olwen: An Edition and Study of the Oldest Arthurian Tale.* Cardiff: Univ. of Wales Press, 1992.

Caesar, Julius. "The Gallic Wars." Translated by McDevitte, William Alexander and Bohn, W.S. Accessed January 31, 2012. *http://www.brainfly.net/html/books/brn0004.htm.*

———. "The Internet Classics Archive | The Gallic Wars by Julius Caesar." Translated by W. A. McDevitte and W. S. Bohn. Accessed January 19, 2012. *http://classics.mit.edu/Caesar/gallic.5.5.html.*

Callimachus. "Classical E-Text: CALLIMACHUS, HYMNS 4 - 6." Translated by Mair, A.W. Accessed January 31, 2012. *http://www.theoi.com/Text/CallimachusHymns2.html.*

Caradoc of Llancarfan. "The Life of Gildas." Translated by Hugh Williams. Accessed February 8, 2012. *http://www.fordham.edu/Halsall/basis/1150-Caradoc-LifeofGildas.asp.*

"Carmina Gadelica Vol. 1: II. Aimsire: Seasons: 70 (notes). Genealogy of Bride. Sloinntireachd Bhride." Accessed November 29, 2012. *http://www.sacred-texts.com/neu/celt/cg1/cg1074.htm.*

Bibliography

Cassius Dio. "Cassius Dio — Epitome of Book 62." Accessed January 19, 2012. *http://penelope.uchicago.edu/Thayer/E/Roman/Texts/Cassius_Dio/62*.html.*

Chadwick, Nora. *The Celts.* London: Penguin, 1991.

Cicero, Marcus. *The Nature of the Gods and, On Divination.* Amherst N.Y.: Prometheus Books, 1997.

Clement of Alexandria. "Logos Virtual Library: Clement of Alexandria: The Stromata." Translated by Wilson, Wiliam. Accessed January 31, 2012. *http://www.logoslibrary.org/clement/stromata/index.html.*

Dictionary.com. "Meanings and Definitions of Words." *Dictionary.com.* Accessed January 23, 2012. *http://dictionary.reference.com/.*

Diodorus Siculus. "LacusCurtius • Diodorus Siculus — Book V Chapters 19-40." Accessed January 31, 2012. *http://penelope.uchicago.edu/Thayer/E/Roman/Texts/Diodorus_Siculus/5B*.html.*

Diogenes Laërtius. "Lives of the Eminent Philosophers/Book I - Wikisource." Translated by Hicks, Robert Drew. Accessed January 31, 2012. *http://en.wikisource.org/wiki/Lives_of_the_Eminent_Philosophers/Book_I#Prologue.*

Egil Skallagrimsson. "Egil's Saga." Translated by Rev. W. C. Green. Accessed January 25, 2012. *http://www.northvegr.org/sagas%20annd%20epics/icelandic%20family%20sagas/egils%20saga/Index.html.*

Ellis, Peter. *The Druids.* Grand Rapids Mich.: W.B. Eerdmans Pub. Co., 1998.

Ellison, Skip. "Divination Books & Tools by Rev. Skip Ellison." Accessed January 25, 2012. *http://www.skipellison.us/dk/Divination_Main.html.*

"Eostre." Accessed April 8, 2013. http://www.englatheod.org/eostre.htm.

Gantz, Jeffrey. *The Mabinogion.* New York: Dorset Press, 1985.

Gildas Bandonicus. "Concerningthe Ruin of Britian." Translated by J. A. Giles & Alan Lupack. Accessed February 8, 2012. *http://www.fordham.edu/Halsall/source/gildas.asp.*

Glenn Hall. "Druid Order of the Sacred Grove," June 4, 2006.

Halsall, Paul. "Internet Medieval Sourcebooks." Accessed February 8, 2012. *http://www.fordham.edu/halsall/sbook.asp.*

Herodotus. "The History of Herodotus Vol. 1." Translated by Macaula, G.C. Accessed January 31, 2012. *http://www.brainfly.net/html/books/brn0098a.htm.*

Hipppolytus. "Philosophumena; or, The Refutation of All Heres..." Translated by F. Legge. Accessed February 7, 2012. *http://www.archive.org/stream/ philosophumenaor01hippuoft#page/62/mode/2up.*

"Home Page of the Black Mountain Druid Order." Accessed December 19, 2012. *http://www.bmdo.org/.*

Hornblower, Simon. *The Oxford Classical Dictionary.* 3rd ed. Oxford; New York: Oxford University Press, 1996.

Hutton, Ronald. *The Stations of the Sun: a History of the Ritual Year in Britain.* Oxford: Oxford University Press, 1997.

John Adlemann. "Brigit, Behind the Veil." *Oak Leaves,* January 1998.

John Michael Greer. "Fwd: Fwd: A Piece About Your Organization for My Book," December 22, 2012.

John Williamson. *The Oak King, the Holly King, and the Unicorn: The Myths and Symbolism of the Unicorn Tapestries.* Olympic Marketing Corp., 1986.

Jones, Mary. "The Red Book of Hergest." Accessed February 8, 2012. *http:// www.maryjones.us/ctexts/hindex.html.*

———. "White Book of Rhydderch." Accessed February 8, 2012. *http:// www.maryjones.us/jce/rhydderch.html.*

Kelly, Fergus. *A Guide to Early Irish Law.* Dublin: Dublin Institute for Advanced Studies, 1988.

Kia Marie Wolfe. *The Wheel of the Year,* n.d.

Koch, John. *The Celtic Heroic Age: Literary Sources for Ancient Celtic Europe and Early Ireland and Wales.* Malden Mass.: Celtic Studies Publications, 1995.

Kondratiev, Alexei. *The Apple Branch: a Path to Celtic Ritual.* Cork [Ireland]: Collins Press, 1998.

"Lebor Gabala Erenn." Accessed April 8, 2013. *http://www.maryjones.us/ctexts/ leborgabala.html.*

Livy. "The History of Rome, Vol. III." Translated by Reverend Canon Roberts. Accessed February 7, 2012. *http://www.brainfly.net/html/books/ brn0131c.htm.*

Loving More®. "Loving More Your #1 Resource for Polyamory." Accessed January 19, 2012. *http://www.lovemore.com/.*

Lucan. "M. Annaeus Lucanus, Pharsalia, Book 3, Line 399." Accessed December 20, 2012. *http://www.perseus.tufts.edu/hopper/text?doc=Perseus%3Atext% 3A1999.02.0134%3Abook%3D3%3Acard%3D399.*

Bibliography

———. "OMACL: Pharsalia: Book I: The Crossing of the Rubicon." Translated by Sir Edward Ridley. Accessed February 7, 2012. *http://omacl.org/Pharsalia/book1.html*.

MacKillop, James. *Dictionary of Celtic Mythology.* Oxford; New York: Oxford University Press, 1998.

Markale, Jean. *Women of the Celts.* 1st U.S. ed. Rochester, Vt.: Inner Traditions International, 1986.

McManus, Damian. *A Guide to Ogam.* Maynooth: An Sagart, 1997.

Multiple. "The Black Book of Carmarthen." Accessed February 8, 2012. *http://www.maryjones.us/ctexts/bbcindex.html*.

"Myths and Legends of the Celtic Race: Chapter I: The Celts in Ancient History." Accessed November 29, 2012. *http://www.sacred-texts.com/neu/celt/mlcr/mlcr01.htm*.

Nennius. "Historia Brittonum." Translated by J. A. Giles. Accessed February 8, 2012. *http://www.fordham.edu/halsall/basis/nennius-full.asp*.

Nilah Foxglove. "The Goddess Eostre and Spring Equinox." *Circle Network News*, 1992 1991.

O'Curry, Eugene. *Lectures on the Manuscript Materials of Ancient Irish History.* Portland, OR: Four Courts Press, 1995.

Occultopedia. "Scapulomancy - Scapulomancy, Divination by Shoulder-blade Bones - Occultopedia, the Occult and Unexplained Encyclopedia." Accessed January 23, 2012. *http://www.occultopedia.com/s/scapulomancy.htm*.

"Odinswifeaecerbot.pdf." Accessed April 8, 2013. *http://www.germanicmythology.com/original/earthmother/odinswifeaecerbot.pdf*.

Paxson, Diana. "Lares and Landwights." presented at the Wiccan Fest, Ontario, Canada, June 6, 2001.

Pennick, Nigel. *The Sacred World of the Celts: An Illustrated Guide to Celtic Spirituality and Mythology.* 1st U.S. ed. Rochester Vt.: Inner Traditions, 1997.

Plato. "The Internet Classics Archive | Laws by Plato." Translated by Benjamin Jowett. Accessed February 7, 2012. *http://classics.mit.edu/Plato/laws.1.i.html*.

Pliny the Elder. "Works of Pliny the Elder - Gaius Plinius Secundus." Translated by John Bostock and H. T. Riley. Accessed February 7, 2012. *http://www.brainfly.net/html/pliny_e.htm*.

Plutarch. "Plutarch • Life of Camillus." Translated by Bernadotte Perrin. Accessed February 7, 2012. *http://penelope.uchicago.edu/Thayer/E/Roman/Texts/Plutarch/Lives/Camillus*.html.*

———. "Plutarch • On the Bravery of Women — Sections I-XV." Translated by Frank Cole Babbitt. Accessed February 7, 2012. *http://penelope.uchicago.edu/Thayer/E/Roman/Texts/Plutarch/Moralia/Bravery_of_Women*/A.html#VI.*

Polybius. "Polybius." Translated by Evelyn S. Shuckburgh. Accessed February 7, 2012. *http://www.brainfly.net/html/polybius.htm.*

Pseudo-Scymnus. "Fjor.net - eTOME." Accessed February 7, 2012. *http://fjor.net/etome/grecoroman/pseudoscymnus.html.*

"Purification | Define Purification at Dictionary.com." Accessed November 28, 2012. *http://dictionary.reference.com/browse/purification?s=t.*

Rankin, David. *Celts and the Classical World.* London [etc.]: Routledge, 1996.

Rees, Alwin, and Rees, Brinley. *Celtic Heritage: Ancient Tradition in Ireland and Wales.* London: Thames and Hudson, 1973.

Rutherford, Ward. *Celtic Lore: The History of the Druids and Their Timeless Traditions.* London: Thorsons, 1995.

Sir James George Frazer. "Chapter 28. The Killing of the Tree-Spirit. § 4. Bringing in Summer. Frazer, Sir James George. 1922. The Golden Bough." Accessed December 12, 2012. *http://www.bartleby.com/196/70.html.*

———. "Chapter 62. The Fire-Festivals of Europe. § 5. The Midsummer Fires. Frazer, Sir James George. 1922. The Golden Bough." Accessed December 12, 2012. *http://www.bartleby.com/196/156.html.*

Squire, Charles. *Celtic Myth and Legend: Poetry & Romance.* Hollywood Calif.: Newcastle Pub. Co., 1975.

"St. Blaise - Saints & Angels - Catholic Online." Accessed November 29, 2012. *http://www.catholic.org/saints/saint.php?saint_id=28.*

stef@polyamory.org. "Alt.polyamory Home Page." Accessed January 19, 2012. *http://www.polyamory.org/.*

Strabo. "Geography." Translated by H. C. Hamilton and W. Falconer. Accessed February 7, 2012. *http://www.brainfly.net/html/strabo.htm.*

———. "LacusCurtius • Strabo's Geography — Book IV Chapter 4." Translated by Jones, H.L. Accessed January 31, 2012. *http://penelope.uchicago.edu/Thayer/E/Roman/Texts/Strabo/4D*.html.*

Bibliography

————. "LacusCurtius • Strabo's Geography — Book IV Chapter 5." Accessed January 19, 2012. *http://penelope.uchicago.edu/Thayer/E/Roman/Texts/Strabo/4E*.html.*

Suetonius. "The Lives of the Caesars." Translated by J. C. Rolfe. Accessed February 7, 2012. *http://www.brainfly.net/html/books/brn0140.htm.*

Tacitus. "Medieval Sourcebook: Tacitus: Germania." Accessed January 23, 2012. *http://www.fordham.edu/halsall/source/tacitus1.html.*

————. "Publius Cornelius Tacitus." Accessed February 7, 2012. *http://www.brainfly.net/html/tacitus.htm.*

Teo Bishop. "Solitary Druid Fellowship." Accessed December 19, 2012. *http://www.solitarydruid.org/.*

Tertullian. "A Treatise on the Soul/De Anima." Translated by Holmes, Peter. Accessed January 31, 2012. *http://www.brainfly.net/html/books/brn0169.htm.*

"The Calendar - Primitive Almanacs." Accessed December 11, 2012. *http://www.thebookofdays.com/misc/primitive_almanacs.htm.*

"The Graduate Center, CUNY - ARIS 2001: Key Findings." Accessed January 19, 2012. *http://www.gc.cuny.edu/Faculty/GC-Faculty-Activities/ARIS--American-Religious-Identification-Survey/Key-findings.*

Ari The Learned. "Landnámabók- THE BOOK OF THE SETTLEMENT OF ICELAND." Translated by Rev. T Ellwood. Accessed January 25, 2012. *http://www.northvegr.org/sagas%20annd%20epics/miscellaneous/landnamabok/index.html.*

"The Loyal Arthurian Warband - Druid Network." Accessed December 20, 2012. *http://druidnetwork.org/node/1000816.*

"The Rainbow Bridge Poem - A Pet Loss Poem." Accessed December 13, 2012. *http://www.rainbowbridge.com/Poem.htm.*

"Traditional Scottish Recipes - Oatcakes/Bannocks." Accessed December 5, 2012. *http://www.rampantscotland.com/recipes/blrecipe_bannocks.htm.*

Unknown. "Aislinge Meic Con Glinne." Accessed February 8, 2012. *http://www.ucc.ie/celt/online/T308002/.*

————. "Annála Connacht." Accessed February 8, 2012. *http://www.ucc.ie/celt/published/G100011/index.html.*

————. "Annals of the Four Masters." Accessed February 8, 2012. *http://www.ucc.ie/celt/online/T100005A/.*

————. "Bethu Brigte - The Life of Brigit." Translated by D. Ó hAodha. Accessed February 8, 2012. *http://www.ucc.ie/celt/published/T201002/index.html.*

————. "Buile Suibhne." Translated by J. G. O'Keeffe. Accessed February 8, 2012. *http://www.ucc.ie/celt/published/T302018/index.html.*

————. "Cath Maige Tuired: The Second Battle of Mag Tuired." Translated by Elizabeth A. Gray. Accessed January 20, 2012. *http://www.ucc.ie/celt/published/T300010/index.html.*

————. "Chronicon Scotorum." Translated by William M. Hennessy & Gearóid Mac Niocaill. Accessed February 8, 2012. *http://www.ucc.ie/celt/published/T100016/index.html.*

————. "Deirdre." Translated by Douglas Hyde. Accessed February 8, 2012. *http://www.ucc.ie/celt/published/T301020/index.html.*

————. "Táin Bó Cúalnge from the Book of Leinster." Translated by Cecile O'Rahilly. Accessed February 8, 2012. *http://www.ucc.ie/celt/online/T301035/.*

————. "The Children of Lir." Accessed January 20, 2012. *http://www.ireland-information.com/articles/thechildrenoflir.htm.*

————. "The Combat of Ferdiad and Cuchulain." Translated by Joseph Dunn & Ernst Windisch. Accessed January 19, 2012. *http://adminstaff.vassar.edu/sttaylor/Cooley/Ferdiad.html.*

————. "The Lebor Gabala Erren - The Book of Invasions." Translated by R. A. S. Macalister. Accessed January 20, 2012. *http://www.ancienttexts.org/library/celtic/irish/lebor.html.*

————. "The Metrical Dindshenchas." Translated by Edward Gwynn. Accessed January 31, 2012. *http://www.ucc.ie/celt/published/T106500A/index.html.*

Valerius Maximus. *Memorable Deeds and Sayings: A Thousand Tales from Ancient Rome.* Translated by Henry John Walker. Hackett Pub Co Inc, 2004.

Valiente, Doreen. *An ABC of Witchcraft: Past and Present.* [1986 ed.]. Blaine, Wash.: Phoenix Pub., 1986.

Wikipedia. "Atargatis - Wikipedia, the Free Encyclopedia." Accessed January 31, 2012. *http://en.wikipedia.org/wiki/Atargatis.*

————. "Badb - Wikipedia, the Free Encyclopedia." Accessed January 31, 2012. *http://en.wikipedia.org/wiki/Badb.*

————. "Georges Dumézil - Wikipedia." Accessed December 22, 2011. *http://en.wikipedia.org/wiki/Georges_Dum%C3%A9zil.*

————. "Liminality - Wikipedia, the Free Encyclopedia." Accessed January 31, 2012. *http://en.wikipedia.org/wiki/Liminality.*

Bibliography

————. "Niall of the Nine Hostages - Wikipedia, the Free Encyclopedia." Accessed January 31, 2012. *http://en.wikipedia.org/wiki/ Niall_of_the_Nine_Hostages.*

Xenophon. "Hellenica." Translated by H. G. Dakyns. Accessed February 7, 2012. *http://www.brainfly.net/html/books/brn0191.htm.*

Index

Index

Index

Made in the USA
San Bernardino, CA
24 April 2020